ADVANCES IN ACCOUNTING EDUCATION
TEACHING AND CURRICULUM INNOVATIONS

ADVANCES IN ACCOUNTING EDUCATION

TEACHING AND CURRICULUM INNOVATIONS

Series Editors: Bill N. Schwartz and J. Edward Ketz

Volume 1: Edited by Bill N. Schwartz and David E. Stout

Volumes 2–3: Edited by Bill N. Schwartz and J. Edward Ketz

ADVANCES IN ACCOUNTING EDUCATION
TEACHING AND CURRICULUM INNOVATIONS VOLUME 4

ADVANCES IN ACCOUNTING EDUCATION

TEACHING AND CURRICULUM INNOVATIONS

EDITED BY

BILL N. SCHWARTZ
School of Business and Economics, Indiana University, South Bend, USA

J. EDWARD KETZ
MBA Faculty Director, Smeal College of Business, The Pennsylvania State University, USA

United Kingdom – North America – Japan
India – Malaysia – China

Emerald Group Publishing Limited
Howard House, Wagon Lane, Bingley BD16 1WA, UK

British Library Cataloguing in Publication Data
A catalogue record for this book is available from the British Library

ISBN: 978-0-7623-0856-9
ISSN: 1085-4622 (Series)

CONTENTS

LIST OF CONTRIBUTORS

Richard E. Baker	Department of Accountancy Northern Illinois University, USA
Daniel Braswell	Department of Accounting University of New Orleans, USA
Steve Buchheit	Rawls College of Business Administration Texas Tech University, USA
Thomas G. Calderon	College of Business Administration University of Akron, USA
Steven V. Campbell	Department of Accounting University of Idaho, USA
Mary York Christ	College of Business Administration Valparaiso University, USA
Denton Collins	Department of Accountancy and Taxation University of Houston, USA
Dean Crawford	Accountancy, Finance and Law Department University of Michigan, Dearborn, USA
Michael F. Foran	Department of Accounting and Finance University of Michigan, Dearborn, USA
Donald W. Gribbin	School of Accountancy Southern Illinois University, Carbondale, USA
Brian Patrick Green	Department of Accounting and Finance University of Michigan, Dearborn, USA
Michael Harkness	Department of Accounting and Finance University of Michigan, Dearborn, USA

Eleanor G. Henry	Accountancy, Finance and Law Department State University of New York, Oswego, USA
Ernest R. Larkins	School of Accountancy Georgia State University, USA
Roberta M. Lipsig	Accountancy, Finance and Law Department State University of New York, Oswego, USA
Lois S. Mahoney	School of Accounting University of Central Florida, USA
Robert C. Maloney	Department of Accounting University of Alaska, Anchorage, USA
Carol J. Normand	Lumpkin College of Business and Applied Sciences Eastern Illinois University, USA
Phillip R. Olds	Department of Accounting Virginia Commonwealth University, USA
Barbara P. Reider	Department of Accounting and Finance University of Montana, USA
Austin Reitenga	Department of Accounting University of Texas at San Antonio Texas, USA
Julie Sobery	School of Accountancy Southern Illinois University, Carbondale, USA
Judith K. Welch	School of Accounting University of Central Florida, USA

EDITORIAL BOARD

James M. Kurtenbach
Iowa State University

Linda M. Lovata
Southern Illinois University, Carbondale

Susan A. Lynn
University of Baltimore

James J. Maroney
Northeastern University

Maureen Mascha
Elmhurst College

James R. Martin
University of South Florida

Gordon S. May
University of Georgia

Steven M. Mintz
Claremont McKenna College

Mark C. Mitschow
SUNY, Geneseo

Gale E. Newell
Western Michigan University

Richard L. Ott
Kansas State University

Sue P. Ravenscroft
Iowa State University

Jane L. Reimers
Florida State University

Alan Reinstein
Wayne State University

Robin W. Roberts
University of Central Florida

Linda V. Ruchala
University of Nebraska

Timothy J. Rupert
Northeastern University

David H. Ryan
Temple University

Georgia Saemann
University of Wisconsin, Milwaukee

Michael S. Schadewald
University of Wisconsin, Milwaukee

Richard G. Schroeder
University of North Carolina, Charlotte

Barbara W. Scofield
University of Texas, Permian Basin

Julie S. Sobery
Southern Illinois University, Carbondale

Kevin D. Stocks
Brigham Young University

Carol F. Venable
San Diego State University

Ralph E. Viator
Texas Tech University

Martha Wartick
University of Northern Iowa

Richard A. White
University of South Carolina

Donald E. Wygal
Rider University

James E. Yardley
Virginia Tech

Marilyn T. Zarzeski
The University of Mississippi

Douglas E. Ziegenfuss
Old Dominion University

STATEMENT OF PURPOSE

Advances in Accounting Education is a refereed academic journal whose purpose is to meet the needs of individuals interested in the educational process. We publish thoughtful, well-developed articles that are readable, relevant and reliable.

Articles may be non-empirical or empirical. Our emphasis is pedagogy, and articles MUST explain how to improve teaching methods or curricula/programs.

Non-empirical manuscripts should be academically rigorous. They can be theoretical syntheses, conceptual models, position papers, discussions of methodology, comprehensive literature reviews grounded in theory, or historical discussions with implications for current and future efforts. Reasonable assumptions and logical development are essential. Most manuscripts should discuss implications for research.

For empirical reports, sound research design and execution are critical. Articles should have well articulated and strong theoretical foundations. In this regard, establishing a link to the non-accounting literature may be desirable. Replications and extensions of previously published works are encouraged. As a means for establishing an open dialogue, responses to or comments on articles published previously are welcomed.

REVIEW PROCEDURES

Advances in Accounting Education will provide authors with timely reviews clearly indicating the review status of the manuscript. The results of initial reviews normally will be reported to authors within *eight* weeks. Authors will be expected to work with an Editor who will act as a liaison between the authors and the reviewers to resolve areas of concern.

See http://www.elsevier.com for Guidelines and additional information regarding manuscript submissions.

A SERVICE-LEARNING APPROACH TO ACHIEVING TAXPAYER COMPLIANCE IN ALASKAN NATIVE COMMUNITIES

Steven V. Campbell, Barbara P. Reider and Robert C. Maloney

ABSTRACT

The Rural Alaska Taxpayer Outreach Program sends senior-level accounting students to remote Alaskan native villages to provide free taxpayer assistance. The Accounting Department at the University of Alaska Anchorage has developed an elective course using this Program as a service-learning project. This paper presents the implementation details and outcome assessments on curricular delivery and student learning. Our experience suggests this service-learning model enhances problem solving, interaction, and communication skills. Further, students participating in the Rural Alaska Taxpayer Outreach Program develop a better understanding of daily life in rural Alaskan villages and a stronger commitment to community service.

Advances in Accounting Education, Volume 4, pages 1–19.

ISBN: 0-7623-0856-7

INTRODUCTION

> "The intricacies and paradoxes in relations between the individual and his actions in the social context have been put very well by the great sage, Rabbi Hillel: 'If I am not for myself, then who is for me? And if I am not for others, then who am I? And if not now, when?'" (Arrow, 1974, p. 15).

Societal demands and our own self-fulfillment require that we be for others as well as for ourselves. Service-learning, a form of active learning involving service to one's community, recognizes public service is not only a noble and worthy end in itself, it is also a means to personal growth and self-fulfillment.

How can accounting students best learn the value of public service and at the same time develop competencies necessary for success as professional accountants? This paper presents implementation details and outcome assessments for the Rural Alaska Taxpayer Outreach Program, a service-learning project that sends senior-level accounting students out into rural Alaska native villages to provide free taxpayer assistance. A distinguishing feature of this service-learning project is that we offer it as a separate elective course. Other distinguishing features include a close working relationship between faculty and students, extended travel away from home, and extensive reflection both in the field and following the service-learning experience.

Our outcome assessments suggest these features enhance certain personal competencies called for in the AICPA Core Competency Framework for Entry into the Accounting Profession (AICPA Core Competency Framework). Specifically, we find this Program promotes student problem solving and decision-making skills, interaction skills, teamwork skills, and communication skills.

The balance of our paper is organized as follows. The next section briefly reviews prior literature concerning the service-learning pedagogy. The subsequent two sections describe the Program's planning and initiation efforts and summarize its operating results for the years 1996–2000. The next two sections discuss the Program's benefits and limitations, respectively. The paper concludes with a discussion of future plans and some final comments.

LITERATURE REVIEW

Bringle and Hatcher define service-learning as a "credit-bearing educational experience in which students: (a) participate in an organized service activity in such a way that meets identified community needs, and (b) reflect on the service activity in such a way to gain further understanding of course content, a broader appreciation of the discipline, and an enhanced sense of civic responsibility"

(1995, p. 112). This definition links formal learning with public service and recognizes student reflection as a necessary component of a service-learning model. Community service involves "providing services to improve the quality of life of residents of a community, especially low-income individuals, or to solve specific problems facing a disadvantaged community" (Rama, 1998, p. 5). Reflection is the "intentional consideration of the service experience in light of particular learning objectives" (Bringle & Hatcher, 1995, p. 115).

While accounting education is a relative newcomer to the service-learning pedagogy, the literature from other disciplines provides a large body of work. In the following sections we summarize this literature according to the effects of service-learning on students, faculty, and universities.

Students

While the community receives the service, more often than not it is the students who benefit the most. Rama et al. (2000) classify desired student outcomes into two categories, intellectual outcomes and personal outcomes, and observe that these categories have considerable overlap with the groupings (functional, personal, and broad business) used in the AICPA Core Competency Framework. Rama et al. define intellectual outcomes as "cognitive competencies, including knowledge of textbook content, relationship of accounting knowledge to the business world, and critical thinking skills" (2000, p. 4). In contrast, personal outcomes include competencies such as personal demeanor, leadership, and communication skills, and a variety of values-related competencies, such as honesty and ethical conduct (Rama et al., 2000, p. 16).

Empirical studies indicate students participating in service-learning projects develop a sense of personal identity, spiritual growth, and moral development (Astin & Sax, 1998; Eyler et al., 1997; Gray et al., 1998). Further, students develop interpersonal, leadership, and communication skills by participating in service-learning projects (Astin & Sax, 1998; Driscoll et al., 1996; Eyler, Giles & Braxton, 1997). Eyler and Giles (1999) found placement quality was most consistently associated with personal outcomes such as leadership, communication, and teamwork skills. The opportunity to work with people from diverse ethnic groups and the extent to which students' service met needs identified by the community were also linked to personal outcomes. These findings suggest researchers can begin to offer faculty guidance on how to structure service-learning experiences to enhance desired outcomes. The present paper follows this purpose and contributes to this body of work.

Service-learning by definition involves working in the community. Recent studies suggest such projects reduce students' stereotypes and foster cultural and racial understanding (Balazadeh, 1996; Keen & Keen, 1998; Western Washington University, 1994). Further, the literature suggests service-learning projects develop citizenship skills, including a commitment to serve the community in the future (Eyler & Giles, 1999). Students who participate in service-learning projects also enjoy a carryover benefit of improved learning in their other academic courses (Cohen & Kinsey, 1994; Fenzel & Leary, 1997; Oliver, 1997). While some studies report no improvement in grade-point average by participation in service-learning activities (Hudson, 1996; Miller, 1994), the probability of a student graduating from college increases by including a service-learning experience (Roose et al., 1997). Students involved in service-learning projects also enjoy stronger relationships with faculty members and increased satisfaction with their university (Astin & Sax, 1998; Berson & Younkin, 1998).

Faculty

Four major research findings address faculty participation in service-learning opportunities. First, once faculty members have successfully introduced service-learning opportunities into their curriculum, they are more likely to integrate such projects in the future (Campus Contact, 1998; Sagaria & Burrows, 1995). Second, faculty members perceive a higher quality of student learning for students who choose to participate in service-learning activities (Hesser, 1995). Third, while the primary focus of service-learning has been in the classroom, faculty participating in service-learning have a higher commitment to research (Driscoll et al., 1996). Fourth, faculty members perceive a lack of campus and community resources as an important barrier to wider implementation of service-learning projects (Wade & Yarborough, 1997).

University

Many colleges and universities have made a commitment to service-learning in recent years (Bringle & Hatcher, 1995; Scott & Ludwigh, 1995) and these institutions report offering a wide range of opportunities for student involvement (Serow et al., 1996). While few universities require service-learning in their curriculum (Sagaria & Burrows, 1995), student retention is higher when service-learning opportunities exist (Astin & Sax, 1998). Finally, Driscoll et al., 1996, used community interviews to assess satisfaction with university interactions and found strong evidence suggesting community relations are judged more favorably when universities support service-learning.

Designing Service-Learning Models

The present study is part of a growing body of literature addressing the problem of designing service-learning projects to enhance desired educational outcomes (Rama et al., 2000, pp. 25–33). Many experts argue service-learning activities should be integrated into course objectives (Howard, 1998; Weigert, 1998; Eyler & Giles, 1999). Astin et al. (2000) found students are more likely to achieve desired outcomes when service is performed as part of a course, rather than as a separate volunteer activity. In the model presented below the service-learning activity is a course, rather than a project within a course or a separate volunteer activity.

PROGRAM PLANNING AND INITIATION EFFORTS

Background

The Rural Alaska Taxpayer Outreach Program has its origins in the Alaska commercial fishing industry, an industry comprised of many small independent fishers who sell their catch to a single processing plant. Since the early 1970s the industry has operated under a limited entry (fishing) permit system that requires the captain of each vessel possess a permit to participate in a given fishery.

Historically, the processors handled almost all of the logistical and financial matters for the fishers, including preparing their tax returns. As the industry changed so did the relationship between the processors and the individual fishers. In the 1990s the canneries stopped taking care of the business and financial matters for the fishers, and many were left without the financial management skills to handle these issues. The remote location of rural Alaska fishing villages compounded the problem and many fishers simply stopped filing their income tax returns.

Commercial harvest records are reported to the Internal Revenue Service (IRS) and for those fishers who did not file returns, the IRS assessed the tax plus penalties and interest based upon the income reported to it. After exhausting most of its collection options, the IRS eventually initiated the process to seize and sell at auction the taxpayers boat and/or fishing permit.

The prospect of seizures created tension between the IRS and the State of Alaska. If a fishing permit was seized and sold at auction, it would likely leave the community and possibly the State. This would cost the community not only the loss of the fisher's income, but the loss of the crew's income as well. The economic consequences to the entire community could be severe if only a few permits were lost. The State of Alaska Division of Investments attempted to provide assistance to Alaskan commercial fishers by creating the Tax Obligation Loan Program. Through this program a commercial fisher facing the loss of his vessel or permit as a result of a substantial tax obligation could qualify for a low interest State loan. The State of Alaska Division of Investments administered the program by working closely with Alaska Business Development Center (ABDC) to identify and assist commercial fishers having substantial tax deficiencies. However, one requirement of the loan program was the fisher had to be compliant in all federal income tax filings.

The Pilot Project

The ABDC is a private, non-profit corporation that assists fishers and other small businesses with business plans and loan applications. Regarding the Tax Obligation Loan Program for commercial fishers, the ABDC found tax compliance was a significant obstacle to qualification. In 1995 representatives from the Alaska Division of Investments, ABDC, and the University of Alaska Anchorage (UAA) Accounting Department developed the idea of sending accounting students to rural Alaska communities to prepare tax returns for commercial fishers. The idea received immediate support from the IRS Pacific-Northwest District, and particularly, the local Taxpayer Education Department, which offered to provide necessary training, software, and technical support. In addition to certifying the students through its Volunteer Income Tax Assistance (VITA) program, the IRS assisted in identifying communities with the highest rates of non-compliance and provided access to taxpayer records.

The Accounting Department selected five students enrolled in its Bachelors Degree Program to participate in the pilot project. Prior to this, accounting students at UAA had participated in the IRS' local VITA program on a voluntary basis, receiving no academic credit toward graduation. The rural village project demanded a much greater commitment and was more in the nature of an internship. Students would work directly with a private business, the ABDC, and they would apply the accounting and tax principles they had learned in the classroom. Therefore, in the first year of the Program the five student volunteers enrolled in an established accounting internship course.

During the spring 1996 semester, teams consisting of two students, one faculty supervisor, and a consultant from ABDC, visited five communities. At the conclusion of the pilot program all participants evaluated the experience and made recommendations for changes and improvements. Without exception the students and faculty who participated in the project judged it to be a positive and worthwhile educational experience that offered significant benefits to the students and the communities. Working and traveling as a team, interviewing taxpayers and examining their source documents, addressing commercial fishing-related tax issues, and responding to a variety of IRS notices and demands for past due taxes were identified as beneficial outcomes of this service-learning project. All stakeholders agreed to continue their participation in the project and to expand the service to more communities in 1997.

Initiating the Rural Alaska Taxpayer Outreach Program

The Accounting Department faculty were comfortable awarding internship course credit to the five students involved in the pilot project because it contained many aspects of on-the-job training. However, faculty also recognized other aspects of the project went beyond the usual internship experience. After considering these aspects, we decided to offer this Program as a separate service-learning course. The separate course format seemed appropriate because the Program: (1) utilized knowledge gained from other classes in the curriculum, (2) addressed a real community need, (3) included a student reflection component, and (4) contained a learning component. Given the amount of training and preparation required, plus the need to achieve a certain level of efficiency in order to make the Program cost effective for the other stakeholders, we felt there was an appropriate expectation for a three credit senior-level elective accounting course. Therefore, in the second year we added the Rural Alaska Taxpayer Outreach Program as a standard course in our spring semester offering.

Classroom Training

The classroom training begins early in the spring semester with a two-hour session covering the history of the Program, the roles of the Program participants, student responsibilities, and student learning objectives and assessments. Also discussed are travel, clothing, food, and lodging arrangements in rural Alaska, and the related liability issues. At this first meeting students must read and sign an *Acknowledgment of Risks & Release of Liability* form.

The next set of classroom sessions involve twelve hours of training by the IRS Taxpayer Assistance staff. Topics include preparing for and completing the VITA exam, entering taxpayer data into the TaxWise software program, and filing returns electronically. Students can take home and practice the TaxWise software using the Accounting Department's laptop computers.

Following the computer training IRS revenue agents and revenue officers present six-hours of traditional classroom instruction. The revenue agents discuss the nature of records and documentation commonly found in rural Alaska, provide a summary of specific tax issues related to the commercial fishing industry, review a completed schedule C tax form for a fisherman, and cover other tax issues common to rural Alaska. The revenue officers also discuss the IRS's role and the taxpayer's rights in the collection of tax deficiencies.

Participant Responsibilities

Village selection, funding, travel, and accommodation arrangements are the responsibility of the ABDC Program Manager. Working from an IRS list of villages most in need of taxpayer assistance, the Program Manager solicits funding from business and government entities in the target communities and regions. Sponsoring entities include major banks, economic development agencies, regional native associations, fish processors, law firms, small businesses, and city governments. Contributions from sponsoring entities consist of both cash and in-kind donations such as accommodations. After the Program Manager obtains the financial support necessary to fund a community visit, she schedules the community for a tax team trip and begins a promotional campaign to inform the community's residents of the free tax preparation service.

Each tax team consists of four members: two UAA accounting students, a supervising accounting professor, and a business consultant from the ABDC. The Program Manager for the ABDC schedules the trips, purchases the plane tickets, and arranges for local transportation, lodging, and a workplace. The responsibilities of the supervising accounting professor include: coordinating travel plans and equipment needs with the students, supervising the students in the field, assisting with complicated tax returns, and contacting the IRS in cases involving delinquent taxes, penalties, missing data, and prior year tax information. Student responsibilities include setting-up the computer equipment in the field, interviewing the clients, preparing the tax returns on the TaxWise software, and filing the returns electronically.

The Program Manager schedules tax team trips on weekends (Friday through Sunday) and during spring break so students avoid missing other classes. After their IRS training, students either take three weekend trips (approximately nine days) visiting one community each weekend, or one 10-day trip over spring break visiting several communities. The trips begin about February 10 and finish shortly before the April 15 income tax filing deadline.

Intended Student Outcomes

At the first class meeting the Accounting Department instructor of record discusses the learning objectives stated on the course syllabus. These are: (1) demonstrating a thorough understanding of personal income tax principles through successful completion of the VITA exam, (2) understanding and applying tax regulations as they relate to the commercial fishing industry, (3) developing effective communication skills in interviewing taxpayers and explaining the application of the Tax Code to their financial circumstances, (4) exercising professional judgment in the interpretation of the Tax Code and establishing reasonable estimates in the case of missing or incomplete information, (5) effectively working with other team members to accomplish a common objective, and (6) effectively using technology to improve efficiency and accuracy and to maintain control over the work flow. Additionally, two other desired outcomes are not stated in the course syllabus: developing a deeper understanding of life in rural Alaska and developing a commitment to serve the community in the future.

Educational Assessment

To evaluate student performance in the field we rely on evaluations of the supervising faculty member and the ABDC consultant. At the end of each trip the faculty supervisor completes an evaluation form and rates the student on the learning objectives stated in the course syllabus. Also, at the completion of each trip, students write a brief paper describing their experience and reporting on what they learned or gained from the experience. These reports help identify areas where students experienced growth or recognized a need to improve. By reviewing student reports from subsequent trips we can identify progress along a continuum in areas such as decision making and problem-solving skills, communication skills, and interaction and teamwork skills. Additionally, these student reports provide insight into what the students are experiencing on an emotional level. The student reports we receive suggest the exposure to rural village life is leaving a vivid impression on the students.

While the class does advance student learning in areas the AICPA Core Competency Framework classifies as functional and broad business perspective competencies, our outcome assessments suggest it advances what are defined as personal competencies in a more direct and significant manner. The development of communication skills is perhaps the most significant issue facing students in successfully performing their responsibilities. Students must deal face-to-face with members of a different culture who do not understand income tax laws and regulations. They must be able to clearly formulate their questions and explain the tax consequences to their client. Problem solving and decision making also play a major role in carrying out their responsibilities. Students perform substantially all of their work in the field in front of the client, and they seldom take problems back to Anchorage for further research. When a problem or unusual circumstance arises, the team members discuss the alternatives and decide on the best solution. These decisions often involve a great deal of ambiguity because the team is often faced with incomplete information. This has been an excellent project for developing professional judgment and problem solving skills.

Our students are immersed in an environment that involves a variety of interactions. In addition to interacting with taxpayers, students often must seek advice and take directions from their supervising professor. After the workday the team members generally prepare their meals together in a relaxed setting and reflect on their day. There are few distractions and no television. Reflection while in the field is an integral part of the learning experience.

Consistent with the results reported by Astin and Sax (1998) and Berson and Younkin (1998), our experience suggests stronger relationships develop between students and faculty who jointly participate in service-learning opportunities. Students made the following comments in their written reports:

> It was a great opportunity to network with the students and faculty of the Accounting Department.
>
> "Professor X" was our faculty advisor on this trip. She was an extremely patient teacher.
>
> Although she was only there to supervise, she always jumped in to help answer questions or solve problems.

Second, consistent with the results reported in Astin and Sax (1998), Driscoll et al. (1996), and Eyler et al. (1997), our experience suggests the educational environment enhances students' communication and interaction skills. The following comments from student reports are representative of what our students tell us:

> I learned a lot about communication and that it varies from person to person.
>
> I think that the program is an awesome experience for students. It gives you hands-on experience dealing directly with people – prying for information – much like the accounting profession.
>
> Not only did I learn how to prepare complicated fishing tax returns, I also had a chance to interact with some very interesting people, and for the first time experience the public/people side of the accounting profession.
>
> I was very nervous during my first trip, but my confidence grew as I realized that I could answer people's questions. I liked educating the taxpayers. New issues developed during each trip, so I was continually learning.

Finally, consistent with the results reported by Balazadeh, (1996), Keen and Keen (1998), and Eyler and Giles (1999), we find the educational environment has a profound influence on fostering cultural understanding and developing a sense of social responsibility. Student comments taken from their written reports support this finding:

> I had never been to any bush communities before this program. I think the experience was a valuable one because I met many Native Alaskans. I was exposed to a completely different type of lifestyle than I am accustomed to.
>
> The trip itself was a great learning experience, as I learned to be flexible and understanding of mother nature. The culture of the villages we went to was fascinating and the people are very kind.
>
> I had a once-in-a-lifetime opportunity to visit native villages in my home state. I found a new appreciation for Alaskan Natives and for Alaska itself.
>
> I thought the people in the villages were very nice and I had more fun with this program than I ever imagined.
>
> I was able to learn a lot about Alaskan Natives.

SUMMARY OF 1996–2000 OPERATIONS

In 1996 we visited five communities; in 2000 we visited 24 communities. Over this same period program expenses – airfare, accommodations, per diem, instructor compensation, and overhead – increased from $25,885 to $78,693. Airfare cost, which constitutes almost one-third of the Program's budget, increased significantly as the Program expanded westward to the Alaska Peninsula and south to the Alaska Panhandle. Only since 1998 has the Program offered students the option of an extended spring-break trip covering several geographically close communities. This grouping of communities saves the Program many thousands of dollars in airfare cost.

Accommodation cost bears no relationship to location, and comfort levels differ considerably among the communities served. In many communities one of the supporting entities owns lodging facilities and donates accommodations as an in-kind contribution. Course overload remuneration to the professor of record is the Program's only fixed cost, and historically the faculty supervisors participating in the Program divide this money. Overhead expenses include salaries and wages paid to ABDC personnel, printing, paper, postage, copying, telephone, facsimile, and ground transportation (snow machine rental) costs.

Table 1 presents a summary of the Program's operating results for years 1996–2000. Over this five-year period student participation has increased from five to fifteen students, the number of returns prepared has increased from 200 to 1,182 and the average cost per return has fallen to $42 per return. The growth of the Program and its increased efficiency suggest the Program has been successful in benefiting the communities we serve as well as the other participants.

Table 1. Summary of Program Results for Years 1996–2000.

	1996	1997	1998	1999	2000
Overall Results					
Student Participants	5	8	12	16	15
Returns Prepared	200	449	684	1,122	1,882
Number of Trips	5	7	9	12	11
Number of Communities	5	11	17	19	24
Clients with Multiple-Year Returns	14	14	20	38	51
Program Expenses	$25,885	$30,537	$70,107	$72,783	$78,693
Average Costs					
Cost Per Return	$129	$68	$102	$65	$42
Cost Per Trip	$5,177	$4,362	$7,789	$6,065	$7,154
Cost Per Community	$5,177	$2,776	$4,124	$3,831	$3,279

BENEFITS

Community

The primary benefit of the Rural Alaska Taxpayer Outreach Program to the Native communities is access to income tax assistance at no charge. A second but equally important benefit is a gradual advancement in tax knowledge and record-keeping practices. As we have returned to the same communities over the years, we have noticed a difference in residents' attitudes toward tax compliance and the IRS. Generally in the first year we visit a village our tax teams observe considerable fear and misunderstanding among the village residents regarding the power and motives of the IRS. In subsequent years the fear level subsides and residents that have used the Program in the past are generally much better prepared when they arrive for their consultation. Returning clients frequently present sorted receipts and in some cases detailed accounting records.

Our students serve as role models for the younger members of the communities we visit. Those residents in the 16–24 year old age group often are surprised to learn that the people assisting them or their parents are actually university students who are studying to become accountants. We use every opportunity to promote post-secondary education and accounting as a career. One of the early goals in this Program was to promote accounting education in the high schools in these communities, but this has proven to be more difficult than originally anticipated. We usually arrive in a community sometime Friday afternoon and have no opportunity to get into a classroom during school hours. Thus we are constrained to use what limited contact we have during the weekend to promote the value of higher education.

Students

One student benefit is the opportunity to apply classroom income tax knowledge to actual clients with real source documents. Students also have the opportunity to expand their income tax knowledge by using the TaxWise software and filing returns electronically. While in the field students learn the value of developing effective interviewing and communication skills. They must word their questions carefully and, in certain cases, must pose a question several different ways to ensure they obtain the needed information. Students also learn the importance of efficiently examining and organizing source documents.

Students usually do not encounter difficult or complex tax issues in this Program; however, they must be prepared to practice their tax research and verification skills. The IRS provides each student with a CD-ROM containing all forms, instructions, and publications, and every student carries a CCH Master Tax Guide into the field. The overriding decision criteria students follow when they are working in the field is that their mission is not to prepare a perfect tax return. The IRS instructors advise the students they will be faced with incomplete information, and that they must occasionally use their judgment and estimation skills to arrive at a reasonable amount to claim for a deduction or asset capitalization. Items such as the cost of meals while on a fishing boat or the cost of a new outboard motor, often are based on the taxpayers' recollection or estimate. The IRS instructors tell the students if they have ninety percent of the documentation needed to complete a tax return, it is much better to have the taxpayer make a reasonable estimate of the missing information than to leave the community without completing the return. This provides students an opportunity to exercise judgment and develop their problem-solving skills.

The exposure the students get to Alaskan Native culture and the harsh realities of life in rural Alaska are perhaps even more valuable in terms of life-long learning. When a tax team lands on a small airstrip on the edge of a community and travels to the village in a wooden sled pulled by a snow-machine, the students quickly realize they are far away from Anchorage. It is not unusual for a village elder to come in for a consultation with a son or daughter whose job it is to translate the conversation into the Yupik language. When students discover the school building where they are staying is one of the only facilities in the village with running water and flush toilets, they gain a new appreciation for just how difficult everyday life can be in rural Alaska.

Finally, students benefit from the personal reward they receive from helping others. Our student learning assessments suggest this Program helps build a foundation for what we hope is a life-long commitment to public service. As we prepare students to enter the accounting profession, we strive to educate them on the responsibilities associated with being a professional. These responsibilities include maintaining technical competence, possessing high ethical standards, and demonstrating a commitment to public service. Examples of written comments students made after completing the Program are the following:

> The VITA program has a lot to offer students in the way of real-life skills. I feel like I have learned a skill that will be useful – particularly as I prepare to enter the workforce.

> This was a very valuable opportunity and I received a lot of knowledge that will greatly help me in the future. I believe that this program is a great real-world experience for students that gives them the opportunity to face challenges and learn from them.

> After having the privilege of participating in the UAA VITA program, I would definitely recommend it to all accounting majors. Not only did I get hands-on experience in preparing tax returns, I also got the opportunity to travel to parts of Alaska that I had not yet seen. The knowledge I have gained from participating in the program is more valuable than anything taught in a textbook. This program is probably the best program I have participated in at UAA and I encourage everyone who has the opportunity to get involved in this program.

> I just want to thank UAA, ABDC, and the IRS for giving me the opportunity to participate in such a wonderful program, not to mention how great it will look on my resume!

> Overall, I was very pleased with the UAA VITA internship. I would definitely recommend it to other students. I think it is a great experience and an important program that allows UAA to be involved in the community.

Faculty

The faculty benefit by interacting with students in a setting far removed from campus. They learn about their students' career goals, their experiences, and their impressions of other accounting classes and instructors. In some respects these trips serve as a form of program assessment and student advising. Our experience is consistent with Astin and Sax (1998) and Berson and Younkin (1998) who found students participating in service-learning projects enjoy stronger relationships with faculty members.

The personal benefit for faculty members involved in service-learning projects has not been previously explored in the literature. Faculty members learn as well as teach and mentor in this Program. Specifically, like their students, faculty supervisors learn about life in rural Alaska and experience the reward associated with community service. Faculty supervisors that do not specialize in taxation, receive the additional benefit of developing their knowledge about personal income taxation. These outcomes are openly discussed among faculty members and are sometimes acknowledged in the written faculty reports.

Consistent with the findings of Hesser (1995), our faculty participants perceive a higher quality of student learning for students who choose to participate in the Program. However, contrary to the results reported in Driscoll et al. (1996), we do not find faculty participation in the Program leads to a higher commitment to research. And, while Wade and Yarborough (1997) report faculty members perceive a lack of campus and community resources as an important barrier to wider implementation of service-learning projects, we have not experienced such a barrier in this Program. Community funding, which is the responsibility of the ABDC Program Manager, has never been a limitation – more communities are willing to fund tax team visits than we are able to serve. Further, the University has been supportive. Over the past two years we have received grants from the University President's Special Project Fund totaling $7,000.

College and University

The primary benefit for the Accounting Department is the enhancement to the bachelors degree program that such a unique learning opportunity represents. Prospective accounting students discover when they near the end of their degree program they will have the opportunity to travel to remote areas of Alaska and apply the knowledge they have gained in the classroom. This is useful for recruiting new students into accounting and it strengthens the tax area within the accounting program. We find students take additional income tax courses and volunteer for local VITA service in anticipation of participating in the Program. Our experience suggests Austin and Sax (1998) were correct in asserting student retention is improved by including a service-learning component in the curriculum.

The most visible benefit to the Accounting Department, the College, and the University is the positive publicity such a program affords. The UAA Accounting Department has gained recognition at the local, state and national level for its participation in this Program. Most recently the Program received special recognition at the presentation of the 1999 Peter F. Drucker Award for Nonprofit Innovation. Thus, we concur with the findings of Driscoll et al. (1996), community relations are judged more favorably when service-learning projects are adopted.

LIMITATIONS

Perhaps the greatest limitation of this Program is the loss of faculty control over the student learning experience. Specifically, having partners limits our ability to control the learning experience. For example, the ABDC and the IRS are production-oriented and village selection, which is controlled by the ABDC and the IRS, reflects this priority. Maximizing the number of returns prepared is the objective of the ABDC and to a lesser extent the IRS. In contrast the UAA Accounting Department is focused on preserving the academic integrity of its accounting course and maximizing the quality of the learning experience. The Accounting Department's ideal program would target villages that give students more exposure to the type of work expected in an advanced tax course. Currently, our students get little exposure to advanced tax issues and instead prepare a large volume of basic, repetitive, individual returns.

Another limitation we have experienced is faculty burnout. Donating several weekends or an entire spring break is a lot to ask of a faculty member on an annual basis. Paying the faculty supervisors a reasonable compensation for their time would probably alleviate this problem.

PLANS FOR THE FUTURE

Given the popularity of the Program with IRS officials, the State of Alaska, and village taxpayers, there is every indication the Program will continue, but improving the Program is an ongoing exercise. Discussed here are a few of the latest developments and plans for the future.

For the first time in the Program's history, the spring 2000 tax season involved recruiting accounting students from the University of Alaska Fairbanks (UAF). This occurred because the spring break at UAA did not coincide with the spring break at UAF, and this meant the Program Manager could plan two different spring break trips, one involving UAA students and the other UAF students. The 10-day spring break trips are a more efficient way of traveling within Alaska due to the cost savings over travel to the same number of villages for a weekend at a time. Future plans call for the involvement of University of Alaska Southeast (UAS) accounting students and faculty. Juneau, Alaska, home to UAS, is a central location for many fishing villages in southeast Alaska. By including UAS in the Program we anticipate better access to villages and future cost savings.

The Program has enjoyed widespread community support since it began in 1996; however, a current problem is that more communities need taxpayer assistance than there are resources to provide the assistance. By including students and faculty from all three major University of Alaska campuses, this need can be better met. Additionally, the IRS recently awarded the Program a $56,000 grant to provide funds for training and travel to villages with insufficient funding. Future plans include seeking additional sources of grant funding to continue services to these villages. Finally, for the fall 2000 semester the Program received a grant from UAA to develop more objective measurement instruments for assessing curricular delivery, student learning, and client satisfaction.

CONCLUSION

As the Rural Alaska Tax Outreach Program begins its sixth year of service, we can begin to assess which aspects of the Program have been successful. Our written student and faculty reports and our field observations suggest the Program has made a positive contribution to the lives of rural Alaskan taxpayers and our accounting students. By traveling to the villages our students develop an understanding of rural life in Alaska and an appreciation for giving something back to the community. Further, our outcome assessments suggest the Rural Alaska Taxpayer Outreach Program enhances the development of certain personal competencies identified in the AICPA Core Competency Framework including: problem solving and decision-making skills, interaction skills, and communication skills.

Ultimately, the value of any curriculum innovation is determined by its ability to improve the educational process for students. The growth of the Program and its popularity among students are perhaps the best evidence of its success. As we strive to maintain the quality of the Program, we continue to look for new ways to enhance educational outcomes and help the communities we serve. We believe the Rural Alaska Taxpayer Outreach Program is a service-learning model that could be applied in other areas of the United States where taxpayer compliance is a problem.

REFERENCES

American Institute of Certified Public Accountants (AICPA) (1999). AICPA *Core Competency Framework for Entry into the Accounting Profession*. New York, NY.

Arrow, K. (1974). *The Limits of Organization*. New York: W.W. Norton & Company.

Astin, A., & Sax, J. (1998). How Undergraduates are Affected by Service Participation. *Journal of College Student Development*, *39*(3), 251–263.

Astin, A., Vogelgesang, L., Ikeda, E., & Yee, J. (2000). *How Service Learning Affects Students*. Los Angeles, CA: Higher Education Research Institute, University of California.

Balazadeh, N. (1996). *Service-Learning and the Sociological Imagination: Approach and Assessment.* Paper presented at the National Historically Black Colleges and Universities Faculty Development Symposium, Memphis, TN.

Berson, J., & Younkin, W. (1998). *Doing Well by Doing Good: A Study of the Effects of a Service-Learning Experience on Student Success.* Paper presented at the American Society of Higher Education Symposium, Miami, FL.

Bringle, R., & Hatcher, J. (1995). A Service-Learning Curriculum for Faculty. *Michigan Journal of Community Service-Learning, 67*(2), 112–122.

Campus Compact (1998). Service Matters: *Engaging Higher Education in the Renewal of America's Communities and American Democracy.* Providence, RI.

Cohen, J., & Kinsey, D. (1994). Doing Good and Scholarship: A Service-Learning Study. *Journalism Educator, 48*(4), 4–14.

Driscoll, A., Holland, B., Gelmon, S., & Kerrigan, S. (1996). An Assessment Model for Service-Learning: Comprehensive Case Studies of Impact on Faculty, Students, Community, and Institutions. *Michigan Journal of Community Service-Learning, 3,* 66–71.

Eyler, J., & Giles, Jr., D. (1999). *Where's the Learning in Service-Learning?* San Francisco, CA: Jossey-Bass, Inc.

Eyler, J., Giles, Jr., D., & Braxton, J. (1997). The Impact of Service-Learning on College Students. *Michigan Journal of Community Service-Learning, 4,* 5–15.

Fenzel, L., & Leary, T. (1997). *Evaluating Outcomes of Service-Learning Courses at a Parochial College.* Paper presented at the Annual Meeting of the American Educational Research Association, Chicago, IL.

Gray, M., Ondaatje, E., Fricker, R., Geschwind, S., Goldman, C., Kaganoff, T., Robyn, A., Sundt, M., Vogelgesang, L., & Klein, S. (1998). *Coupling Service and Learning in Higher Education: The Final Report of the Evaluation of the Learn and Serve America, Higher Education Program.* RAND.

Hesser, G. (1995). Faculty Assessment of Student Learning: Outcomes Attributed to Service-Learning and Evidence of Changes in Faculty Attitudes about Experiential Education. *Michigan Journal of Community Service-Learning, 2,* 33–42.

Howard, J. P. (1998). Academic Service-Learning: A Counternormative Pedagogy. In: R. A. Rhoads & J. P. Howard (Eds), *Academic Service-Learning: A Pedagogy of Action and Reflection, New Directions for Teaching and Learning No. 73* (pp. 21–29). San Francisco, CA: Jossey-Bass Publishers.

Hudson, W. (1996). Combining Community Service and the Study of American Public Policy. *Michigan Journal of Community Service-Learning, 2,* 33–42.

Keen, C., & Keen, J. (1998). *Bonner Student Impact Survey.* Bonner Foundation.

Miller, J. (1994). Linking Traditional and Service-Learning Courses: Outcome Evaluation Utilizing Two Pedagogically Distinct Models. *Michigan Journal of Community Service-Learning, 1,* 29–36.

Oliver, H. (1997). *Taking Action in Rural Mississippi: Uniting Academic Studies and Community Service through Project D.R.E.A.M.S.* Paper presented at the Annual International Conference of the International Partnership for Service-Learning, Kingston, Jamaica.

Rama, D. V. (1998). Service-Learning: An Active Learning Approach for Accounting Education. In: D. V. Rama (Ed.), *Learning by Doing: Concepts and Models for Service-Learning in Accounting* (pp. 3–18). Washington, DC: American Association of Higher Education.

Rama, D. V., Ravenscroft, S., Wolcott, S., & Zlotkowski, E. (2000). Service-Learning Outcomes: Guidelines for Educators and Researchers. *Issues in Accounting Education, 15*(4), 657–692.

Roose, D., Daphne, J., Miller, A., Norris, W., Peacock, R., White, C., & White, G. (1997). *Black Student Retention Study: Oberlin College*. Oberlin College.

Sagaria, M., & Burrows, J. (1995). *Higher Education Urban Community Service: From Periphery to Core?* Paper presented at the Annual Meeting of the American Educational Research Association, San Francisco, CA.

Scott, J., & Ludwigh, M. (1995). Community Service at Urban Public Institutions: A Report on Conditions and Activities. *Metropolitan Universities: An International Forum*, *6*(3), 55–70.

Serow, R., Calleson, D., Parker, L., & Morgan, L. (1996). Institutional Support for Service-Learning. *Journal of Research and Development in Education*, *29*(4), 220–225.

Wade, R., & Yarbrough, D. (1997). Community Service-Learning in Student Teaching: Toward the Development of an Active Citizenry. *Michigan Journal of Community Service-Learning*, *4*, 42–55.

Weigert, K. M. (1998). Academic Service-Learning: Its Meaning and Relevance. In: R. A. Rhoads & J. P. Howard (Eds), *Academic Service-Learning: A Pedagogy of Action and Reflection, New Directions for Teaching and Learning No. 73* (pp. 3–10). San Francisco, CA. Josser-Bass Publishers

Western Washington University. (1994). *Community Service Activity by Western Washington Students: Its Extent, Nature, and Impact on the Surrounding Community*. Western Washington University, Bellingham, WA.

USING THE *WALL STREET JOURNAL* AND THE INTERNET TO IMPLEMENT THE AECC'S INTRODUCTORY ACCOUNTING RECOMMENDATIONS

Michael F. Foran and Phillip R. Olds

ABSTRACT

The challenge for improving introductory accounting is to develop ways instructors can implement the AECC's recommendations with available resources. This paper discusses an experimental course that attempted to accomplish this objective.

We offered a multimedia approach to teaching introductory accounting at a large mid-western university during the Fall 1997 semester. Each class period had three parts: (1) a traditional presentation of accounting, (2) a discussion of the Wall Street Journal, *and (3) the use of the Internet.*

This course emphasized to business students that accounting takes place within a challenging and changing environment, and that they need to understand that environment. In addition, we sought to expand the students' vocabulary and to improve their reading comprehension. The course stressed the use of accounting information. It showed students that introductory accounting is relevant and is widely used in the real world of business.

Advances in Accounting Education, Volume 4, pages 21–39.

ISBN: 0-7623-0856-7

INTRODUCTION

Accounting education is changing constantly. The articles, special conferences, and sessions at meetings of the American Accounting Association (AAA) that are devoted to accounting curriculum and pedagogical issues seem countless. Prior to the establishment of the Accounting Education Change Commission (AECC) in 1989 this was certainly not the case. Smith and Usry (1989) reviewed changes in accounting courses from 1962 to 1987 and found little significant change. No course underwent less change than introductory accounting.

Since the AECC's creation, and as a result of its initiatives, some schools have revamped their entire accounting curriculum [for example, see Ainsworth and Plumlee (1993)]. Others have at least changed the way they structure and/or teach introductory accounting [for example, see Abdolmohammadi (1998), DeBerg, Adams and Lea (1998), and Saudagaran (1996)]. Perhaps the first accounting course has received special attention because the AECC devoted its *Position Statement No. 2* (1992) entirely to this course, or because of the large number of students that take this course.

The purpose of this paper is to suggest ways that instructors can change the introductory financial accounting course to incorporate some of the AECC's recommendations using resources that students will use throughout their careers. The methods we advocate will also work in large classes in which instructors do not have graduate student assistance.

BACKGROUND

The AECC was not the first group to advocate significant and comprehensive changes in accounting education. Needles and Powers (1990) identified 17 different models from seven different accounting organizations regarding the structure of accounting education.

Two committee reports were particularly important in the establishment of the AECC. Accounting academicians addressed the need for changes through the AAA's committee report Future Accounting Education: *Preparing for the Expanding Profession* (AAA, 1986), commonly referred to as the "Bedford Committee Report." The public accounting profession spoke out with *Perspectives on Education: Capabilities for Success in the Accounting Profession* (Perspectives, 1989), commonly referred to as "the Big-8 White Paper." Both of these reports advocated more emphasis on developing students' problem-solving and communication skills. The AECC's formation resulted from funding provided by the Big-8 accounting firms. It was intended to encourage the changes in accounting education called for by the Bedford committee and by the Big-8 White Paper.

The AECC's first position statement (1990) focused primarily on the educational objectives for accounting majors (versus non-accounting majors who must take introductory accounting), but it did note that:

> The introductory accounting course should be given special attention. It must serve the interest of students who are not going to enter the profession as well as those who are. The broad approach recommended in these objectives serves the interests and needs of both groups (p. 3).

This broad approach emphasized teaching students to learn on their own, using unstructured problems that require multiple sources of information, and using technology, among others.

The AECC devoted their second position statement (1992) entirely to the introductory accounting course, which it noted is actually two courses at most schools. Their recommendations for the first course in accounting are summarized below. They believed that students should:

- Have a broad view of accounting's role in satisfying society's need for information . . .
- Understand the basic features of accounting and reporting . . .
- Understand fundamental accounting concepts in addition to the elements of financial statements . . .
- Possess enhanced analytical skills and the ability to confront unstructured problems . . .
- Gain an appreciation that accounting as a discipline is the focus of constructive debate and intensive rethinking . . .

The committee stated that the first course ". . . should be a rigorous course focusing on the relevance of accounting information to decision making (use) as well as its source (preparation)" (p. 2).

Others also concluded that a revamped introductory accounting course could better meet the needs of accounting majors and non-majors alike. Baldwin and Ingram (1991) argued that introductory accounting should be viewed as the ". . . last accounting course in the business major" rather than the ". . . *first course in the accounting major*" (italics original). They further concluded that ". . . the needs of the 80% [non-accounting majors] are more relevant than the needs of the 20% [accounting majors] . . ." (p. 4).

Baldwin and Ingram, like the authors of the Big-8 White Paper, expressed concern over the decline in the number of accounting majors. They believed that the traditional structure of introductory accounting might be part of the reason for the decline. Cohen and Hanno (1993) examined this view empirically. They concluded that "... a traditional quantitative and rules-based approach will perpetuate and foster a parochial view of accounting, while inhibiting the desired increased emphasis on people skills and communication skills" (pp. 235–236).

Beyond simply not attracting a sufficient number of majors to accounting to meet the needs of the profession, a greater concern may be that the traditional structure of introductory accounting is discouraging the best students from majoring in accounting. Adams et al. (1994) found that, based on grades received in the first accounting course, the top 25% of those who chose not to major in accounting received higher grades in the course than those who did major in accounting. They concluded that "... presenting accounting as an interesting and vital profession throughout the curriculum might be an effective retention strategy for high-aptitude students" (p. 57).

The faculty in most accounting departments probably have discussed the importance of balancing the needs of accounting majors and non-accounting majors in introductory accounting. Some faculty believe that a "users" approach will put accounting majors at a disadvantage in intermediate accounting, but accounting majors typically represent as little ten percent of the students in the class (Adams et al., 1994). Recall that both the AECC, in *Position Statement No. 1,* and Baldwin and Ingram (1991) contended that the needs of accounting majors and non-majors are the same for the first accounting course. Bernardi and Bean (1999) investigated this hypothesis and found that students who took a preparer-oriented introductory course did not perform better in intermediate accounting courses than other students who took a user-oriented course.

As discussed above, the AECC and others have advocated that introductory accounting should be changed to include a more user-oriented focus. While the Bernardi and Bean study does not prove that a user's focus is best, it does suggest that it does not harm those who chose accounting as a major. Therefore, we might attract more and better students into accounting if the first course has more of a user's orientation without reducing their success in the upper-level accounting courses.

LITERATURE REVIEW

Many have proposed ways to accomplish some or all of the recommendations in AECC Position Statement No. 2. Table 1 identifies studies that addressed various recommendations made by the AECC regarding the first course in accounting.

Table 1. Studies Addressing AECC Recommendations.

AECC Recommendation	Studies
Broad view of accounting's role in society	Basu & Cohen, 1994
	Saudagaran, 1996
	Abdolmohammadi, 1998
	DeBerg. Adams & Lea, 1998
	Bernardi & Bean, 1999
Understanding basic features of accounting and reporting	All studies cited
Understanding accounting concepts	Edmonds & Edmonds, 1994
Possesses skills to confront unstructured problems	Ainsworth, 1994
	Basu & Cohen, 1994
	Knechel & Rand, 1994
	Rankine & Stice, 1994
	Saudagaran, 1996
	Abdolmohammadi, 1998
	DeBerg. Adams & Lea, 1998

These proposals typically have as one objective the enhancement of students' critical thinking skills. Interestingly, neither AECC *Position Statement No. 1* nor No. 2 used the phrase "critical thinking." However, many of the skills and teaching techniques these statements did call for, such as being able to solve unstructured problems, certainly relate to critical thinking skills. Cunningham (1996, pp. 58–59) described several specific ways students' critical thinking skills can be enhanced. These include: using Socratic discussion, having students analyze articles, having students work in groups, using research projects, and using role-playing.

Most of the recommended changes for introductory accounting have included one or more of the activities mentioned above. Table 2 shows studies that used one or more of the pedagogues for improving these critical thinking skills.

The studies referenced in Tables 1 and 2 are summarized briefly in the following paragraphs. However, several articles described multiple pedagogues the authors used in their respective introductory accounting classes.

Rankine and Stice (1994) suggested ways to incorporate articles from the popular press into introductory accounting classes. They emphasized that students should receive specific questions to answer regarding the articles that are assigned.

Knechel and Rand (1994) proposed a teaching technique that might be classified as a role-playing simulation as a way of achieving some of the objectives stated in the AECC's *Position Statement No. 1.* Extending a method proposed previously by one of the authors (Knechel, 1989), they had three classes use the board game of Monopoly to simulate operating a business (playing the role

Table 2. Studies That Examine Various Pedagogical Techniques That Improve Critical Thinking Skills.

Technique	Studies
Socratic discussion	DeBerg. Adams & Lea, 1998
Analyzing articles	Rankine & Stice, 1994
	Saudagaran, 1996
	Abdolmohammadi, 1998
Working in groups	Ainsworth, 1994
	Basu & Cohen, 1994
	Edmonds & Edmonds, 1994
	Saudagaran, 1996
	Cermignano et al., 1998
	Bernardi & Bean, 1999
Research projects	Ainsworth, 1994
	Basu & Cohen, 1994
	Saudagaran, 1996
	Abdolmohammadi, 1998
Role playing	Ainsworth, 1994
	Knechel & Rand, 1994
	DeBerg. Adams & Lea, 1998

of managers) while students in two other classes completed a traditional practice set. Their project also involved group work.

Basu and Cohen (1994) used a research project that required students to work in groups to analyze a publicly traded company. This assignment went beyond simply analyzing the company's annual report by requiring them to use library and database information as a part of their research.

Edmonds and Edmonds (1994) describe a teaching approach they use to focus students' learning on understanding accounting concepts, one of the recommendations of the AECC. Their suggestions centered mostly on restructuring the delivery of course content with strategies such as "progressive differentiation," and "integrative reconciliation." They implemented these strategies, in part, by having students work in groups.

Some use rather unusual approaches to stimulate students. For example, Cermignano et al. (1998) use variations of popular television game shows to keep students interested. These games, are called "Accounting Jeopardy," The Accounting Pyramid," and "The Accounting Feud."

Some schools have sought to completely restructure their introductory accounting courses. Kansas State University changed from one course of financial accounting and one of managerial accounting to an approach that integrated financial and managerial accounting throughout both courses (Ainsworth, 1994).

The pedagogy for these courses included group work, written assignments, and cases.

Santa Clara University, which is on the quarter system, has a three-course sequence for introductory accounting. The first of these courses uses a research project, business articles, and cases in an effort to develop students' critical thinking skills, communication skills, ability to work in groups, and their ability to learn on their own. (Saudagaran, 1996)

Abdolmohammadi et al. (1998) described a revised introduction to accounting course offered at Bentley college. This course sought to accomplish many of the AECC's recommendations by using cases, unstructured problems, computers, written and oral assignments, group work, and research projects. To accomplish this, they reduced the size of the classes from 140 students to 25 to 40 students, with 25 being the ideal.

DeBerg et al. (1998) explained how the faculty at California State University, Chico restructured the introduction to accounting course to accomplish three objectives: (1) "... introduce accounting students to decision-making processes involving financial data, (2) bring about *accounting literacy,* and (3) develop students' *problem-solving* skills" (p. 163). The revised course incorporates cases, group work, unstructured problems, simulations, and extensively uses personal computer applications. However, special training of the faculty was necessary to implement these pedagogues, and "... would have been impossible without substantial, external funding, along with the support of an administration that encourages experimentation and collaboration" (p. 179)

While the revised introductory accounting course described by DeBerg et al. (1998) used a Socratic approach as one of many changes to the way the course had been taught previously, readers seeking a more comprehensive Socratic approach should read Hoyle (1996). He describes a comprehensive Socratic methodology that he uses in his intermediate accounting classes. However, his method would certainly work in introductory accounting as well.

MOTIVATION FOR THIS PROJECT

There are a variety of ways to address the AECC's concerns. One potential drawback is the significant increase in the instructor's effort that they require. Many instructors need formal training to use some of the proposed methods effectively, and most of the approaches increase significantly the time spent grading. Cunningham (1996) noted that "Grading may be more difficult and time consuming in a course emphasizing creative and critical thinking than it is in a traditional course" (p. 64). The research project used by Basu and Cohen

(1994) took students an average of about 25 hours to complete. Grading a project of this complexity takes considerable time.

The discussion above demonstrates that many accounting instructors have used various strategies to implement the recommendations of the AECC. While effective in the view of the instructors who used them, several of these approaches require considerable time and/or resources. The experimental course described below seeks to address some of the concerns raised by the AECC in a way that is effective and efficient.

THE EXPERIMENTAL COURSE

In the spring of 1997, the committee on financial accounting at a major midwestern university was discussing various approaches to the introductory accounting course. With some of the AECC's ideas still fresh, one of the authors volunteered to teach a course that stressed business applications and the use of accounting information as opposed to the traditional emphasis on the generation and reporting of financial data.

The course was an experimental offering of introductory accounting during the 1997 fall semester. Each class period was divided into three parts: (1) a traditional presentation of accounting, (2) a discussion of the *Wall Street Journal* (*WSJ*), and (3) the use of the Internet. There was no formal textbook used. The objective of the approach was to demonstrate the application of accounting in its natural business environment and to emphasize its relevance to the user of accounting information. The basic plan was to incorporate the most beneficial aspects of this course into the regular course during the following year.

ADVANTAGES OF THE MULTIMEDIA APPROACH

We used the *WSJ* and the Internet materials as a complement to the traditional methods of presenting accounting topics. They did not require the use of separate skills or knowledge. The use of these materials required very little additional grading because they were always related to the topics being studied in class (marketable securities, debt, dividends, etc.). When we conducted formal assessment of the *WSJ* and Internet materials, it consisted of questions included on the regular exams given throughout the course.

A broad approach such as this points out to students that the business core is really integrated. Working students particularly enjoyed the practical approach taken in the course and reported that they shared some of the class assignments with their colleagues.

THE MULTIMEDIA APPROACH

The basic materials used in the course follow:

(1) Anthony, R. N., (1996). *Essentials of Accounting, 6th Edition*, Addison-Wesley
(2) Anthony, R. N., (1996). *A Review of Essentials of Accounting, 6th Edition*, Addison-Wesley
(3) Morris, K. M., & Siegal, A. M., (1993), *The Wall Street Journal Guide to Understanding Money & Investing*, Lightbulb Press
(4) *The Wall Street Journal*
(5) The Internet

Essentials of Accounting, 6th Edition, a self-study program manual provided the basic background information for the traditional accounting part of the course. *WSJ Guide to Understanding Money & Investing* helped students learn to read and study the option markets, currency markets, bond markets, index markets, foreign stock markets, interest rate markets, and mutual funds. The *WSJ* part of the course emphasized such things as finding market values and following the performance of various companies that are listed on the New York, American and NASDAQ stock exchanges. We also regularly discussed major articles concerning current accounting and business issues, such as the derivatives controversy relative to the FASB. The Internet part of the course focused both on making students aware of various accounting and business sites and on the richness and diversity of the information available there. Table 3 provides a detailed list of the topics covered in the course and indicates whether the *WSJ* or the Internet was used to cover a given topic.

We hoped that exposure to the diverse *WSJ* articles and Internet sites would improve the students' reading comprehension and expand their business vocabularies. The use of these media provided students with the opportunity to enhance these skills by exposing them to business terminology within the context of actual business transactions, exchanges, and perspectives. The *WSJ* and Internet assignments helped students integrate and apply their book learning. Students read articles with new terms such as derivatives, debt and equity financing, mergers and acquisitions, initial public offerings, etc., in which actual corporations were participants. In addition, they were given the opportunity to create their own views of the subjects studied and to share their views with others. From our perspective, this background helped students obtain a better understanding of the environment within which the choices that underlie financial reporting must be made.

Table 3. Topics Covered in the Experimental Course.

	Teaching Methods Used	
	WSJ	Internet
Topics Covered		
Accounts Receivable		
Notes Receivable		
Factoring		X
Cash and Cash Equivalents	X	X
Bank Reconciliation		
Electronic Funds Transfer		X
Securities	X	X
Inventory		X
Non-current Assets		X
Depreciation		X
Liabilities and Equity	X	X
Stockholders' Equity	X	X
Statement of Cash Flows		X
Analysis of Financial Statements	X	X
Balance Sheets		X
Income Statements	X	X
Statement of Stockholders' Equity		X
International Markets and Foreign Currency	X	X
Equity and Index Options	X	
Corporate Dividend News	X	
Money Rates	X	
Futures Prices	X	
Mutual Funds	X	

GETTING STARTED

This experiment included two sections of introductory accounting (out of eight). A third section was added later because of a change in instructors. The students were aware that these sections were going to be different from the other introductory accounting sections because of the difference in assigned materials and because of a notice that all students enrolled in those sections would be required to subscribe to the *WSJ* for fifteen weeks. Approximately 70% of the students enrolled in the courses were non-accounting majors, mostly sophomores. Both part-time and full-time students were in the classes, and their average age was about 23.

On the first day of class, students were informed of the experimental nature of the course. The objective would be to cover the same material that was covered in the other sections, but in a different way. Each class session lasted for 75 minutes. The classrooms contained multimedia equipment with access to the Internet. A course web page with syllabus, assignments, web links, and announcement sections was posted on the Internet.

USING THE *WALL STREET JOURNAL* IN CLASS

We regularly posted notices in the announcement section of the class web page identifying *WSJ* articles and items of interest that the students needed to read and be prepared to discuss in class.

The major focus of our attention with respect to the *WSJ* was on the Money and Investing (Sect. C) portion of the paper. Specifically, the goal was to make the students aware of the various types of accounting and business information available there and to teach them how to read and understand the tables and the quotes. In the first five weeks, we examined the first 10–12 pages of Section C of the *WSJ*. This coverage included examining the stock quotes and market values on the major stock exchanges, introducing the Dow Jones Averages and the component organizations that make up those averages, reviewing the Market Diary and the Stock Market Data Bank.

After everyone began receiving the *WSJ*, usually about the second week of class, we told the students to bring it to each class meeting. As a general rule, they were to bring the prior day's issue to class. On the first day we looked at the general layout of the *WSJ*, examined how it was organized and reviewed the information contained in the different sections. The following days we went directly to Sect. C and discussed the information on stocks, international stocks, bonds, interest, currency prices, and commodities prices that are provided in the Markets Diary (p. 1) and on the major indexes, most active issues, diaries, price percentage gainers and losers, and volume percentage leaders provided in the Stock Market Data Bank (usually p. 2). In addition, we identified and discussed the names and types of articles and the columns on the first two pages of Sect. C (Daily Market, Abreast of the Market, Heard on the Street, etc.).

During the next class, we looked at the Dow Jones Averages (p. 3) and the stocks that comprise those averages. We then examined the explanatory notes and footnotes provided below the averages. Finally, we selected several well-known corporations, such as Boeing, General Electric and Berkshire Hathaway (this stock always generates student interest because of its huge price per share), which are listed on the New York Stock Exchange. We discussed the meaning of the numbers and stock market valuations listed in the table by using the headings at the top of the column. These headings include 52 Weeks Hi and

Lo, Stock, Symbol, dividend, yield percent, PE, volume of trades in 100 share lots and the Hi, Low and Close of the stock for that particular day.

On subsequent days, we used the *WSJ Guide to Understanding Money and Investing* in conjunction with Sect. C of the *WSJ* to help students understand the remaining tables (World Stock Markets, Treasury Bonds, Notes & Bills, Foreign Exchange, Listed Options Quotations, etc.). Again, the emphasis was on data availability and on the use of the information in reporting market values, etc. We did not expect students to be experts on interpreting a given table at the end of the course.

We usually started coverage of the tables in the *WSJ* by giving a lecture that emphasized how the data in a particular table related to a current accounting or business problem. For example, stock tables gave the market values for marketable securities on the balance sheet. Option tables gave an introduction to derivatives and the market value used for valuing puts and calls.

In addition, as we found articles of interest in the *WSJ*, we would notify students through the class web page and/or in class that they should be prepared to discuss those articles at the next class meeting. At that class meeting, we would ask students to answer specific questions about the article. The following are examples:

(1) What is the accounting or business issue involved?
(2) What are some possible solutions?
(3) How does this issue relate to what we have studied previously or are studying currently in class?

We usually directed the questions to the class as a whole and volunteers responded. Occasionally, we asked individual students to answer the questions or formed discussion groups where a spokesperson would give the answer that the group had chosen. Peer pressure, general interest in the subject matter, and the possibility of being called on in class motivated the students to complete the *WSJ* and Internet assignments. Students were also motivated by the fact that the information they learned in this class could be used in their other business courses (particularly finance and economics) and for class projects.

This multimedia approach creates an environment that is conducive to learning, because it involves searching for new and relevant experiences in a changing business world. Students quickly see that accounting takes place in an economic, financial and political context, and that it does not exist in a vacuum separated from outside influences and distractions. It also makes everyone aware that GAAP is not perfect.

Using the *WSJ* to examine world stock markets, foreign currency markets, and foreign corporations being traded in the United States helps to impress students with the international nature of accounting problems. Seeing the data in the *WSJ* currency trading and currency cross rate tables makes the accounting for foreign currency transactions and translations much more meaningful.

Instructors wishing to integrate ethics into their introductory accounting classes can also benefit from the multimedia approach. Instructors can demonstrate the ethical dilemmas of business decisions easily through numerous *WSJ* articles on fraud and bankruptcy. Additionally, SEC actions requiring companies to restate earnings, and fining accountants, stockbrokers, or management demonstrate the consequences of unethical behavior.

During the final three weeks of the course, topics covered in the *WSJ* were the Listed Options Quotations (puts and calls), Index Options Trading, Futures Prices, Futures Options Prices, Commodities, Cash Prices and Mutual Fund Quotations. After examining these tables in general, we selected an item in each one for further examination. Students learned about the different types of financial instruments and how to read the quotes in the table related to that instrument. The class discussed almost every table in the Money and Investing section of the *WSJ* by the end of the course.

USING THE INTERNET IN CLASS

The specific purpose of using the Internet was to familiarize students with a convenient, contemporary source of real world financial information. The information from the Internet helped us accomplish the bigger objective of teaching students about the role of accounting in the business environment.

Because using the Internet was just one of many aspects of the revised course, most of the assignments were exploratory in nature and the time necessary to obtain the required information was relatively short. The following were the most beneficial Internet sites. Although Internet sites often disappear, most of these sites are associated with major organizations, and should be relevant for the foreseeable future. (Except for quote.yahoo.com, each begins with www.):

fasb.org	sec.gov	aicpa.org
iasc.org.uk	irs.gov	nasdaq.org
yahoo.com	checker-llp.com/cashman.htm	nyse.com
amex.com	bonds-online.com	quote.yahoo.com
toysrus.com	xe.net/currency	mcdonalds.com
disney.com	microsoft.com	

For instance, we assigned the FASB page and asked the class to find the number of FASB members, to identify two current issues or projects, and to discover the subject matter covered in Statements 115, 121, and 125. We also assigned the SEC page and asked the class to use EDGAR to find an item, such as the amount of cash or inventory, on the latest 10Q or 10K of a major company such as Boeing or General Electric.

The first Internet assignments dealt with accounting organizations and the availability of information at those sites. For instance, we visited the home-pages of the FASB, SEC, AICPA, IASC, and the IRS. We asked students to determine the basic mission of these organizations, their structure, the name of their associated standards (if applicable) and the type of information available at that site.

The next set of Internet assignments related to the topic being discussed in class. For example, the discussion of marketable securities and derivatives included visits to the websites of the NYSE, AMEX, and NASDAQ. Also, we visited the SEC's website to examine companies' 10K and 10Q reports. The "education" and "market regulation" sections, among others, of the NYSE web site and the "site map" and "equity & index options" sections of the NASDAQ web site contain interesting and useful information.

Students selected several companies on each exchange and followed them for several weeks. They obtained stock quotes from the Internet in order to determine the market value of securities for the companies selected. These sources also provided other relevant information about the companies.

We covered other topics similarly. For example, the class visited a factoring Internet site during the discussion of accounts receivable. We also demonstrated FIFO, LIFO, and average cost methods of accounting for inventories. Then we examined the balance sheet and notes of Toys-R-Us on the Internet in class since that corporation used both the FIFO and LIFO methods.

We examined specific liabilities on the Internet using Toys-R-Us. Students encountered debt denominated in foreign currency, debt with different interest rates, off-balance sheet leases and terms such as LIBOR. In class we visited an online bond site that gave quotes and information on corporate bonds, treasuries and zero coupons [bonds-online.com].

Next we discussed common stock, preferred stock, dividends and the cash flow statement in general. Then, we examined those topics using the annual report of Toys-R-Us on the Internet.

During the last three weeks of the course, the class analyzed the financial statements of Toys-R-Us, Microsoft, and McDonalds on the Internet. The goal was to enhance students' critical thinking skills. We developed and gave a simple questionnaire to the students. This questionnaire covered topics related to the companies' inventory methods, depreciation methods, types of fixed assets and related lives, the amount of off-balance sheet leases, the amount of debt denominated in foreign currencies, par values of stock and dividends paid. The class calculated various financial ratios in answering the questions. We assigned these questionnaires before we discussed them in class. All students answered the same questions. The questions for each company were slightly different, depending on unique aspects of the company.

During class, we divided the students into groups and assigned questions to each group. The members of each group were to agree on the answers. Once they agreed, a rotating spokesperson gave the group's answer, and stated where in the annual report they found it. If an answer was difficult to find or was controversial, we would look for the answer on the Internet during class. We discussed each company individually, compared them, and discussed possible reasons for differences between them.

WSJ AND INTERNET INTERACTION

We designed the *WSJ* and Internet coverage to reinforce the traditional accounting. For instance, when we examined areas in the *WSJ*, such as the Corporate Dividend News and the Digest of Earnings Reports, we asked students to find the date of declaration, the date of record, and the date of payments of various companies' dividends. We also asked them to interpret the meaning of the term ex-dividend. Students picked one of the companies with dividend information in the *WSJ* and compared that information with the news release distributed on the Internet.

Similarly, we used the *WSJ* Digest of Earnings to find the way companies report discontinued operations, extraordinary items and accounting adjustments. We also looked for restructurings, write-offs, stock splits and stock dividends. Again, we selected one corporation, and students compared the information available in the *WSJ* to that found on the Internet.

The class examined and discussed the World Stock Markets and associated Dow Jones Global Indexes, Foreign Markets and Foreign Stock Market Indexes as shown in the *WSJ*. Students also analyzed the Foreign Exchange column, the Currency Trading section and the Key Currency Cross Rates. They learned the currencies of major nations and the necessity of foreign currency transactions and translations. We also taught the foreign currency topic using annual reports posted on the Internet, which show that many companies have subsidiaries and stores all over the world, that their debt is payable in foreign currencies, and that they have to translate foreign currency amounts into dollars. Finally, we demonstrated the ability to follow foreign markets and their stock market indexes on the Internet. We also visited web sites for foreign currency conversion [xe.net/ucc/]. The timing of this aspect was very good since the

Asian economic problems started becoming significant in October 1997, and the students' interest in this subject was very high.

COURSE ORGANIZATION

The original intent of the course was to spend an equal portion of each class session (about 25 minutes) on each of the three parts of the course (traditional accounting, use of the *WSJ* and use of the Internet). After getting started, we found that most of the students did not have the accounting background to get as much out of the *WSJ* and the Internet as we had desired. Thus, we made a change to put more emphasis on the essentials of accounting and relevant terminology at the beginning of the course. During the first five weeks of the semester, the class spent about 55 minutes of each session on accounting concepts and only about 10 minutes on each of the other two areas.

In the second part of the course, we reduced the time spent on the essentials of accounting since we had already covered the majority of the Anthony primer. The time spent in each class session on each of the three parts of the course was about equal. Using the basic information available in the primer, the topics discussed included cash and cash equivalents, bank reconciliations, marketable securities, accounts receivable, notes receivable, bad debts, inventory, fixed assets, depreciation, intangible assets, and amortization.

In the third part of the course, we examined the liability and equity sections of the balance sheet along with the statement of cash flows. We started by introducing current liabilities and long-term liabilities in general. Then we introduced present value concepts. In conjunction with the *Guide to Understanding Money and Investing*, we used the *WSJ* to read quotes from the Treasury Bonds, Notes & Bills, New York Exchange Bonds, Amex Bonds, Government Agency & Similar Issues, Money Rates and Credit Markets sections.

The final part of the course dealt with analysis of the Internet financial statements of selected corporations. This part addressed issues such as consolidations, foreign currency, ratios, etc.

PROBLEMS ASSOCIATED WITH THE MULTIMEDIA APPROACH

Internet sites are constantly being added, deleted, and changed. When teaching multiple sections on different days, the *WSJ* quotes, rates, etc. change, and they must be re-examined every day before class. It is necessary to find new examples.

An instructor must be flexible. The authoritarian role of the instructor is diminished because we cover material for which the instructor may not have expert knowledge. For example, instructors may have no personal experience with Treasuries, future contracts or options. On the other hand, getting involved with unknown areas can serve as an example to the student that acquiring knowledge (even for the instructor) is the purpose of education.

Students were exposed to a lot of new information that, in some cases, was probably overwhelming. They continually wanted to limit the scope of the exams and then to do only what was testable. To some extent this attitude was understandable, and we did specify the scope of each exam. Several students also mentioned their desire for a textbook to use for background information.

ASSESSMENT

The first exam was very similar to the first exam used with the traditional approach the previous year, except for a matching question based on Internet information about the accounting organizations. The emphasis of this exam was on the basic accounting model.

On three later tests, questions concerning the Internet and the *WSJ* materials were on a basic or introductory level. For example, one matching question required students to match nations with their currencies. We also used multiple-choice questions that required students to know the definition of a put or call. Questions related to traditional accounting concepts were similar to those we used in prior introductory accounting classes.

The committee on financial accounting at the University that experimented with this course decided to use both the *WSJ* and the Internet as supplemental material in subsequent introductory courses. Today, the *WSJ* portion covers basic markets (NYSE, AMEX, NASDAQ, Foreign Currencies) and quotations. Instructors assign relevant accounting or related articles as they appear. Also, the *WSJ* is now being used in some sections of the second semester of introductory accounting (managerial accounting). The Internet portion emphasizes organizations (SEC, FASB, IASC, AICPA, etc.) at the beginning of the course. Students then use the Internet to analyze one or more sets of financial statements toward the end of the course. Individual instructors can expand on these areas if they desire and if it is relevant to the topics being covered. We now use a text that emphasizes the basic accounting concepts and the use of accounting information (*Using Financial Accounting: An Introduction*, by Murray, Newman & Elgers, 1997).

CONCLUSION

The AECC has established several objectives that it believes introductory accounting should achieve. In the "real-world of accounting academe," it is doubtful a single course can accomplish all of the AECC's objectives, but the challenge is to accomplish as many as is reasonably possible. The purpose of this multimedia experimental course was to emphasize to business students that accounting takes place within a challenging and changing environment, and that it is important to understand that environment. A related objective was an attempt to improve reading comprehension and to expand the students' vocabulary. To accomplish these objectives, this course integrated current *WSJ* articles, Internet assignments, financial statement analysis, and group work into introductory accounting. It focused on real world tools to demonstrate the relevance and applicability of accounting to the students.

We believe the course accomplished its objectives and also emphasized to the student that introductory accounting is relevant and that it can be used in the real world. We also believe instructors at other schools can implement the pedagogues used in this course with reasonable ease, even if those instructors teach large classes.

REFERENCES

Abdolmohammadi, M. J. et al. (1998). Designing and implementing an AECC complying introductory accounting course: a four-year perspective. *Advances in Accounting Education, 1*, 147–162.

Accounting Education Change Commission (1990). *Position Statement No. 1: Objectives of Education for Accountants*. Torrance, CA: Accounting Education Commission.

Accounting Education Change Commission (1990). AECC urges priority for teaching in higher education. *Issues in Accounting Education*, *5*(2), 330–331.

Accounting Education Change Commission (1992). *Position Statement No. 2: The First Course in Accounting*. Torrance, CA: Accounting Education Commission.

Adams, J. A., Pryor, L. J., & Adams, S. L. (1994). Attraction and retention of high-aptitude students in accounting: An exploratory study. *Issues in Accounting Education*, *9*(1), 45–58.

Ainsworth, P. L., & Plumlee, D. R. (1993). Restructuring the accounting curriculum content sequence: the KSU experience. *Issues in Accounting Education*, *8*(1), 112–127.

Ainsworth, P. L. (1994). Restructuring the introductory accounting course: The Kansas State University experience. *Journal of Accounting Education*, *12*(4), 305–323.

American Accounting Association, Committee on the Future Structure, Content, and Scope of Accounting Education (1986). Future accounting education: Preparing for the expanding profession. *Issues in Accounting Education*, *1*, 168–195.

Anthony, R. N. (1996). *Essentials of Accounting* (6th ed.). Addison-Wesley.

Anthony, R. N. (1996). *A Review of Essentials of Accounting* (6th ed.). Addison-Wesley.

Baldwin, B. A., & Ingram, R. W. (1991). Rethinking the objectives and content of elementary accounting. *Journal of Accounting Education, 9*, 1–14.

Baldwin, B. A. (1993). Teaching introductory financial accounting in mass-lecture sections: Longitudinal evidence. *Issues in Accounting Education, 8*(1), 97–111.

Basu, P., & Cohen, J. (1994). Learning to learn in the accounting principles course: Outcome assessment of an integrative business analysis project. *Journal of Accounting Education, 12*(4), 359–374.

Bernardi, R. A., & Bean, D. F. (1999). Preparer versus user introductory sequence: the impact on performance in Intermediate Accounting I. *Journal of Accounting Education, 17*, 141–156.

Cermignano, G. P., Hargadon, J. M., & McMullen, D. A. (1998). The "games accounting professors play": Communicating with generation x. *Advances in Accounting Education, 1*, 133–146.

Cohen, J., & Hanno, D. M. (1993). An analysis of underlying constructs affecting the choice of accounting as a major. *Issues in Accounting Education, 8*(2), 219–238.

Cunningham, B. M. (1996). How to restructure an accounting course to enhance creative and critical thinking. *Accounting Education, 1*(1), 49–66.

DeBerg, C. L., Adams, S. J., & Lea, R. B. (1998). Curricular revision starting at ground zero: the case of introductory accounting. *Advances in Accounting Education, 1*, 163–188.

Edmonds, C. D., & Edmonds, T. P. (1994). A concepts approach to teaching the first course in accounting. *Advances in Accounting, 12*, 123–142.

Hill, M. C. (1998). Class size and student performance in introductory accounting courses: further evidence. *Issues in Accounting Education, 13*(1), 47–64.

Hoyle, J. (1996). Using the Socratic method to teach a traditionally lecture-based class. *Accounting Education, 1*(1), 37–47.

Knechel, R. W., & Rand, R. S. (1994). Will the AECC's course delivery recommendations work in the introductory accounting course? Some preliminary evidence. *Journal of Accounting Education, 12*(3), 175–191.

Knechel, R. W. (1989). Using a business simulation game as a substitute for a practice set. *Issues in Accounting Education, 4*(2), 411–424.

Murray, D., Neumann, B. R., & Elgers, P. (1997). *Using Financial Accounting: An Introduction.* Cincinnati, OH: South-Western College Publishing.

Morris, K. M., & Siegal, A. M. (1993). *The Wall Street Journal Guide to Understanding Money & Investing.* Lightbulb Press.

Needles, B. E., & Powers, M. (1990). A comparative study of models for accounting education. *Issues in Accounting Education, 5*(2), 250–267.

Perspectives on Education: *Capabilities for Success in the Accounting Profession* (1989). New York: Arthur Andersen & Co., Arthur Young, Coopers & Lybrand, Deloitte Haskins & Sells, Ernst & Whinney, Peat Marwick Main & Co., Price Waterhouse, and Touche Ross.

Rankine, R., & Stice, E. K. (1994). Using articles from the popular press in the introductory accounting course. *Issues in Accounting Education, 9*(1), 142–150.

Saudagaran, S. M. (1996). The first course in accounting: An innovative approach. *Issues in Accounting Education, 11*(1), 83–94.

Smith, J. M., & Usry, M. F. (1989). Changes in accounting education. *Journal of Accounting Education, 8*, 1–7.

DEVELOPING INTERMEDIATE ACCOUNTING STUDENTS' ANALYTICAL AND COMMUNICATION SKILLS THROUGH THE ANNUAL REPORT PROJECT

Mary York Christ

ABSTRACT

This paper describes a course project developed for the Intermediate Accounting sequence. The Annual Report Project in an unstructured assignment that requires drawing information from different sections of a company's annual report and 10K. Essentially, students recreate, in summary form, all the entries that were made by the company in the most recent year. They must draw the information from the balance sheet, income statement, statement of cash flows, footnotes, and 10K. In many instances, students must make logical assumptions where adequate data are not available.

The project is intended to develop students' analytical, problem solving, and communication skills while solidifying their understanding of Intermediate Accounting topics. The instructor may base a large portion of the grade on how well the students present and explain their data. This approach stresses the analytical and communication aspects of the assignment. An appendix includes an example Annual Report Project assignment.

Advances in Accounting Education, Volume 4, pages 41–57.

ISBN: 0-7623-0856-7

INTRODUCTION

In recent years, accounting educators have focused increased attention on identifying skills that accounting graduates need to succeed in today's workplace and on how best to develop those skills. Publications from a variety of sources have delineated a fairly consistent list of desired skills (AICPA, 1999; AECC, 1990; Arthur Andersen et al., 1989; AAA, 1986). Virtually every such list includes analytical thinking, problem solving, and communication skills. The Accounting Education Change Commission (AECC) Position Statement No. 1 (1990, p. 310) also states:

> Students must be active participants in the learning process, not passive recipients of information. They should identify and solve unstructured problems that require the use of multiple information sources. Learning by doing should be emphasized.

The purpose of this paper is to describe a course project I developed for the Intermediate Accounting sequence. The Annual Report Project is an unstructured assignment that requires drawing information from different sections of a company's annual report and 10K. It is intended to develop students' analytical, problem solving, and communication skills while solidifying their understanding of Intermediate Accounting topics. The next section summarizes literature and materials related to annual report usage in the accounting curriculum. The objectives of the Annual Report Project are then described, followed by a detailed discussion of the project requirements. A discussion of grading issues and student reactions to the project follow in the next section. An appendix presents an example of the Annual Report Project assignment.

ANNUAL REPORT USAGE IN THE ACCOUNTING CURRICULUM

Previous Literature

For many years, educators have recognized that incorporating real company annual reports into the accounting curriculum can add relevancy to the material and help develop student skills.

Harkins and Mills (1985, pp. 150–152) argue that Intermediate Accounting textbooks do not adequately make the link between the accounting process and financial reporting. Consequently, students do not develop an adequate appreciation for the aggregation and terminology found in annual reports or the significance of annual report disclosures. They (Harkins & Mills 1985, pp. 155–157) describe three alternative approaches for introducing annual reports into Intermediate Accounting. Each approach involves using annual report examples and integrating them with discussions of textbook material throughout the course.

Amernic and Elitzur (1992, pp. 31–36) take a different approach to integrating annual reports into Intermediate Accounting. They use historical reports to illustrate the evolving nature of accounting standards and to stress how corporate accountability responds to changing legal, social, and economic environments. Specifically, students use a 1925 and a 1990 annual report of the same company, identify differences, and speculate on the reasons for the differences. Secondly, students use 1924 and 1925 annual reports and construct a cash-flow statement for the company.

Pasewark (1997, p. 80) maintains that there are three reasons to use annual reports in the accounting curriculum. First, he agrees with Harkins and Mills (1985, pp. 150–152) that students do not recognize the difference between the accounting process and the reporting and disclosure process. Second, use of annual reports provides students with opportunities to see how financial statement information is used in business decisions. Third, annual reports can enhance topic areas that are difficult to cover in a textbook. Pasewark (1997, pp. 81–84) then discusses a variety of ways to integrate annual reports into Intermediate Accounting. These include using textbooks that incorporate annual reports, bringing annual reports into the classroom for illustration, annual report practice sets, examination and quiz questions based on real annual report information, and financial database projects.

Finally, international companies provide another opportunity for integrating annual reports into the curriculum. As a means of comparing U.S. accounting rules to those of other countries, international annual reports may be used throughout upper-level accounting courses or during a focussed component of one course (Tondkar et al., 1994, 273–275). Within a separate International Accounting course, Bloom and Schirm (2000, 135–142) require that students select a foreign company, study the country and its accounting framework, develop a financial reporting conceptual framework for that country, and use the annual report to prepare a financial statement analysis of the company.

Current Intermediate Accounting Textbooks

The literature cited above is generally critical of Intermediate textbooks for not integrating annual reports into the text and assignment material. Recent editions of texts, however, have responded to these types of criticisms and have added significant material related to real company reports. I reviewed six Intermediate Accounting textbooks to evaluate the level and nature of their usage of annual report information. The texts reviewed were Dyckman, Davis and Dukes (2001); Hartman, Harper, Knoblett and Reckers (2000); Kieso, Weygandt and Warfield (2001); Nikolai and Bazley (2000); Skousen, Stice and Stice (2000); and Spiceland, Sepe and Tomassini (2001).

Each textbook includes recent annual report information for a real company. Spiceland, Sepe and Tomassini (2001) and Hartman, Harper, Knoblett and Reckers (2000) include just the financial statements, footnotes, and the auditors' and management's reports.[1] The other four texts include this information as well as the financial review, selected financial data, management's discussion and analysis, and quarterly data. Additionally, the text web sites for all but Dyckman, Davis and Dukes (2001) include links to company web pages that are used for assignments that are presented either in the text or at the text web site. Kieso, Weygandt and Warfield (2001) also comes with a CD that includes annual reports for more than 20 companies.

All of the textbooks have incorporated extensive excerpts from annual reports as illustrations in almost every chapter. Frequently, these illustrations include examples of footnote disclosures. Furthermore, all of the textbooks have incorporated a variety of end-of-chapter assignments that utilize annual report information. The data for these assignments are obtained in one of three ways: (1) Most chapters of all the texts have a problem that relates to the annual report that is included in the book. (2) Some problems provide excerpted annual report information in the body of the assignment. (3) Some assignments require that the student access annual report information from a company web site. The majority of the assignment material requires the student to find information and then analyze and interpret that information. Sometimes the analysis includes the calculation of ratios. Generally speaking, these assignments are very good at focusing the student on how companies report and use accounting information. A small minority of the text assignments also ask the student to piece together summary entries or to solve for missing information.

Published Annual Report Practice Sets

Published practice sets provide another means of integrating annual reports into the curriculum. Two such practice sets include Baldwin's (1999) The Financial Reporting Project and Readings and Pasewark's (2000) Understanding Annual Reports. While there are differences between these two projects, they are similar to many of the textbook problems just described, only on a much larger scale. The stated purpose of the Baldwin (1999, p. v) project is for the student to experience "live" financial statements and to become familiar with common sources of business and financial information. Pasewark's (2000, p. 1) stated objective is for students to understand and analyze an annual report. Both projects require the student to obtain an annual report, retrieve information from that report, and analyze and interpret that information. They are both quite extensive and include all areas of the financial statements. The Baldwin project also incorporates readings and addresses topics such as the accounting environment and the accounting profession.

OBJECTIVES OF THE ANNUAL REPORT PROJECT

Objective No. 1: Cognitive Development

Bloom's taxonomy (Bloom, 1956) provides a useful framework for considering the cognitive development of accounting students (Brazelton 2000, pp. 72–73). Bloom defined six levels of cognitive development: knowledge (recall and memory), comprehension (use of facts or ideas without relating them), application (remembering information and applying it to specific situations), analysis (taking apart information and identifying relationships), synthesis (using component parts of an idea to develop new ideas), and evaluation (making judgments and selecting among competing alternative solutions). The taxonomy is hierarchical with higher-level skills building on lower-level ones.

Traditional textbook exercises and problems require straightforward recall of definitions and application of rules. These assignments primarily focus on the knowledge, comprehension, and application objectives. While these levels of cognition are important, given the changing nature of the accounting profession, it is also critical that students complete assignments that push them to the higher order levels of cognitive development (Ainsworth & Plumlee, 1993, p. 116; Brazelton, 2000, pp. 69–74).

As discussed above, current Intermediate Accounting textbooks have all incorporated a number of cases that require understanding, interpreting, and using actual financial statement data. Published practice sets involve similar assignments, but on a larger scale. These kinds of problems and projects focus more on the three higher-level objectives of analysis, synthesis, and evaluation (Bonner, 1999,[2] p. 28; Brazelton, 2000, p. 68). The Annual Report Project requires that students work backwards from published financial statement information to recreate summary source entries. While this assignment is quite different from the majority of those in textbooks or published practice sets, it also requires the higher-level skills. Therefore, the first objective of the Annual Report Project is:

> To provide students with an assignment that encourages the development of their analytical and problem-solving skills by requiring the use of analysis, synthesis, and evaluation.

Objective No. 2: Real World Examples

The majority of textbook problems still use information and data developed for the assignment rather than figures taken from real financial statements. As a result, students tend to learn topics with "artificial" illustrations. While this is a good starting point, one unintended outcome may be that students believe topics covered in class are not representative of the "real world." When a course uses actual company financial statements as a basis for problems (whether from the textbook or other sources), students come to recognize that GAAP in practice reflects what is presented in the hypothetical textbook examples. They also learn to bridge the gap from accounting process to financial reporting and are exposed to varying reporting choices (Harkins & Mills, 1985, p. 152). Topics may, in fact, become more relevant and interesting to students the more they are exposed to actual annual report data.

Textbook examples and problems typically use terminology that is straightforward and preferred but may or may not be the terminology used in the financial statements of actual companies. For example, most textbooks use account titles like "Bad Debt Expense" and "Income Tax Expense" whereas many companies use "Provision for Uncollectible Accounts" or "Provision for Income Taxes." Some companies make common use of the term "reserve" and use assorted names for their Retained Earnings account. While these are not major differences, students need to recognize that companies may use a variety of terms to describe the same underlying concept.

As discussed above, Intermediate books now include at least one complete annual report in the text as well as problems or cases that reference real statements. Since these problems tend to be end-of-chapter problems, they focus on a small set of issues or topics. To assist students in seeing the "big picture," it is also important to include assignments that focus on multiple sections of the annual report. Furthermore, as future preparers and users of financial statements, students can benefit from being exposed to a variety of real annual reports. Thus, the second objective of the Annual Report Project is:

> To provide students with detailed exposure to the financial statements of an actual company.

Objective No. 3: Communication Skills

Communication skills are another area where students need to develop proficiency. Effective communication skills consist of a variety of dimensions, including the ability to locate, organize, and use information from a variety of sources and the ability to present and defend views through written language

(AECC, 1990). According to Brazelton (2000, p. 61), the construction of clear, logical arguments requires complete understanding of the material. Consequently, the third objective of the Annual Report Project is:

> To provide students with a major assignment that requires organizing and analyzing information from different sources and presenting their conclusions in a clear and persuasive manner.

ANNUAL REPORT PROJECT REQUIREMENTS

Basic Project Requirements

The basic requirements of the Annual Report Project are to take the financial statements of a real company and recreate entries the company made during the last year related to essentially all of the balance sheet accounts (see example assignment in the Appendix). I exclude accounts not covered in Intermediate Accounting. Typically this omission only leaves out the foreign currency translation adjustment in the stockholders' equity section. In a traditional, two-term Intermediate Accounting sequence, the instructor may assign the project each term and include only the topics from that course. Alternatively, I assign the project in the second Intermediate class, with all topics from both terms included. This latter approach has the advantage of requiring students to recall and use knowledge from a previous class. Additionally, students may begin working on the project at the beginning of the second course rather than waiting until coverage of additional topics.

I have used this project for five years at my current institution, which is a small, private, residential, Midwestern University. Students are full-time, traditional age, and, with rare exception, all students in the Intermediate class are accounting majors. Class size ranges from about 15 to 25 and students complete the assignment individually. I initially assigned the project each semester but for the last three years, I have assigned the Annual Report Project in Intermediate Accounting II only, with all topics from both semesters included. Depending on other projects and course requirements, the Annual Report Project has counted anywhere from 10% to 20% of the course grade. Generally, the project is due during the last two weeks of the semester. For the topics I have included, students can complete the project shortly after we cover Stockholders' Equity. Typically, Intermediate texts have two to three chapters after Stockholders' Equity, which allows adequate time for students to complete the project before the end of the term. The assignment could be submitted in sections. I do not do that because I want the students to assemble the entire project into a polished professional report.

Selecting Companies and Obtaining Annual Reports

I allow students to choose their own company. However, an instructor may prefer to assign companies to the students. When students choose their own company, the instructor should approve the choice to ensure that the selected report includes a sufficient quantity of the topics covered in Intermediate Accounting. For example, companies in a service industry or banking will not have inventory, and some companies do not have leases or long-term debt. Having students select their own company frequently increases their interest level as they choose one that has particular appeal to them (potential employer, hometown company, interesting products, etc.). However, as discussed later, assigning a company can ease the grading burden by having multiple students complete the project using the same annual report. Requiring that the company be publicly traded ensures that a recent 10K is accessible from the SEC EDGAR web site.

Students may obtain copies of the financial statements through a variety of means. They may download the 10K directly from the SEC EDGAR site (http://www.sec.gov/edgar.shtml), with the help of tools for accessing EDGAR (e.g. 10K Wizard, http://www.10kwizard.com), or via a database such as Disclosure. If the instructor wants students to have experience working with actual "glossy" annual reports, they can be ordered free of charge from a variety of web sites (e.g. http://www.annualreportservice.com or http://public.wsj. com/ home.html) or by writing directly to the company. Reports generally arrive in the mail within one to two weeks. Finally, many companies put their complete annual report on their web sites in pdf format. I allow students to use any of these options. If an instructor would like to develop particular skills, he or she might require that a specific approach be used for acquiring the report.

I discuss the project on the first or second day of class and usually require that the students submit their company reports for approval by the third week of class. This time frame has not presented a problem. I tell the students what I am looking for (i.e. inclusion of most of the topics in the assignment in the annual report) and many submit more than one company for approval.

Working Backwards – An Unstructured Exercise

The project is relatively unstructured and requires drawing information from the balance sheet, income statement, statement of cash flows, footnotes, and in some instances, the 10K. Students traditionally work from textbooks, complete some calculations, develop journal entries; and, occasionally, develop footnote disclosures. This project forces them to work backwards from the end product (financial statements and footnotes) and stresses the interrelationships between the various components of the statements – an exercise that requires analysis and synthesis cognitive skills (Brazelton, 2000, p. 68). Arya, Fellingham and Schroeder (2000, p. 395) describe a similar assignment that uses matrix algebra to solve for the journal entries.

My experience has been that even with direction (see Appendix), the volume of information in the annual report and the level of aggregation overwhelm students (Harkins & Mills, 1985, p. 155). In the end, students are frequently amazed at how readily information from each of the statements and the footnotes fits together. They have to struggle to get to this point because they simply are not used to working backwards (Arya, Fellingham & Schroeder, 2000, pp. 394–395). I stress that what I am asking students to do is not something they are likely to do in practice. Rather, the primary purpose of the project is to enhance their understanding of financial statements and their analytical and communication skills.

In many ways, this project complements the trend in Intermediate texts where cases challenge the students to interpret and understand the financial statements. In the Annual Report Project, that increased understanding should aid the student in working backwards from the end product. The following paragraphs illustrate some of the links and analyses students must make to complete the project.

Examples of Issues Addressed in the Assignment

Accounting students may not grasp the purpose or usefulness of the statement of cash flows. Furthermore, some students never understand the significance of cash versus accrual accounting. For this project, the cash flow statement helps students see the cash-accrual link. For example, in analyzing the activity in the property, plant, and equipment accounts, the investing cash flows may identify the acquisition of assets as an outflow as well as inflows from the sale of assets. Students must recognize that the cash inflow probably does not equal the book value of the disposed assets since there may have been sold at a gain or loss. Companies may not disclose depreciation expense separately on the income statement but it probably appears when it is added back in the operating section of an indirect method cash flow statement. The instructor may consider providing guidance to students by suggesting they create t-accounts for the area they are working on and fill in the t-accounts with information from the statements and notes. Missing information is either "plugged" or I make alternative suggestions if too much data are missing.

In some instances, the 10K provides more detailed information than the annual report, e.g. when analyzing Accounts Receivable. Unless the amounts are immaterial, the 10K will provide a detailed analysis of valuation and qualifying accounts, including the Allowance for Doubtful Accounts. In analyzing the 10K disclosure, students will likely be exposed to new terminology. First, the use of the term "valuation and qualifying account" is probably new to them. Second, the 10K schedule frequently presents information on a variety of valuation accounts and uses generic terminology. The schedule might label increases to the account as "charged to expense" and describe deductions as "for the purpose for which the account was created." My experience has been that, for many students, it is not trivial to recognize that the increase charged to expense is Bad Debt Expense and the deduction is for write-offs.

Students may encounter other accounts that textbooks either do not cover or only cover briefly, such as a LIFO reserve account. When analyzing taxes and debt, they will learn that companies disclose cash paid for interest and taxes, either in the cash flow statement or somewhere in the footnotes. If their company is involved in capital leases, the lease (or debt) footnote will detail future lease payments and subtract the portion related to interest to arrive at the liability on the balance sheet. To analyze this footnote the student must focus on time value of money concepts. The tax, pension, post-retirement benefits, and options footnotes will provide detailed information calculated and disclosed but not necessarily recorded in the statements. These footnotes may also use varying terminology that the student must interpret.

Finally, because published financial statements may be quite aggregated, adequate detailed information is not always available. This forces students to develop plausible explanations for the missing numbers. They need to draw on their accounting knowledge to provide reasonable explanations for why account balances changed from one year to another. Potential complications arise if the reported financial statement information is not consistent or articulated (Bahnson, Miller & Budge, 1996, p. 2). In some instances, students must simply say they do not know why the available information does not agree. This situation can be a learning experience as it puts the student in a position of dealing with ambiguity – a circumstance many accounting students do not like!

The third stated objective of this project relates to communication skills. As described more fully below, I assign a large portion of the grade to how students present the information. The end product is a report. It is not necessarily long. However, I evaluate very critically whether the student tells me where they obtained the information from in the annual report or 10K, and how they present and explain their analysis and any "missing" information or assumptions they made. They are also encouraged to present the report in a very professional manner, but I give them complete freedom on how they do that. Most students submit reports either bound or in binders and incorporate graphics and color to enhance the presentation of the material.

GRADING THE PROJECT

Grading is more onerous if each student works with a different company. For large classes, it may be preferable to assign everyone the same company or to use a few companies with a set number of students assigned to each. If only a few companies are used, the instructor can develop an answer key with "correct" analyses. An alternative approach is to evaluate accuracy, but also to focus heavily on the students' analytical and communication skills. This approach is consistent with objectives No. 1 and No. 3 delineated earlier and is the approach I use. The following is an excerpt from the grading information I give students.

> Everyone is analyzing a different company for this project; obviously, there is no answer key. Consequently, a key part of this assignment revolves around how you present your analysis. In many respects, this is analogous to a project you might be assigned on the job. I have given you a task to perform. As your "supervisor," I am available as a consultant while you work on the project. Upon completion of the task, you need to present your results to me in a professional, well organized, coherent manner so that I can understand what you did and what conclusions you have reached. I will then evaluate the quality of your work.
>
> The final product you turn in should be typed and presented in the same order as the requirements are listed in the assignment. You also must turn in either the original or a copy of the company's financial statements (including footnotes). Your project will be graded on the following criteria.

	% of Points
Presentation & Explanation of Analysis	40%
Identification of Relevant Data	20%
Analysis & Interpretation of GAAP	35%
Writing Style: Grammar, Punctuation, Spelling, etc.	5%
Total	100%

To illustrate my grading approach further, assume the project is worth 100 points. I allocate those 100 points among the topics the chosen company reports in its financial statements. In allocating the 100 points, I assign more points to the more difficult topics. Typically, a given topic is worth 10–15 points. If a topic is worth 10 points, I then assign those 10 points based on the breakdown above. That is, four points for presentation and explanation (40%), two points for identifying relevant data (20%), three and a half points for GAAP (35%), and a half point for writing style (5%). I grade each topic separately and use a spreadsheet to summarize the total grade. In a typical class, the grades for the complete project range from 66% to 98%. There have been two semesters where an individual student scored in the 30% range. Over all the semesters, the average project grade is in the 80%–83% range.

At least two problems in grading are worth noting. First, if each student chooses a different company, the level of difficulty of the analysis may vary considerably across students. Careful review and approval by the instructor of the chosen annual reports can help to minimize this problem. Second, a common complication in reconstructing entries arises if the chosen company participated in any acquisitions or disposals of other companies during the year. In this case, the makeup of the consolidated entity has changed from one year to the next. The instructor may choose not to allow companies where this situation occurred. Given the frequency of acquisitions this may be difficult. Students must be made aware of the issue and recognize that part of the entries made during the year relate to an acquisition or disposal. Footnotes vary considerably in the detail they provide on these transactions. The acquisition problem is compounded if the financial statements are, in fact, not well articulated (Bahnson, Miller & Budge, 1996, pp. 6–7).

Finally, with respect to grading, because the project is due at the end of the semester and graded as one unit, there is a large end-of-semester grading burden. I generally have three weeks (factoring in final's week) to complete the process and I also have relatively small classes. Nevertheless, it usually takes me an hour or more to grade each project. Faculty with larger classes or time constraints could address this burden in a variety of ways. As mentioned earlier, students might be assigned one or a small number of companies, thereby creating some efficiency in grading. This approach would also have the advantage of allowing the instructor to compare the work of different students on the same company. Alternative due dates or submitting the project in sections also might alleviate the grading burden.

STUDENT REACTIONS

Anecdotal evidence suggests that students struggle with the project and find it ambiguous and unstructured. As is typical with semester projects, many students procrastinate and put in long hours at the end of the semester to complete the project on time. Upon completion, students frequently say that they enjoyed the assignment and felt it was a good learning experience. In reflecting back, students often are amazed at how much they have learned about financial reporting through the Intermediate courses.

Limited student feedback data also are available from the end-of-semester student evaluations. No specific questions on the evaluation form relate to the Annual Report Project. But there are two open-ended questions that ask, "What was the most beneficial aspect of this course?" and "What was the least beneficial aspect of this course?" Over six semesters of using the project, 23% of the students have listed the Annual Report Project as the most beneficial while only 3% have listed it as the least beneficial. As the project has evolved and become better defined, student reactions have also become more positive. During the last two semesters of use, 41% have identified the Annual Report Project as the most beneficial aspect of the course with no one listing it as the least beneficial.

CONCLUSION

The Annual Report Project is a useful addition to the Intermediate Accounting course sequence. It stresses analytical, problem solving, and written communication skills and exposes students to the real-world reporting of most of the topics covered in the Intermediate course. Furthermore, by using examples and assignments in class with other annual reports, the development of analytical skills is enhanced. The instructor has a fair amount of flexibility in how the assignment is handled from the selection of a company to the accounts to analyze and the grading approach. This assignment is different from published practice sets or textbook assignments and, therefore, complements materials that are already available for Intermediate Accounting instructors.

APPENDIX

THE ANNUAL REPORT PROJECT

EXAMPLE ASSIGNMENT

The purpose of this project is to give you experience reading and interpreting actual financial statements. The project is NOT a financial statement analysis. Rather, it is an analysis and explanation of the company's accounting practices. After you have selected a real company and obtained a copy of their most recent annual report or 10K, answer the following questions. You will need to use the Balance Sheet, Income Statement, Statement of Cash Flows, and Notes to the Financial Statements.

- What industry is the company in? What is its primary source of revenue? What are their revenue recognition policies?

- *Review the basic financial statements.*
  Does the company use a single-step or multi-step income statement format? Are there any "special" items reported in their income statement? Is the balance sheet a classified or unclassified one? Do they use the direct or indirect method on their statement of cash flows?

- *Accounts Receivable*
  Review the information on accounts receivable and uncollectible accounts. Reconstruct all the entries that were made during the year related to receivables and bad debts. (Hint: the 10K usually has a section that reconciles the activity in the allowance for doubtful accounts.)

- *Inventory*
  What inventory cost flow method does the company use? If they use LIFO, how did the choice of LIFO versus FIFO impact their income this year? Reconstruct all of the inventory entries that were made during the year (if the company uses LIFO, use a LIFO reserve account).

- *Property, Plant, and Equipment (PPE)*
  What makes up the company's PPE? What depreciation method(s) do they use? Did they acquire or dispose of any assets during the year? Reconstruct all entries related to PPE. (Hint: Remember that disposals involve removing both the original cost and the accumulated depreciation; disposals may also involve gains or losses).

- *Intangible Assets*
  Does the company have any intangible assets? If so, explain the nature of their intangibles. Reconstruct all entries related to intangibles for the year.

- *Investments*
  Has the company invested in any debt or equity securities? If so, how have they classified them? Reconstruct all the entries related to investments for the year.

- *Current Liabilities*
  Review the activity in the current liability accounts. Describe the nature of the company's current liabilities.

- *Long-Term Debt*
  Does the company have any long-term debt? If so, describe the nature and terms of the debt. Reconstruct all the journal entries that appear to have been made with respect to long-term debt (don't forget interest).

- *Leases*
  Is the company involved in any leases as either a lessee or lessor? If so, how are they classified? Reconstruct all the journal entries that appear to have been made with respect to leases.
- *Pensions and Other Post-retirement Benefits*
  Does the company have any pension or other post-retirement benefit plans? Describe those plans. Is the funded status of these plans different than any accrued or prepaid cost on the balance sheet? If so, explain in your own words the reconciliation of the two. Explain, in your own words, what was included in the current year's expense related to these plans. Reconstruct all the journal entries that appear to have been made with respect to pension and post-retirement benefit plans.
- *Options*
  Does the company have any employee stock option plans? If so, describe those plans. Explain, in your own words, the current year's activity in the plans. Reconstruct all the journal entries that appear to have been made with respect to options during the year.
- *Taxes*
  What did the company report as total tax expense for the year (don't forget any intraperiod tax allocation)? Does the company have deferred taxes? If so, identify their total CURRENT deferred tax ASSET, total CURRENT deferred tax LIABILITY, total NON-CURRENT deferred tax ASSET, and total NON-CURRENT deferred tax LIABILITY. Read the tax footnote to the financial statements. Explain, in your own words, any schedules found in the note. Reconstruct all the journal entries that appear to have been made with respect to taxes.
- *Stockholders Equity*
  Describe fully the capital structure of the company. Review the Statement of Stockholders' Equity and explain the changes that occurred during the year. Were dividends declared during the year? If so, how much was paid to each class of stock? Reconstruct all the journal entries that appear to have been made with respect to all stockholder equity accounts (you may exclude any foreign currency translation entries).

NOTES

1. Hartman, Harper, Knoblett, and Reckers (2000) also include a brief financial highlights section.
2. Bonner (1999) uses a different taxonomy developed by Gagné, but relates it to Bloom's taxonomy in an appendix.

REFERENCES

Accounting Education Change Commission (AECC) (1990). Objectives of education for accountants: Position Statement No. 1. *Issues in Accounting Education*, (Fall), 307–312.

Ainsworth, P. L., & Plumlee, R. D. (1993). Restructuring the accounting curriculum content sequence: the KSU experience. *Issues in Accounting Education*, (Spring), 112–127.

American Accounting Association (AAA), Committee on the Future Structure, Content, and Scope of Accounting Education (the Bedford Committee) (1986). Future accounting education: preparing for the expanding profession. *Issues in Accounting Education*, (Spring), 168–196.

American Institute of Certified Public Accountants (AICPA) (1999). *AICPA Core Competency Framework for Entry into the Accounting Profession*. New York: AICPA.

Amernic, J., & Elitzur, R. (1992). Using historical annual reports in teaching: letting the past benefit the present. *The Accounting Historians Journal*, *19*(1), 29–50.

Arthur Andersen & Co., Arthur Young, Coopers & Lybrand, Deloitte Haskins & Sells, Ernst & Whinney, Peat Marwick Main & Co., Price Waterhouse, and Touche Ross (1989). *Perspectives on Education: Capabilities for Success in the Accounting Profession*. New York: Authors.

Arya, A., Fellingham, J. C., & Schroeder, D. A. (2000). Estimating transactions given balance sheets and an income statement. *Issues in Accounting Education*, (August), 393–410.

Bahnson, P. R., Miller, P. B. W., & Budge, B. P. (1996). Non-articulation in cash flow statements and implications for education, research and practice. *Accounting Horizons*, (December), 1–15.

Baldwin, B. A. (1999). *The Financial Reporting Project and Readings* (2nd ed.). Cincinnati: South-Western College Publishing.

Bloom, B. S. (Ed.). (1956). *Taxonomy of Educational Objectives: The Classification of Educational Goals, by a Committee of College and University Examiners*. Handbook I. Cognitive Domain. New York: Longmans, Green.

Bloom, R., & Schirm, D. (2000). Analyzing and international annual report as a course project. *Advances in Accounting Education*, *2*, 131–163.

Bonner, S. E. (1999). Choosing teaching methods based on learning objectives: an integrative framework. *Issues in Accounting Education*, (February), 11–39.

Brazelton, J. K. (2000). Students may blossom using Bloom's taxonomy in the accounting curriculum. *Advances in Accounting Education*, *2*, 57–85.

Dyckman, T. R., Davis, C. J., & Dukes, R. E. (2001). *Intermediate Accounting* (5th ed.). New York: Irwin-McGraw-Hill.

Harkins, J. L., & Mills, J. (1985). Annual reports: a pedagogical tool for intermediate accounting. *Advances in Accounting*, *2*, 149–166.

Hartman, B., Harper, R., Knoblett, J. A., & Reckers, P. M. (2000). *Intermediate Accounting* (3rd ed.). New York: South-Western.

Kieso, D. E., Weygandt, J. J., & Warfield, T. D. (2001). *Intermediate Accounting* (10th ed.). New York: Wiley.

Nikolai, L., & Bazley, J. (2000). *Intermediate Accounting* (8th ed.). New York: South-Western.

Pasewark, W. R. (2000). *Understanding Annual Reports* (4th ed.). New York: Irwin-McGraw-Hill.

Pasewark, W. R. (1997). Integrating corporate annual reports into the accounting curriculum. *Accounting Education: A Journal of Theory, Practice & Research*, *2*(1), 79–94.

Skousen, K. F., Stice, J. D., & Stice, E. K. (2000). *Intermediate Accounting* (14th ed.). New York: South-Western.

Spiceland, J. D., Sepe, J., & Tomassini, L. A. (2001). *Intermediate Accounting* (2nd ed.). New York: Irwin-McGraw-Hill.

Tondkar, R. H., Adhikari, A., & Coffman, E. N. (1994). Adding an international dimension to upper-level financial accounting courses by utilizing foreign annual reports. *Issues in Accounting Education*, (Fall), 271–281.

EXPANDING THE GLOBAL MARKET: A CASE STUDY FOR EVALUATING ALTERNATIVES

Ernest R. Larkins

ABSTRACT

Students may study international taxation in introductory tax, international accounting, or multijurisdictional tax courses. The complexity of international tax law often obscures important relationships and makes it difficult for students to apply their new knowledge in decision contexts. This case study enhances student comprehension of the "big picture," requires students to consider both tax and non-tax factors of doing business abroad, and encourages students to use multiple sources of information to conduct their research. The project involves a domestic company interested in "going international." Students receive projected sales and profit information for five alternative ways of conducting business abroad, select a country in which to invest, and evaluate each method. Eighty percent of students concluded that the overall project was a worthwhile learning experience. Teaching notes facilitate the project's use in class. Accounting professors can expand or reduce the project's scope to tailor it to a given course or level.

Advances in Accounting Education, Volume 4, pages 59–85.

ISBN: 0-7623-0856-7

INTRODUCTION

Accounting students may study international taxation in an introductory tax (e.g. the second undergraduate tax course), international accounting, or multijurisdictional tax course.[1] For most students, the topic of international taxation involves many new terms, concepts, and rules. Students often fail to integrate international tax rules and visualize how all the parts affect decision making.

Textbooks, which often cover international taxation in distinct modules, account for part of their difficulty. For example, one chapter (or section of a chapter) might deal with the foreign tax credit, while another covers anti-deferral rules (e.g. the controlled foreign corporation provisions), and still another covers sources of income. The lecture approach is not always successful in synthesizing these separate modules; students too often cannot assimilate the voluminous materials in the allotted time to see the "big picture" clearly. Also, the lecture approach alone often encourages sub-optimal passive learning, which is not conducive to the study of complex tax rules. In contrast, this project allows students to become more active in the learning process and develop the higher cognitive levels of synthesis and evaluation.

The primary learning objectives are for students to synthesize international tax concepts and evaluate alternative means for doing business abroad. Secondary learning objectives of this project are to synthesize tax planning ideas with non-tax considerations, familiarize students with sources of international tax law for research (especially web sites), develop students' oral and written communication skills, and encourage cooperative learning through teams. Mullis (1995, pp. 130–134) observes that cooperative projects emphasize the importance of "learning to learn," establish patterns for lifelong learning, encourage students to be active learners, and foster accountability among group members. Since team decision making is often the norm in public accounting, industry, and government, cooperative learning helps prepare students for these work environments.

These objectives are consistent with important skills Albrecht and Sack (2000, p. 56) identify and AICPA (1999, pp. 1–10) recommendations that educators foster a global perspective and develop research, decision making, and communication skills of accounting students. In particular, the AICPA (1999, 1–10) recommends that those entering the profession should be able to analyze the financial implications of entering new markets, use research skills to identify relevant information to support decisions, leverage technology to obtain decision-supporting information from electronic databases, evaluate alternative solutions to problems, identify the strengths and weaknesses of specific scenarios or cases, and organize and report findings clearly and concisely, both orally and in writing. This project provides the opportunity for students to develop each of these essential skills.

INTERNATIONAL TAX CASE

This section describes the hypothetical case study the author uses to develop students' abilities to synthesize international tax concepts and evaluate alternative methods for conducting business abroad. The author uses the case study in a masters-level international tax course. Other than short question-and-answer sessions and the semester's end group presentation, the course does not devote specific in-class hours to the project. Students complete the project outside regular class time, which normally requires 15 to 20 hours. However, as explained later, professors can reduce the project's scope in several ways to reduce the overall time commitment. Twenty percent of students' final grades depends on the project.

The international tax course at the author's university is elective. To enroll in the course, students must satisfy the prerequisites, consisting of two introductory tax courses (one undergraduate and one graduate) and a masters-level tax research course. The number of students enrolled in the international tax course each year varies from 10 to 35.

To assure relevancy of content and completeness, three international tax experts reviewed the case study. All three experts are international tax partners who have taught international tax courses and seminars. Generally, their comments confirmed that the project addresses the most important and relevant issues. They did recommend coverage of a few issues that the project did not clearly address (e.g. the foreign tax credit recapture possibility).

Alternatives for Going Global

Burpee, Inc., a U.S. C corporation producing infant formulas, recently sought professional advice about doing business abroad in Country X. According to a market study that a company specializing in identifying foreign consumer bases just completed, 60% of Burpee's potential foreign customers reside in Country X. The remaining customers reside in countries near Country X. This expansion is Burpee's first significant venture into the international market, and the board is considering five alternatives for going global:

(1) Manufacturing their product in the United States and shipping it abroad as Burpee receives orders (i.e., exporting)

Required initial investment: $1 million
Discount rate for cash flows: 9%

(2) Licensing their know-how and product formulas to Rugrat, an unrelated resident of Country X, for production and distribution abroad
Required initial investment: $1.1 million
Discount rate for cash flows: 12%

(3) Entering a 50–50 joint venture in Country X with Rugrat, for which Rugrat will be responsible for marketing and distribution[2]
Required initial investment: $1.2 million
Discount rate for cash flows: 12%

(4) Establishing branch operations in Country X to coordinate sales[3]
Required initial investment: $1.3 million
Discount rate for cash flows: 14%

(5) Organizing Hiccup, a wholly-owned subsidiary in Country X, which will control all aspects of foreign production and distribution[4]
Required initial investment: $1.6 million
Discount rate for cash flows: 14%

The alternatives are listed in ascending order of expected return, capital investment, and risk. Ceteris paribus, the greater the commitment to the foreign market, the greater the expected market penetration, and the higher the expected return. Similarly, the greater the commitment, the more likely the early years will result in net losses and the higher the risk. Varying the discount rates among the five alternatives considers the loss of purchasing power over time and the riskiness of conducting business in different ways or forms. The discount rate does not reflect country-specific risks such as the possibility a foreign government might expropriate business assets. Thus, students evaluate each alternative in light of its expected net present value and non-tax factors (including country-specific risks). The marketing and accounting departments collaborated to develop pro forma income statements for Burpee's domestic operations and each of the five global expansion alternatives over the next five years.[5] Table 1 provides these statements.

Personnel Transfers

Some of the alternatives require that Burpee transfer U.S. personnel abroad, while others involve training foreign personnel in the United States. To reduce the project's scope, professors can omit personnel issues from the case if they wish.

Table 1. Pro Forma Income Statement (millions).

U.S. Profits Before Considering Global Expansion Alternatives	2001	2002	2003	2004	2005
Net Domestic Sales	$20.0	$22.0	$22.0	$21.0	$20.0
Cost of Goods Sold	13.0	14.3	14.3	13.7	13.0
Gross Profit	$ 7.0	$ 7.7	$ 7.7	$ 7.3	$ 7.0
Operating Expenses	2.5	2.7	2.8	2.6	2.6
Net Income Before Tax	$ 4.5	$ 5.0	$ 4.9	$ 4.7	$ 4.4
Alternative 1: Export Profits					
Net Export Sales	$ 3.0	$ 4.6	$ 5.3	$ 8.0	$ 9.2
Cost of Goods Sold	2.0	2.9	3.4	5.2	6.0
Gross Profit	$ 1.0	$ 1.7	$ 1.9	$ 2.8	$ 3.2
Operating Expenses .	0.5	0.7	0.8	0.9	0.9
Net Income Before Tax	$ .5	$ 1.0	$ 1.1	$ 2.0	$ 2.3
Alternative 2: Licensing Profits					
Royalty Income	$ 1.5	$ 1.7	$ 2.3	3.0	$ 3.5
Operating Expenses	0.7	0.7	0.5	0.5	0.5
Net Income Before Tax	$ .8	$ 1.0	$ 1.8	$ 2.5	$ 3.0
Alternative 3: Share of Joint Venture Profits					
Net Sales	$ 6.9	$ 9.0	$11.6	$12.1	$14.1
Cost of Goods Sold	4.6	6.0	7.5	7.8	9.1
Gross Profit	$ 2.3	$ 3.0	$ 4.1	$ 4.3	$ 5.0
Operating Expenses[a]	3.3	2.1	1.1	0.9	0.9
Net Income (Loss) Before Tax	($ 1.0)	$ .9	$ 3.0	$ 3.4	$ 4.1
Alternative 4: Sales Branch Profits					
Net Branch Sales	$ 5.0	$ 7.0	$13.0	$16.2	$18.0
Cost of Goods Sold	3.3	4.7	9.1	10.7	11.7
Gross Profit	$ 1.7	$ 2.3	$ 3.9	$ 5.5	$ 6.3
Operating Expenses	3.0	2.5	1.0	1.4	1.6
Net Income (Loss) Before Tax	($ 1.3)	($ .2)	$ 2.9	$ 4.1	$ 4.7
Alternative 5: Foreign Subsidiary Profits					
Net Sales	$ 5.5	$ 7.5	$15.0	$21.6	$23.0
Cost of Goods Sold	3.6	5.1	9.8	13.2	14.0
Gross Profit	$ 1.9	$ 2.4	$ 5.2	$ 8.4	$ 9.0
Operating Expenses[a]	5.2	3.7	1.2	1.2	1.1
Net Income (Loss) Before Tax	($ 3.3)	($ 1.3)	$ 4.0	$ 7.2	$ 7.9

[a] Operating expenses do not include interest and royalty expense from contracting with Burpee (if any).

Under alternative 1, Burpee sends a U.S. sales representative to Country X for between two and four years to establish and develop the export market. The representative solicits business but is not authorized to conclude sales; only the U.S. home office can approve sales orders. Under alternative 2, Burpee brings two Rugrat employees to the United States for three months to observe U.S. production of the infant formula. Also, U.S. personnel make short, periodic trips to Country X to observe production and distribution activities and to act as Rugrat's consultants. In alternative 3, five Rugrat employees visit the U.S. plant for six months, and Burpee transfers a U.S. manager and a team of three U.S. technicians to Country X for two years. Alternative 4 requires a U.S. manager and a team of four U.S. sales representatives to live in Country X for three to five years. In alternative 5, Burpee transfers seven U.S. technicians and four U.S. sales representatives to Country X for three to five years and three U.S. managers to Country X for three to seven years.

The average annual salaries during the most recent year of a U.S. manager, technician, or sales representative living in the United States are $120,000, $80,000, and $60,000, respectively. Also, Burpee must pay a $3,000 average monthly salary to a Rugrat employee visiting the United States. Burpee bears the costs of these transfers, including any additional taxes resulting to the individuals involved. Under each global alternative, the pro forma income statements already include the before-tax compensation expenses to Burpee. Students determine whether individuals involved incur additional taxes because of their transfers and, thus, how much Burpee must reimburse transferred personnel.

Project Requirements

Each student group selects a country with a sophisticated tax system (e.g. the Cayman Islands is not acceptable). Students bring different experiences and skills to the project that, when combined with the experiences and skills of others, improve decision making, often dramatically. Though students can complete this case study working independently, the author believes a higher quality project results when assigned to student teams. One approach might be for each group member to complete the analysis for one or two global alternatives. The final report then becomes a patchwork of analyses, each completed by a different group member. This "divide and conquer" approach is a bad idea since it largely defeats the purpose of working as a team. Instead, groups should meet initially to discuss overall approaches to each alternative (e.g. what are the major tax issues that they must investigate and from where can they obtain information). Then, each group member should conduct an independent analysis for all five alternatives, after which the entire group meets to resolve differences in results and reach consensus.

As a rule, groups should select countries for which they can find sufficient research materials relating to income and withholding tax rates, tax treaties with the United States, allowable business forms, and other nontax issues. University libraries and internet resources often contain relevant information on Australia, Canada, and countries in Western Europe. However, the author accepts many other country selections, which often result in very interesting analyses (e.g. one group recently chose Azerbaijan). Nonetheless, students may be unable to find reliable and up-to-date information for some developing countries in Africa, Eastern Europe, and Latin America.

Based on the country selection, students research the tax implications of the five alternatives above, write a report to Burpee describing their conclusions and recommendations, and present their results to the class.[6] Reports emphasize the net present value of each global alternative. The calculation of these cash flows provide students with opportunities to design spreadsheets that facilitate their analyses. Students also consider country-specific nontax factors that might play a significant role in the decision to conduct business in Country X. For example, regulatory requirements may preclude Burpee from establishing a wholly-owned subsidiary. Some countries may routinely ignore intangible property laws (if they exist at all), suggesting that any formulae or know-how shared with a licensee or partner might be infringed. In other countries, cultural and social mores may make market penetration difficult without Rugrat's participation. Political and economic risks in some jurisdictions might cause Burpee to prefer alternatives involving fewer "assets on the ground" in Country X, particularly if the risk of plant and equipment expropriation is high. In some locations, such non-tax factors can outweigh the tax considerations.[7] Student groups in the author's course often recommend strategies for going global that explicitly consider such non-tax factors. In fact, student groups regularly forgo the expansion alternative resulting in the highest expected return (e.g. the wholly-owned subsidiary) because they believe the risk involved does not justify the additional return.

If professors require students to address personnel issues, the latter briefly discuss the tax implications for the Burpee and Rugrat employees involved under each alternative. Students need not perform detailed calculations for each employee. The professor's objective might be for students to identify the relevant tax provisions and explain the additional tax costs that Burpee can expect to incur. Of course, students should consider the impact (if any) of existing income tax treaties and totalization agreements in force. The "commercial traveler" article in U.S. income tax treaties generally exempts individuals from host country income taxation if their stays abroad do not exceed 183 days and they meet certain other requirements. United States' totalization agreements usually exempt transferred personnel from the host country's social security tax system if their visits do not exceed five years. Specific requirements often vary from one treaty or agreement to the next.[8]

International Resource Materials

International tax research requires knowledge of the international aspects of the U.S. tax law, tax treaties, and foreign tax laws. The U.S. tax law and tax treaties are readily available from a variety of sources. Up-to-date English versions of foreign tax laws, on the other hand, are more difficult to find in the United States. Thus, tax professionals often rely on summaries and narratives of foreign tax laws for a general understanding of the likely impact that foreign taxes have on the bottom line. In practice, professionals usually consult local counsel in the target country early in the process.

Table 2 lists many resources that students should find helpful in completing their projects.

TEACHING NOTES

This section contains teaching notes for each of the five alternatives for going global. Appropriate conclusions and recommendations depend on the foreign countries students select. Thus, these teaching notes suggest general approaches to selecting the optimal business strategy rather than specific solutions.

Professors may wish to assign this article (or the tables illustrating the analysis) to student groups to guide their analyses. If so, they may wish to change the profit projections for some or all alternatives. Alternatively, professors might choose to illustrate the economic analyses a few weeks before final reports are due. Thus, professors could select a country that the student groups do not choose and demonstrate an approach using calculations similar to those in Tables 4 through 8.

Professors not specializing in international tax law may feel uncomfortable about evaluating student projects and assigning grades. A detailed knowledge of international tax law is not essential. It may be entirely appropriate, especially in a course where most students will not pursue international tax careers, to emphasize issue identification. Thus, the evaluation of projects might focus on whether students raise the relevant issues more than whether students offer reasonable or optimal solutions. Knowing that an issue exists

Table 2. Resources for Conducting International Tax Research.

Loose-Leaf Services

Foreign Tax and Trade Briefs (Diamond 2000) – Helpful for obtaining tax and withholding rates.

Tax Management Portfolios: Foreign Income – A separate BNA portfolio exists for many foreign countries. This resource is very good, though one need not read through the entire portfolio for this project. Students can use portfolios as references, perusing the index for the information they need. As a word of caution, BNA has not updated some portfolios for a while. Portfolios also are available on LEXIS.

Tax Treaties (CCH 2000) – An excellent, highly-recommended collection of tax treaty documents.

Tax Treaties (RIA 2000) – Another excellent, highly-recommended collection of treaties and related documents.

Accounting Firm and IRS Publications

International Tax and Business Guides (Deloitte Touche 2000) – Excellent collection of soft-bound booklets for many countries, which also are available on LEXIS.

U.S. Tax Treaties (IRS 1999) – Good summary of withholding tax rates and personal service income rules.

Worldwide Summaries (PricewaterhouseCoopers 1999) – Excellent hard-bound collection of foreign tax laws.

Web Sites

Doing Business In (Ernst & Young)	www.doingbusinessin.com
Export Hotline – excellent non-tax reports	www.exporthotline.com
International Tax and Legal (KPMG)	www.tax.kpmg.net
Office of International Policy (SSA)- totalization agreements	www.ssa.gov/international
PricewaterhouseCoopers Global	www.pricewaterhousecoopers.com
Tax and Accounting Sites Directory (Dennis Schmidt)	www.taxsites.com
Tax Resources (Frank McNeil)	www.taxresources.com
Tax Resources Site Seeker (Kent Information)	www.kentis.com/siteseeker/taxlink.html
Tax World (Thomas Omer)	www.taxworld.org
Taxes Around the World (Paradine)	www.paradine.com/worldtax/index.html
Taxman International (Ed Visser)	www.xs4all.nl/~edvisser/taxman.html

may be the most important objective in some courses or with some groups of students.

The assumptions below apply to the example analyses that follow:

- If Country X is a low-tax (high-tax) nation, its effective corporate income tax rate is 25 (45)%.
- Country X's withholding tax rates for dividends, interest, and royalties are five, 15, and 30%, respectively.
- Country X does not impose a branch profits tax.

Table 3. Summary of Issues and Authorities.

Issues	Authorities
Alternative 1: Exporting	
What is Burpee's effective tax rate?	I.R.C. § 114
How much of the Burpee representative's compensation does Country X tax?	Foreign law; income tax treaty; totalization agreement
How much of the Burpee representative's compensation does the U.S. tax?	I.R.C. §§ 911, 3121
Alternative 2: Licensing	
How much is Burpee's royalty withholding tax?	Foreign law; income tax treaty
How much is Burpee's incremental U.S. tax?	I.R.C. §§ 903, 904
How much of the Rugrat employees' compensation does the U.S. tax?	I.R.C. §§ 861, 864; income tax treaty; totalization agreement
How much of the Burpee consultants' compensation does Country X tax?	Foreign law; income tax treaty; totalization agreement
How much of the Burpee consultants' compensation does the U.S. tax?	I.R.C. §§ 911, 3121
Alternative 3: Marketing Joint Venture	
How is the venture classified for U.S. tax purposes?	Treas. Reg. § 301.7701-2, 3
Can Burpee deduct early year losses?	I.R.C. §§ 702, 704
Is the joint venture a controlled foreign corporation?	I.R.C. § 957
How much is Burpee's Country X tax?	Foreign law
How much is Burpee's dividend withholding tax?	Foreign law; income tax treaty
How much is Burpee's incremental U.S. tax?	I.R.C. §§ 78, 901-904
How much of the Rugrat employees' compensation does the U.S. tax?	I.R.C. §§ 861, 864; income tax treaty; totalization agreement
How much of the Burpee employees' compensation does Country X tax?	Foreign law; income tax treaty; totalization agreement
How much of the Burpee employees' compensation does the U.S. tax?	I.R.C. §§ 901, 904, 911, 3121
Alternative 4: Sales Branch	
Can Burpee deduct early year losses?	I.R.C. § 165
How much is Burpee's Country X income tax and branch profits tax?	Foreign law; income tax treaty
How much is Burpee's incremental U.S. tax?	I.R.C. §§ 901, 904
How much of the Burpee employees' compensation does Country X tax?	Foreign law; income tax treaty; totalization agreement
How much of the Burpee employees' compensation does the U.S. tax?	I.R.C. §§ 901, 904, 911, 3121

Table 3. Continued.

Issues	Authorities
Alternative 5: Wholly-Owned Subsidiary	
Is Burpee's subsidiary a controlled foreign corporation?	I.R.C. § 957
Do the subsidiary's profits constitute Subpart F income?	I.R.C. § 952
How much is the subsidiary's Country X tax?	Foreign law
How much is Burpee's dividend withholding tax?	Foreign law; income tax treaty
How much is Burpee's incremental U.S. tax?	I.R.C. §§ 78, 902-904
How much of the Rugrat employees' compensation does the U.S. tax?	I.R.C. §§ 861, 864; income tax treaty; totalization agreement
How much of the Burpee employees' compensation does Country X tax?	Foreign law; income tax treaty; totalization agreement
How much of the Burpee employees' compensation does the U.S. tax?	I.R.C. §§ 901, 904, 911, 3121

Other assumptions appear later as they relate to particular global expansion alternatives. Table 3 summarizes the issues, authorities, and necessary information for each alternative.

Alternative 1: Exporting

Alternative 1 offers the lowest before-tax return ($6.9 million over 5 years per Table 1) and is often the entry strategy of choice when expanding abroad because of exporting's relatively low risk. Usually, the extraterritorial income exclusion in I.R.C. § 114 (effective September 30, 2000) minimizes the effective tax rate on such profits.[9] However, U.S. multinationals with excess foreign tax credits from conducting business in high-tax countries or domestic net operating losses should not claim the exclusion. Since the facts characterize this proposal as Burpee's first significant global venture, students can assume that Burpee has no excess credits. Also, the pro forma financial statements do not indicate or suggest the presence of domestic losses.

Another possibility is to establish a domestic international sales corporation (DISC). Under I.R.C. § 995, a DISC provides a tax deferral benefit, and the U.S. Treasury charges firms interest on their deferred taxes at a relatively low T-bill rate. Thus, the DISC benefit resembles a low-interest loan, so the DISC might be a good choice for exporters with high costs of capital. The greater the spread between a company's cost of capital and the T-bill rate, the greater the deferred tax. Though inexpensive to establish and maintain, relatively few U.S. companies use a DISC for exporting. Thus, this article does not consider the DISC further.

Entity Analysis

The extraterritorial exclusion provides a permanent 15% tax benefit (illustrated below) when the net export profit margin is 8% or more, between 15 and 30% when the margin is 4% or more but less than 8%, and 30% when the margin is below 4%. The pro forma income statement for the exporting alternative in Table 1 projects profit margins that exceed the 8% threshold each year. For example, the expected margin in 2001 is 16.7% (0.5/3.0). Thus, the extraterritorial exclusion reduces the effective tax rate on the export profit from the normal corporate rate of 34% (based on taxable income of $4.5 million from domestic operations and $0.5 million from exporting) to 28.9% [0.34 × (1 − 0.15)], a 15% tax benefit. If instead the net export profit margin had been less than 4% each year, the effective tax rate would have been 23.8% [0.34 × (1 − 0.3)].

Based on the Table 1 data and the assumptions above, the calculations in Table 4 indicate that the net present value of alternative 1 is $2.6 million. The analysis treats each year's before-tax profit and tax payment as separate cash flows, one positive and one negative, and converts each cash flow to a present

Table 4. Exporting Cash Flow Analysis (millions).

Year	Description	Profit/Loss		Tax Rate[a]		Discount	
2001	Profit before tax	$ 0.5			÷	(1+0.09)	= $ 0.46
2001	U.S. income tax	−0.5	×	0.289	÷	(1+0.09)	= −0.13
2002	Profit before tax	1.0			÷	$(1+0.09)^2$	= 0.84
2002	U.S. income tax	−1.0	×	0.289	÷	$(1+0.09)^2$	= −0.24
2003	Profit before tax	1.1			÷	$(1+0.09)^3$	= 0.85
2003	U.S. income tax	−1.1	×	0.289	÷	$(1+0.09)^3$	= −0.25
2004	Profit before tax	2.0			÷	$(1+0.09)^4$	= 1.42
2004	U.S. income tax	−2.0	×	0.289	÷	$(1+0.09)^4$	= −0.41
2005	Profit before tax	2.3			÷	$(1+0.09)^5$	= 1.49
2005	U.S. income tax	−2.3	×	0.289	÷	$(1+0.09)^5$	= −0.43
Present value of after-tax cash flow							$ 3.60
Required initial investment							−1.00
Net present value							**$ 2.60**

[a] The effective tax rate is equal to the otherwise applicable corporate rate for Burpee's taxable income (see Table 1) reduced by the 15% extraterritorial exclusion [0.34 × (1 − 0.15)].

value amount at the applicable discount rate. The analytical approach followed in Tables 5 through 8 for the other global alternatives is similar. Though the format of the analysis might be more compact, students often grasp the fundamental approach quicker from this more detailed presentation. Also, this approach encourages students to complete their analyses using spreadsheets.

Personnel Analysis

Under the case facts, Burpee does not authorize the sales representative to conclude sales contracts on its behalf. Otherwise, Country X might treat this employee as a dependent agent, which effectively treats Burpee as though it has a permanent establishment in Country X. In this event, Burpee incurs foreign income tax on a portion of its export profits. Avoiding permanent establishment status simplifies the calculation of Burpee's cash flow since it means the foreign income tax usually is zero.

The representative can exclude his or her $60,000 salary each year since a two-to-four year stay meets the I.R.C. § 911(d)(1) foreign residency or physical presence requirements. Thus, the sales representative should pay only Country X income tax (though a U.S. return is still required). If the Country X individual tax exceeds the tax the sales representative would otherwise pay if working in the United States, Burpee reimburses the additional tax cost. Since this "tax reimbursement" might also be taxable income in Country X, the individual might incur still more Country X tax, necessitating Burpee to reimburse such tax. This further reimbursement leads to more Country X tax and so on. Thus, the total reimbursement might be considerably higher than the simple difference in tax on a fixed amount of taxable income. Several "rounds" of reimbursements might be necessary to solve the "simultaneous equation problem" and keep the employee whole.

Likewise, the employee is usually not liable for social security tax in Country X, but it depends on that country's internal laws. For more definitive guidance, the U.S.-Country X totalization agreement (if one exists) should exempt the employee from Country X's social security tax under the "temporary assignment" exception (visits less than five years). Regardless of liability to Country X, the representative continues to pay social security tax in the United States under I.R.C. § 3121(b) or under any applicable totalization agreement.

Alternative 2: Licensing

Licensing know-how and product formulas to an unrelated party involves more risk than exporting since Burpee relinquishes control over some business processes. For example, Rugrat's quality control in producing and its vigor in marketing the infant formula may fall below Burpee's expectations. Further, legal recourse may be expensive or limited if either party terminates the licensing agreement but Rugrat continues to exploit the know-how and formula illegally or otherwise violates the licensing agreement. Just as the risk is greater, however, the expected returns also are higher. For example, the expected before-tax return in 2001 (2005) is \$300,000 (\$700,000) greater for licensing than exporting.

Entity Analysis

While exporting (alternative 1) rarely attracts foreign income or withholding tax, Burpee may be subject to a foreign withholding tax on royalties it receives. A treaty (if any) between Country X and the United States may reduce the withholding tax otherwise payable under Country X's tax law. The royalty received is gross income in the United States. However, Burpee can claim a foreign tax credit for withholding tax remitted to Country X.

Like Table 4's exporting analysis, Table 5 lists the before-tax profit and tax payments as separate cash flows. In contrast to the exporting analysis, the licensing arrangement usually results in some U.S. income tax for the difference

Table 5. Licensing Cash Flow Analysis (millions).

Year	Description	Profit/Loss		Tax Rate		Discount		
2001	Profit before tax	\$0.8			÷	(1+0.12)	=	\$0.71
2001	Country X royalty tax withheld	−0.8	×	0.30	÷	(1+0.12)	=	−0.21
2001	Incremental U.S. income tax	−0.8	×	(0.34−0.30)	÷	(1+0.12)	=	−0.03
2002	Profit before tax	1.0			÷	$(1+0.12)^2$	=	0.80
2002	Country X royalty tax withheld	−1.0	×	0.30	÷	$(1+0.12)^2$	=	−0.24
2002	Incremental U.S. income tax	−1.0	×	(0.34−0.30)	÷	$(1+0.12)^2$	=	−0.03
2003	Profit before tax	1.8			÷	$(1+0.12)^3$	=	1.28
2003	Country X royalty tax withheld	−1.8	×	0.30	÷	$(1+0.12)^3$	=	−0.38
2003	Incremental U.S. income tax	−1.8	×	(0.34−0.30)	÷	$(1+0.12)^3$	=	−0.05
2004	Profit before tax	2.5			÷	$(1+0.12)^4$	=	1.59
2004	Country X royalty tax withheld	−2.5	×	0.30	÷	$(1+0.12)^4$	=	−0.48
2004	Incremental U.S. income tax	−2.5	×	(0.34−0.30)	÷	$(1+0.12)^4$	=	−0.06
2005	Profit before tax	3.0			÷	$(1+0.12)^5$	=	1.70
2005	Country X royalty tax withheld	−3.0	×	0.30	÷	$(1+0.12)^5$	=	−0.51
2005	Incremental U.S. income tax	−3.0	×	(0.34−0.30)	÷	$(1+0.12)^5$	=	−0.07
Present value of after-tax cash flow								\$4.02
Required initial investment								−1.10
Net present value								**\$2.92**

between the U.S. rate and the foreign withholding rate. If the withholding rate is the lesser of the two, their summation is always the same (i.e., the U.S. rate of 34%). For example, a royalty withholding rate of 15 (rather than 30%) results in the same total tax payments and net present value ($2.92 million). When the withholding rate exceeds the U.S. rate (a rare but occasional occurrence), the foreign tax credit eliminates the incremental U.S. tax liability.

As one might expect, the net present value is higher under a licensing contract than when exporting ($2.92 vs. $2.60 million). However, students must remember that these numbers do not tell the whole story. Potential non-tax factors under the licensing alternative, such as a weakly-enforced legal system or concerns about Rugrat's reliability, might create a preference for exporting.

Personnel Analysis
Assuming no U.S.-Country X income tax treaty, the two Rugrat employees incur U.S. tax since they do not satisfy the de minimis requirements in I.R.C. §§ 861(a)(3) and 864(b)(1). Specifically, their compensation for this period exceeds $3,000. Also, a three-month visit may exceed the 90 days allowed. If the U.S. individual tax rate exceeds the Country X individual tax rate, Burpee reimburses them for any incremental tax liability they incur. If a U.S.-Country X treaty exists, it might allow more than $3,000 to be earned and extend the allowable visit beyond 90 days so that Rugrat employees avoid U.S. tax.

Short, periodic visits of U.S. consultants in most countries do not expose them to tax in the host country. Assuming such visits, no special tax issues arise for these individuals. However, Country X tax law controls.

Alternative 3: Marketing Joint Venture

Joint ventures involve different risks than licensing arrangements since the contractual responsibilities and rights of the partners differ from those of leasing agreements. Also, joint ventures requiring a transfer of physical assets to countries experiencing economic or political turmoil may risk expropriation. As a permanent establishment in Country X, the joint venture pays foreign income tax on its profits (unless Country X grants a tax holiday or other concessions). When the United States taxes these profits and when Burpee can claim a foreign tax credit depend on the joint venture's tax classification under U.S. law.

Foreign limited liability companies listed in Treas. Reg. § 301.7701–2(b)(8) (e.g. public limited companies in Australia) are "per se corporations." Treas. Reg. § 301.7701–3 allows all other business entities to select their tax classifications. If not listed as a "per se corporation," Burpee can treat the joint venture as either a corporation or partnership under U.S. law.

Table 6. Joint Venture: Cash Flow Analysis (millions).

Panel A: Treated as a Corporation in a Low-Tax Country (25% Rate)

Year	Description	Profit/Loss		Tax Rate	Discount	
2001	Loss from operations	$ −1.0			÷ (1+0.12) =	$−0.89
2002	Profit before tax	0.9			÷ $(1+0.12)^2$ =	0.72
2003	Profit before tax	3.0			÷ $(1+0.12)^3$ =	2.14
2003	Country X income tax	−(3.0−1)	×	0.25	÷ $(1+0.12)^3$ =	−0.52
2004	Profit before tax	3.4			÷ $(1+0.12)^4$ =	2.16
2004	Country X income tax	−3.4	×	0.25	÷ $(1+0.12)^4$ =	−0.54
2005	Profit before tax	4.1			÷ $(1+0.12)^5$ =	2.33
2005	Country X income tax	−4.1	×	0.25	÷ $(1+0.12)^5$ =	−0.58
2005	Country X dividend tax withheld	−7.8[a]	×	0.05	÷ $(1+0.12)^5$ =	−0.22
2005	Incremental U.S. income tax	−10.4[b]	×	0.0525[c]	÷ $(1+0.12)^5$ =	−0.31
Present value of after-tax cash flow						$4.28
Required initial investment						−1.20
Net present value						**$3.08**

Panel B: Treated as a Corporation in a High-Tax Country (45% Rate)

Year	Description	Profit/Loss		Tax Rate	Discount	
2001	Loss from operations	$ −1.0			÷ (1+0.12) =	$−0.89
2002	Profit before tax	0.9			÷ $(1+0.12)^2$ =	0.72
2003	Profit before tax	3.0			÷ $(1+0.12)^3$ =	2.14
2003	Country X income tax	−(3.0−0.1)	×	0.45	÷ $(1+0.12)^3$ =	−0.93
2004	Profit before tax	3.4			÷ $(1+0.12)^4$ =	2.16
2004	Country X income tax	−3.4	×	0.45	÷ $(1+0.12)^4$ =	−0.97
2005	Profit before tax	4.1			÷ $(1+0.12)^5$ =	2.33
2005	Country X income tax	−4.1	×	0.45	÷ $(1+0.12)^5$ =	−1.05
2005	Country X dividend tax withheld	−5.72[d]	×	0.05	÷ $(1+0.12)^5$ =	−0.16
Present value of after-tax cash flow						$3.34
Required initial investment						−1.20
Net present value						**$2.14**

Panel C: Treated as a Partnership in a Low-Tax Country (25% Rate)

Year	Description	Profit/Loss		Tax Rate	Discount	
2001	Loss from operations	$ −1.0			÷ (1+0.12) =	$−0.89
2001	Reduction in U.S. income tax	1.0	×	0.34	÷ (1+0.12) =	0.30
2002	Profit before tax	0.9			÷ $(1+0.12)^2$ =	0.72
2002	U.S. income tax	−0.9	×	0.34	÷ $(1+0.12)^2$ =	−0.24
2003	Profit before tax	3.0			÷ $(1+0.12)^3$ =	2.14
2003	Country X income tax	−(3.0−0.1)	×	0.25	÷ $(1+0.12)^3$ =	−0.52
2003	Incremental U.S. income tax	−2.9	×	(0.34−0.25)	÷ $(1+0.12)^3$ =	−0.19
2004	Profit before tax	3.4			÷ $(1+0.12)^4$ =	2.16
2004	Country X income tax	−3.4	×	0.25	÷ $(1+0.12)^4$ =	−0.54

Table 6. Continued.

Year	Description	Profit/Loss		Tax Rate	Discount		
2004	Incremental U.S. income tax	−3.4	×	(0.34−0.25)	÷ $(1+0.12)^4$	=	−0.19
2005	Profit before tax	4.1			÷ $(1+0.12)^5$	=	2.33
2005	Country X income tax	−4.1	×	0.25	÷ $(1+0.12)^5$	=	−0.58
2005	Incremental U.S. income tax	−4.1	×	(0.34−0.25)	÷ $(1+0.12)^5$	=	−0.21
Present value of after-tax cash flow							$4.28
Required initial investment							−1.20
Net present value							**$3.08**

Panel D: Treated as a Partnership in a High-Tax Country (45% Rate)

Year	Description	Profit/Loss		Tax Rate	Discount		
2001	Loss from operations	$ −1.0			÷ (1+0.12)	=	$−0.89
2001	Reduction in U.S. income tax	1.0	×	0.34	÷ (1+0.12)	=	0.30
2002	Profit before tax	0.9			÷ $(1+0.12)^2$	=	0.72
2002	U.S. income tax	−0.9	×	0.34	÷ $(1+0.12)^2$	=	−0.24
2003	Profit before tax	3.0			÷ $(1+0.12)^3$	=	2.14
2003	Country X income tax	−(3.0−0.1)	×	0.45	÷ $(1+0.12)^3$	=	0.93
2004	Profit before tax	3.4			÷ $(1+0.12)^4$	=	2.16
2004	Country X income tax	−3.4	×	0.45	÷ $(1+0.12)^4$	=	−0.97
2005	Profit before tax	4.1			÷ $(1+0.12)^5$	=	2.33
2005	Country X income tax	−4.1	×	0.45	÷ $(1+0.12)^5$	=	−1.05
Present value of after-tax cash flow							$3.56
Required initial investment							−1.20
Net present value							**$2.36**

[a] The dividend paid equals net profit less Country X income taxes over the entire five years or $7.8 [(1−0.25) ($−1.0 + $0.9 + $3.0 + $3.4 + $4.1)].

[b] U.S. taxable income is equal to the grossed-up dividend received or $10.4 ($−1.0 + $0.9 + $3.0 + $3.4 + $4.1).

[c] The incremental U.S. tax rate is equal to 5.25% [0.34 −0.25 −0.05 (1−0.25)].

[d] The dividend paid equals net profit less Country X income taxes over the entire five years or $5.72 [(1−0.45) ($−1.0 + $0.9 + $3.0 + $3.4 + $4.1)].

Entity Analysis If Corporation

If Burpee treats the joint venture as a corporation, it is not a controlled foreign corporation (CFC) since Burpee's ownership does not exceed the 50% threshold of I.R.C. § 957(a). (Of course, Burpee might increase its ownership in a manner acceptable to Rugrat if it desires CFC status.) Thus, Burpee defers U.S. taxation on its share of the profits in Country X until the joint venture corporation repatriates dividends; the arrangement avoids Subpart F income since the joint venture is not a CFC. Burpee reports dividends as gross income on its U.S. return but receives a deemed paid credit for the underlying foreign income tax the joint venture paid to Country X on the distributed profits. Also, Burpee receives a foreign tax credit for any dividend tax Country X withholds.

Panel A (B) of Table 6 shows the net present value calculation when: (1) U.S. law treats the joint venture as a corporation, (2) Country X also treats the joint venture as a separate taxable entity, (3) Country X permits the joint venture to carry forward net operating losses so that the 2001 loss offsets all profits in 2002 and some profits in 2003, and (4) Country X has a low (high) income tax rate. In Panel A, the joint venture corporation does not pay dividends until 2005 to maximize the deferral, resulting in a net present value of $3.08 million. Of course, the benefits increase as the deferral period lengthens. For the high-tax example in Panel B, the timing of dividend payments does not significantly affect the net present value since Burpee never pays a residual U.S. tax. However, for consistency of presentation, I again assume that dividends occur in 2005. The resulting $2.14 million net present value is substantially less than the result in Panel A when Country X's income tax rate is lower. Guidance for decreasing tax liability with loans (i.e., deductible interest) appears later under the wholly-owned subsidiary alternative.

Entity Analysis If Partnership

Most foreign jurisdictions permit the partnership form but may vary in whether they: (1) limit the liability of partners, and (2) treat partnerships as either flow-through or taxable entities. To illustrate the cash flow implications, the following analysis assumes that Country X permits partnerships and treat such business forms as flow-through entities. Under the latter assumption, Country X taxes Burpee (in its capacity as a partner) on its share of the joint venture's profits.

Assuming Burpee treats the joint venture as a partnership, it reports its share of the joint venture's annual losses (or profits) on its U.S. return (even if the partnership does not repatriate profits). For example, $1 ($4.1) million is deductible (taxable) in 2001 (2005). Treas. Reg. § 1.702-1(a)(8) allows Burpee to claim a foreign tax credit for any Country X income tax paid or accrued on its share of the joint venture's profits.

Panel C (D) in Table 6 provides the cash flow analyses when both U.S. and Country X treat the joint venture as a partnership and Country X is a low-tax (high-tax) country. Of course, Country X may treat the joint venture as a corporation even though the United States treats it as a partnership. Among other things, this hybrid characterization of the joint venture means that Country X may impose a dividend withholding tax on remitted profits, which Burpee can claim as a foreign tax credit. However, this article does not explore hybrid characterizations. As in Panels A and B, the 2001 loss offsets all 2002 profits and some 2003 profits. The net present values are $3.08 and $2.36 in Panels C and D, respectively. As when the joint venture is a corporation, treatment as a partnership results in a substantially larger net present value when Country X's income tax rate is lower. However, under the facts and assumptions given, the partnership form does not yield after-tax cash flows that are very different from the corporate form. When the Country X income tax rate is 25%, the net present value is $3.08 million regardless of whether U.S. law treats the joint venture as a corporation or partnership (Panels A and C). When the Country X income tax rate is 45%, the net present value is $2.14 million (Panel B) for a corporate joint venture and $2.36 million (Panel D) for a partnership joint venture.

Personnel Analysis

The issues regarding the Rugrat employees visiting the United States are similar as those for the inbound transfers under the licensing arrangement. The transfers of the U.S. manager and technicians abroad are similar to those discussed for the exporting alternative. However, the manager's $120,000 salary exceeds the I.R.C. § 911(b)(2)(D) excludable limit. Thus, additional calculations might be necessary to determine whether the I.R.C. § 911 exclusion with a foreign tax credit for income not excluded or the foreign tax credit alone minimizes worldwide taxes for this individual.

Alternative 4: Sales Branch

As an extension of the home office, a sales branch is not a separate entity. Thus, establishing a sales branch in Country X does not provide limited liability protection as would a subsidiary and some partnerships. This unlimited liability is a chief reason that U.S. multinationals, except in certain specialized industries, avoid conducting foreign business through a branch.

Entity Analysis

As a permanent establishment, the sales branch is subject to Country X income tax. In addition, a branch profits tax may apply to remittances, depending on Country X law and any U.S.-Country X treaty. I.R.C. § 901(a) allows a foreign tax credit for any Country X income tax and branch profits tax after 2002.

Branch profits and losses flow through to Burpee. Thus, the losses in 2001 and 2002 are deductible against profits from U.S. operations, an advantage of the branch form. Also, Country X carries these losses forward to reduce 2003 taxable profits. In 2003, the branch turns profitable. To preclude a double tax benefit, the I.R.C. § 904(f) recapture provisions may reduce the foreign tax

Table 7. Sales Branch: Cash Flow Analysis (millions).

Panel A: Low-Tax Country (25% Rate)

Year	Description	Profit/Loss	Tax Rate	Discount	
2001	Loss from operations	$-1.3		÷ (1+0.14) =	$-1.14
2001	Reduction in U.S. income tax	1.3	× 0.34	÷ (1+0.14) =	0.39
2002	Loss from operations	−0.2		÷ $(1+0.14)^2$ =	−0.15
2002	Reduction in U.S. income tax	.2	× 0.34	÷ $(1+0.14)^2$ =	0.05
2003	Profit before tax	2.9		÷ $(1+0.14)^3$ =	1.96
2003	Country X income tax	−(2.9−1.3−0.2)	× 0.25	÷ $(1+0.14)^3$ =	−0.24
2003	Incremental U.S. income tax	−2.9	× (0.34-.025)	÷ $(1+0.14)^3$ =	−0.18
2004	Profit before tax	4.1		÷ $(1+0.14)^4$ =	2.43
2004	Country X income tax	−4.1	× 0.25	÷ $(1+0.14)^4$ =	−0.61
2004	Incremental U.S. income tax	−4.1	× (0.34-0.25)	÷ $(1+0.14)^4$ =	−0.22
2005	Profit before tax	4.7		÷ $(1+0.14)^5$ =	2.44
2005	Country X income tax	−4.7	× 0.25	÷ $(1+0.14)^5$ =	−0.61
2005	Incremental U.S. income tax	−4.7	× (0.34-0.25)	÷ $(1+0.14)^5$ =	−0.22
Present value of after-tax cash flow					$3.90
Required initial investment					−1.30
Net present value					**$2.60**

Panel B: High-Tax Country (45% Rate)

Year	Description	Profit/Loss	Tax Rate	Discount	
2001	Loss from operations	$-1.3		÷ (1+0.14) =	$-1.14
2001	Reduction in U.S. income tax	1.3	× 0.34	÷ (1+0.14) =	0.39
2002	Loss from operations	−0.2		÷ $(1+0.14)^2$ =	−0.15
2002	Reduction in U.S. income tax	0.2	× 0.34	÷ $(1+0.14)^2$ =	0.05
2003	Profit before tax	2.9		÷ $(1+0.14)^3$ =	1.96
2003	Country X income tax	−(2.9−1.3−0.2)	× 0.45	÷ $(1+0.14)^3$ =	−0.43
2004	Profit before tax	4.1		÷ $(1+0.14)^4$ =	2.43
2004	Country X income tax	−4.1	× 0.45	÷ $(1+0.14)^4$ =	−1.09
2005	Profit before tax	4.7		÷ $(1+0.14)^5$ =	2.44
2005	Country X income tax	−4.7	× 0.45	÷ $(1+0.14)^5$ =	−1.10
Present value of after-tax cash flow					$3.36
Required initial investment					−1.30
Net present value					**$2.06**

credit in 2003. However, assuming that Country X allows Burpee to carry forward its 2001 and 2002 losses as deductions to 2003, the recapture provisions may have little or no impact.

The $2.60 million net present value in Panel A of Table 7 compares unfavorably with the joint venture alternative in a low-tax country. Similarly, the $2.06 million net present value in Panel B compares unfavorably when doing business in a high-tax country. Also, recall that conducting business abroad through a branch exposes the U.S. parent company to unlimited liability for the branch's activities.

Personnel Analysis
The issues for the outbound transfer of the U.S. manager and sales representatives are similar to those discussed earlier. However, Burpee should be aware that extended visits (exceeding five years when a totalization agreement is in force) may expose its employees to social security taxation in Country X.

Alternative 5: Wholly-Owned Subsidiary

In the last alternative of Table 1, Burpee expects operating losses in 2001 and 2002 if it decides to establish a wholly-owned subsidiary in Country X. Burpee's early losses under alternative 5 exceed the early losses under alternative 4 (foreign branch). Similarly, the later profits under alternative 5 are greater than the profits under alternative 4. The cash flow differences are attributable to the different functions transferred to Country X. Under alternative 4, Burpee only engages in sales activities abroad. Under alternative 5, the foreign subsidiary both manufactures and sells the baby formula. Burpee decided that curbing the extra risk involved in manufacturing its formula abroad would necessitate incorporation of its foreign operations. Foreign manufacturing results in heavier losses in the early years but larger expected profits later. The losses do not flow through to Burpee and, thus, do not reduce U.S. taxes in 2001 and 2002. However, assuming Country X allows net operating loss deductions, the early losses do offset all 2003 profit and some 2004 profit when calculating Country X's income tax.

Entity Analysis
As a wholly-owned company, Burpee's subsidiary is a controlled foreign corporation under I.R.C. § 957(a). However, since the subsidiary produces the infant formula within Country X, none of the subsidiary's profits are Subpart F income. Thus, any profits the subsidiary remits as a dividend is gross income to Burpee, but the retention of profits in Country X defers U.S. tax. When Burpee receives dividends, it includes the grossed-up dividend in gross income under I.R.C. § 78 and claims an I.R.C. § 902 deemed paid credit.

Deferral may be a worthwhile strategy if the corporate tax rate in Country X is less than the U.S. tax rate of 34%. The spread between these two rates is one measure of the deferral benefit (though any dividend withholding tax reduces this benefit). The larger the spread, the greater the benefit. In Panel A

Table 8. Subsidiary: Cash Flow Analysis (millions)

Panel A: Low-Tax Country (25% Rate)

Year	Description	Profit/Loss		Tax Rate		Discount	
2001	Loss from operations	$−3.3			÷	(1+0.14) =	$−2.89
2002	Loss from operations	−1.3			÷	$(1+0.14)^2$ =	−1.00
2003	Profit before tax	4.0			÷	$(1+0.14)^3$ =	2.70
2004	Profit before tax	7.2			÷	$(1+0.14)^4$ =	4.26
2004	Country X income tax	−(7.2−0.6)	×	0.25	÷	$(1+0.14)^4$ =	−0.98
2005	Profit before tax	7.9			÷	$(1+0.14)^5$ =	4.10
2005	Country X income tax	−7.9	×	0.25	÷	$(1+0.14)^5$ =	−1.03
2005	Country X dividend tax withheld	−10.9[a]	×	0.05	÷	$(1+0.14)^5$ =	−0.28
2005	Incremental U.S. income tax	−14.5[b]	×	0.0525[c]	÷	$(1+0.14)^5$ =	−0.40
Present value of after-tax cash flow							$4.49
Required initial investment							−1.60
Net present value							**$2.89**

Panel B: High-Tax Country (45% Rate)

Year	Description	Profit/Loss		Tax Rate		Discount	
2001	Loss from operations	$−3.3			÷	(1+0.14) =	$−2.89
2002	Loss from operations	−1.3			÷	$(1+0.14)^2$ =	−1.00
2003	Profit before tax	4.0			÷	$(1+0.14)^3$ =	2.70
2004	Profit before tax	7.2			÷	$(1+0.14)^4$ =	4.26
2004	Country X income tax	−(7.2−0.6)	×	0.45	÷	$(1+0.14)^4$ =	−1.76
2005	Profit before tax	7.9			÷	$(1+0.14)^5$ =	4.10
2005	Country X income tax	−7.9	×	0.45	÷	$(1+0.14)^5$ =	−1.85
2005	Country X dividend tax withheld	−8.0[d]	×	0.05	÷	$(1+0.14)^5$ =	−0.21
Present value of after-tax cash flow							$3.36
Required initial investment							−1.60
Net present value							**$1.76**

Panel C: High-Tax Country (45% Rate) and Loan Contract

Year	Description	Profit/Loss		Tax Rate		Discount	
2001	Loss from operations	$−3.3			÷	(1+0.14) =	$−2.89
2002	Loss from operations	−1.3			÷	$(1+0.14)^2$ =	−1.00
2003	Profit before tax	4.0			÷	$(1+0.14)^3$ =	2.70
2004	Profit before tax and interest	7.2			÷	$(1+0.14)^4$ =	4.26
2004	Country X income tax	−(7.2−0.6−1.2)	×	0.45	÷	$(1+0.14)^4$ =	−1.76
2004	Country X interest tax withheld	−1.2	×	0.15	÷	$(1+0.14)^4$ =	−0.11
2005	Profit before tax and interest	7.9			÷	$(1+0.14)^5$ =	4.10
2005	Country X income tax	−(7.9−1.2)	×	0.45	÷	$(1+0.14)^5$ =	−1.57
2005	Country X interest tax withheld	−1.2	×	0.15	÷	$(1+0.14)^5$ =	−0.09
2005	Country X dividend tax withheld	−6.7[e]	×	0.05	÷	$(1+0.14)^5$ =	−0.17
Present value of after-tax cash flow							$3.47
Required initial investmen							−1.60
Net present value							**$1.87**

Table 8. Continued.

Notes:

[a] The dividend paid equals net profit less Country X income taxes over the entire five years or $10.9 [(1−0.25) ($-3.3−$1.3 + $4.0 + $7.2 + $7.9)].

[b] U.S. taxable income is equal to the grossed-up dividend received or $14.5 ($-3.3−$1.3 + $4.0 + $7.2 + $7.9).

[c] The incremental U.S. tax rate is equal to 5.25% [0.34−0.25−0.05 (1−0.25)].

[d] The dividend paid equals net profit less Country X income taxes over the entire five years or $8.0 [(1−0.45) ($−3.3−$1.3 + $4.0 + $7.2 + $7.9)].)].

[e] The dividend paid equals net profit less Country X income taxes over the entire five years or $6.7 [(1−0.45) ($−3.3−$1.3 + $4.0 + $7.2−$1.2 + $7.9−$1.2)].

of Table 8, Burpee defers U.S. income of $14.5 million until 2005, resulting in a net present value of $2.89 million. When Country X's corporate tax rate exceeds the U.S. rate (as in Panel B), no deferral benefit results. Under the facts given, the $1.76 million net present value in Panel B when Country X imposes a 45% tax is substantially less than the $2.89 million in Panel A when the Country X income tax rate is only 25%.

If the Country X corporate income tax rate equals or exceeds the U.S. tax rate, no U.S. tax advantage results from deferring dividend payments. However, Burpee may be able to increase its net present value using either loans to or licensing contracts with its wholly-owned subsidiary. Any such loans or licensing contracts should be bona fide and provide for arm's length interest and royalty payments. Otherwise, the United States or Country X might treat the arrangement as an artificial means to shift income.

For example, assume the same facts as Panel B's high-tax scenario and that interest expense is fully deductible under Country X's income tax law. Deductible interest, in effect, exempts a portion of profits from the 45% income tax and, instead, substitutes the interest withholding tax of 15% (see initial assumptions). The tax savings can be substantial in some cases. Panel C reflects Burpee's expectation that its foreign subsidiary can remit $1.2 million of profits as interest in both 2004 and 2005. The fully deductible interest expense reduces the tax paid to Country X in 2004 and 2005, and the net present value increases from $1.76 million (Panel B) to $1.87 million (Panel C). If the interest is not fully deductible, the increase in after-tax cash flow is less. For example, thin capitalization rules (i.e. limits on acceptable debt-to-equity ratios) in Country X might restrict otherwise deductible interest expense. Country X tax provisions also might limit deductions when a subsidiary pays interest to a nonresident parent company. These latter restrictions are common in some Latin American countries. Finally, if Country X has transfer pricing rules similar to

I.R.C. § 482, it might seek to disallow some of the interest deduction as artificial income shifting that does not clearly reflect taxable income.

In addition to using loan or royalty contracts, Burpee might increase the net present value through mixing the five global expansion alternatives. For example, Burpee might decide to establish a sales branch in Country X initially to take advantage of the anticipated losses. In 2003 or 2004, Burpee might incorporate the branch operations. Mixing the alternatives in this manner complicates any cash flow analysis (e.g. it triggers the I.R.C. § 904(f) branch loss recapture rules) and also might require the marketing and accounting departments to revise their projected income numbers in the later years based on the changes.

Personnel Analysis

The outbound personnel transfers when establishing a wholly-owned subsidiary are similar to those discussed elsewhere. As under the sales branch alternative, visits that exceed five years can increase exposure to social security tax in Country X.

EVALUATION AND ADAPTABILITY

Based on the presentations and final reports in two of the author's international tax classes, about 80% of the students accomplished all the project's pedagogical objectives. Students especially demonstrated evidence of synthesizing international tax concepts, evaluating alternative means of conducting business abroad, and consulting a variety of international tax resources in their research.

Twenty students in the author's course completed an anonymous, in-class questionnaire following their projects. Before leaving the room, the author requested that the last student to finish shuffle the completed questionnaires to preserve anonymity. Ninety percent of the students found the project challenging. Eighty-five percent indicated that the project helped them understand the course materials better. Sixty percent believed the project provided a good opportunity to develop communication and interpersonal skills, while 70% said the project helped them to become more familiar with resources for international tax research. Eighty percent indicated that the overall project was a worthwhile learning experience.

In open-ended responses, two students indicated that their group experiences were less than ideal though another student specifically praised the group setting since it was "beneficial to have to convince group members."

Three students noted that the project required a lot of time. The most positive comment stated: "Great project! One of the most beneficial I have done in grad school. Project helped me think through the different alternatives thoroughly."

Professors can adapt this project to introductory tax, international accounting, or multijurisdictional tax courses. As presented, the project touches on most major tax issues of conducting business abroad. The author's students usually take 15 to 20 hours to complete the project, which they complete over several weeks as a term-long assignment. This significant time commitment may exceed the available time in some courses, particularly in introductory tax courses in which professors devote only one or two class periods to multijurisdictional topics.

To scale down the project, the professor might drop some of the tax issues. For example, eliminating the information about personnel transfers reduces the project's scope moderately. Similarly, the professor might decide to focus on only three of the alternatives for doing business rather than all five or only one of the joint venture forms (corporation or partnership) under alternative 3. Another means of reducing the project's size is to provide students with basic data, such as income tax and withholding rates, rather than expect them to locate the information themselves. The professor also might eliminate the requirement that students investigate the nontax factors to narrow the project's scope even further. Finally, as suggested earlier, the professor might require students to identify the relevant issues rather than to develop solutions. Each of these suggestions scales down the project, requiring less student time. However, narrowing the project's scope substantially might mean that the professor cannot achieve some of the pedagogical objectives discussed earlier to the same degree.

Professors can reuse this project year after year. If desired, they can assign countries rather than allow groups to choose their own. However, allowing students to choose their own countries often increases their enthusiasm for the project, particularly if they already have a personal or business interest in some area. Ideally, some groups should select high-tax countries while others choose low-tax countries since the in-class comparison and contrast often leads to helpful insights (e.g. why Burpee would decide to invest in a high-tax country). It is common for groups with an international student to select that person's home country as the group's Country X. In these cases, the international student may become the "expert," especially about the nontax factors of conducting business in Country X. This scenario often increases the level of participation and contribution of all students and is another benefit of permitting groups to select their own countries.

Another easy way to keep the project "fresh" is to change some of the accounting numbers. Also, some professors might wish to change Burpee's industry. The results may differ for information technology and service companies. To summarize, simple changes in the project's facts or in the countries analyzed produce a nearly endless variety of reasonable solutions from one year to the next.

CONCLUSION

This project allows students to synthesize international tax concepts and evaluate alternative ways of conducting business abroad. In addition, it familiarizes students with resources for conducting international tax research, provides the opportunity for students to work in teams, and develops their oral and written communication skills. Taxes are a very real cost of doing business abroad. Professionals who understand not only how to conduct business globally but how to minimize the tax cost while incorporating non-tax factors into their analyses are much in demand, and this project develops such an understanding.

NOTES

1. Schadewald (1999, 76–77) makes the case for covering multijurisdictional topics in introductory tax courses. The author uses the full case study in an international tax course. To use the case study in an introductory tax course, its scope can be narrowed. A later section suggests various means of scaling back the assignment.

2. Burpee makes a check-the-box decision about its joint venture. Thus, students specify whether the joint venture should be established as a partnership or corporation.

3. Branch operations generally involve higher risks than other alternatives since the home office's legal liability is not limited. In contrast, incorporation abroad limits liability to the foreign investment.

4. Producing the formula in Country X exposes Burpee to more foreign risk. Thus, in contrast to alternative 4 involving only sales activities abroad, foreign production necessitates incorporation in Country X to limit liability.

5. Professors can lengthen the project's time horizon. However, five years is sufficient to expose students to the importance of present value analysis in multi-year decision contexts.

6. Students become familiar with the tax issues related to the five alternatives for going global through reading assignments. International tax chapters in tax textbooks or international tax books such as Doernberg (1999) introduce students to the issues. This article's case study helps students to synthesize the textbook material and use it to make decisions.

7. The author directs students to Folsom et al. (2000), Oakley, III et al. (1999), and Tung (1999) for general guidance and the Export Hotline (www.exporthotline.com) for excellent country and industry reports on non-tax factors.

8. On request, the author will send the more detailed instructions he provides to students. Send requests to elarkins@gsu.edu.

9. On June 29, 2001, a World Trade Organization (WTO) dispute panel released an interim report announcing that the extraterritorial income exclusion is an illegal export subsidy. Likely, the United States' appeal will extend the dispute into 2002 before its final resolution. Throughout 2001 and 2002, U.S. exporters probably can rely on the extraterritorial income exclusion. If the United States loses its appeal, many international tax practitioners believe that the existing I.R.C. § 114 qualification requirements will be modified to comply with WTO directives. Thus, the analysis in this article will not change if either the U.S. prevails in its appeal or, as many expect, any subsequent change in the extraterritorial exclusion affects only the qualification requirements, not the exclusion benefit.

ACKNOWLEDGMENTS

The author thanks Greg Geisler, two anonymous reviewers, and the editor for many helpful suggestions that significantly improved the manuscript. GSU's Center for Teaching and Learning provided financial support for the development and classroom implementation of this project.

REFERENCES

Albrecht, W. S., & Sack, R. J. (2000). *Accounting Education: Charting the Course through a Perilous Future*. Sarasota, FL: AAA.

American Institute of Certified Public Accountants (1999). *The AICPA Core Competency Framework for Entry into the Accounting Profession*. New York, NY: AICPA.

Commerce Clearing House (2000). *Tax Treaties*. Chicago, IL: CCH.

Deloitte Touche Tohmatsu International (2000). *International Tax and Business Guides*. New York, NY: Deloitte Touche.

Diamond, W. H. (2000). *Foreign Tax and Trade Briefs*. New York, NY: Matthew Bender.

Doernberg, R. L. (1999). *International Taxation in a Nutshell* (4th ed.). St. Paul, MN: West Information Publishing.

Folsom, R. H., Gordon, M. W., & Spanogle, Jr., J. A. (2000). *International Business Transactions in a Nutshell* (6th ed.). St. Paul, MN: West Information Publishing.

Internal Revenue Service (1999). *U.S. Tax Treaties*. (Publication 901).

Mullis, B. J. (1995). Introducing faculty to cooperative learning. In: W. A. Wright (Ed.), *Teaching Improvement Practices: Successful Strategies for Higher Education* (pp. 127–54). Bolton, MA: Anker.

Oakley, III, E. F., Larkins, E. R., & Winkle, G. M. (1999). Issues in managing the multinational corporation. *CPA Journal*, *69*(January), 49–52.

PricewaterhouseCoopers (1999). *Worldwide Summaries*. New York, NY: John Wiley & Sons.

Research Institute of America (2000). *Tax Treaties*. New York, NY: RIA.

Schadewald, M. S. (1999). Integrating multijurisdictional issues into the introductory tax courses. *Journal of the American Taxation Association*, *21*(Spring), 76–93.

Tung, R. L. (1999). *The Handbook of International Business*. London, UK: International Thomson Business Press.

DEVELOPMENT OF TEACHING SKILLS IN DOCTORAL PROGRAMS VS. FACULTY PERFORMANCE EVALUATION: A SURVEY STUDY

Donald W. Gribbin, Julie Sobery and Daniel Braswell

ABSTRACT

This study reports the results of a survey measuring the attention given to the development of teaching skills in doctoral programs, and the attention given to teaching skills in faculty hiring, promotion, and tenure decisions. It compares these results to a 1981 study by Edwards, Ingram and Sanders. Responses were obtained from 39 doctoral program coordinators regarding teaching skills training in doctoral programs, and from 356 departmental administrators regarding criteria concerning faculty hiring, promotion, and tenure decisions. Results indicate that training in teaching effectiveness is a minor portion of doctoral program emphasis, whereas teaching effectiveness is claimed to be a major consideration in hiring, promotion, and tenure decisions.

Advances in Accounting Education, Volume 4, pages 87–104.

ISBN: 0-7623-0856-7

INTRODUCTION

Albrecht and Sack (2000) portray a very bleak state of accounting education. They note many of the problems in accounting education are related to pedagogy. Such problems may be due to the lack of attention given to teaching preparation in doctoral programs. Given that accounting faculty members typically regard teaching as a primary responsibility (in addition to research and service), why is this issue often ignored (or at least minimized) in doctoral programs? Possibly, teaching is viewed as a "hygiene" factor; i.e. good teaching does not lead to tenure but bad teaching can cause one to not receive tenure. The accounting education literature has discussed this issue of "research vs. teaching" for many years. One of the first survey studies to collect data regarding this issue was a 1981 study by Edwards, Ingram and Sanders (hereafter EIS, 1981).

The study by EIS (1981) indicated that teaching received minor coverage in accounting doctoral programs, that departmental administrators felt that accounting doctoral programs gave too little time to teaching skills and that training was inadequate. A major conclusion of their study was that accounting academicians should give more explicit consideration to developing teaching skills in doctoral programs.

Since EIS, 1981, the dimension of teaching effectiveness has received increased attention. In 1990, the Accounting Education Change Commission (AECC) issued *Position Statement Number One: Objectives of Education for Accountants*. In that Statement, the AECC stresses that:

> Faculty must be trained to apply appropriate instructional methods. Doctoral programs therefore should give more attention to teaching methods. Faculty who are effective teachers and those who develop and implement new or innovative approaches to teaching and curriculum design should be recognized and rewarded for such scholarly activities (AECC, 1990a).

Further to emphasize its position, the AECC issued a call for increased emphasis on teaching in higher education (AECC, 1990b). The Commission argued that an increased emphasis on teaching and curriculum and course development is vital to the future of accounting education. It urged everyone concerned with education ". . . to become involved in helping academia reorder its priorities and place renewed emphasis on teaching and curriculum and course development" (AECC, 1990b).

In 1993, the AECC issued *Position Statement Number Five: Evaluating and Rewarding Effective Teaching*. It listed five characteristics of effective teaching, urged effective teaching to be rewarded, and gave six strategies for evaluating and improving teaching. It concluded that "every party with a stake in improving accounting education has a stake in improving accounting professors' teaching . . ." (AECC, 1993).

The primary purpose of this study is to compare the current coverage of teaching skills in doctoral programs and departmental administrator views of that coverage with the results of EIS, 1981. This comparison is an attempt to assess whether there has been any reported change in teaching emphasis since 1981 in light of the AECC recommendations. This study also reports the degree to which teaching skills faculty are currently teaching in accounting doctoral programs and looks at whether they perceive that the current level of training is adequate for future accounting academics.

RESEARCH DESIGN[1]

This study replicates the two questionnaires used in EIS, 1981. The purpose of the first questionnaire (available upon request) was to assess the extent to which doctoral program curricula includes teacher training (EIS, 1981). We sent it to the doctoral program coordinators (hereafter Coordinators) of all universities listed in Hasselback (1997) as offering doctoral studies in accounting. The questionnaire contained multiple choice questions concerning six areas of interest: (1) teacher training techniques used in doctoral programs, (2) specifics on any teaching courses, (3) reasons for not including teaching courses in doctoral programs, (4) emphasis placed on general subject areas, (5) teaching skills taught in doctoral programs, and (6) perceived change in emphasis on teacher training in doctoral programs. As in EIS, 1981, we asked subjects to indicate both their perceptions of attributes of the program which involved teacher training and the approximate weight given to the various subjects in the doctoral curriculum. We received usable responses from 39 universities, a 42% response rate[2] (13 [33%] were from private and 26 [67%] were from public universities).

The purpose of the second questionnaire (available upon request) was to assess departmental administrators' (hereafter Administrators) perceptions of the importance of various factors in the selection of new faculty members and their perceived need for teacher training needed by accounting faculty. We sent it to the departmental administrators of the 795 universities listed in Hasselback (1997) as offering degree programs in accounting. The questionnaire contained multiple choice items concerning five areas of interest: (1) the relative importance of specific criteria in faculty selection, (2) the relative emphasis placed on specific topics in doctoral curricula, (3) the adequacy of teacher training in doctoral programs, (4) the relative importance of specific criteria in promotion and tenure decisions, and (5) the degrees offered in accounting.[3]

We received responses from 356 administrators, a 45% response rate[4] (146 (41%) were from private and 210 (59%) were from public universities). Three hundred thirty-seven (95%) reported having a bachelors program in accounting, eight reported having no bachelors program, and 11 did not respond. One hundred seventy-nine (50%) schools reported having a masters program, 144 schools reported having no masters program, and 33 schools did not respond. Finally, 35 (10%) schools reported having a doctoral program, 273 schools reported having no doctoral program, and 48 did not respond. Of the 35 respondents from doctoral granting institutions, seven (20%) were private universities and 28 (80%) were public universities. We dated and sequentially numbered responses as received, separately for each sample. We made comparisons between early and late responses to test for non-response bias. A chi-square test revealed no statistically significant differences ($p = 0.05$), indicating that the samples should be representative of the populations, assuming late respondents do not differ significantly from non-respondents (Armstrong and Overton, 1977).

TEACHER TRAINING

Teacher Training Techniques Used

Twenty-eight percent of the Coordinators indicated the integration of formal, independent courses in teaching, 5% indicated a teaching course integrated within a practicum, and 41% indicated the implementation of individualized assistance in teaching. Only 7% of the EIS, 1981 respondents had a formal

Table 1. Teacher Training Techniques used in Accounting Doctoral Programs.

Technique	Current Study Percent Response	Current Study Number Response ($n = 39$)	EIS, 1981 Study Percent Response	EIS, 1981 Study Number Response ($n = 46$)
A formal, independent course in teaching	28	11	7	3
A teaching course integrated with a practicum	5	2	4	2
Individualized assistance in teaching	41	16	37	17
Teaching experience as a degree requirement	56	22	41	19
Other	23	9	20	9
None of the above	5	2	28	13

Note: Percentage response total does not equal 100 because respondents may have indicated more than one answer.

teaching course (see Table 1). Fifty-six percent of the respondents indicated that teaching experience is a degree requirement, compared to only 41% of the EIS 1981 respondents. Only 5% indicated that they integrated none of the listed teaching training techniques into their program, down from 28% in the EIS 1981 study.

Of 22 schools that require teaching experience, six reported a formal course, one reported a course integrated within a practicum, and eleven reported individualized teaching assistance. Of 17 schools that did not require teaching experience, five reported a formal course, one reported a course integrated within a practicum, and five reported individualized teaching assistance.

Of 22 schools that require teaching experience, 17 are public and five are private institutions. One private institution has no undergraduate accounting program. Of 17 schools that did not require teaching experience, 13 are public and four are private institutions. Three private institutions have no undergraduate accounting program.

Of 13 schools that have either a formal teaching course in or a course integrated within a practicum, eight reported these as credit courses, nine reported them as required, eight reported them as "open to business students only," seven reported them taught by business (non-accounting) faculty, and six reported them taught by non-business faculty.

Reasons for No Teaching Course

Similar to EIS, 1981, we asked respondents who indicated the absence of formal courses to indicate the primary reasons for that absence (see Table 2). Twenty-eight respondent schools did not have a formal course. They gave the following

Table 2. Reasons for not Including Teaching Course in Doctoral Program.

Reason	Current Study Percent Response	Current Study Number Response ($n = 28$)	EIS, 1981 Study Percent Response	EIS, 1981 Study Number Response ($n = 42$)
Inadequate marginal benefits	18	5	31	13
Lack of faculty interest	21	6	28	12
Lack of student interest	4	1	11	5
Inadequate resources	25	7	22	9
Insufficient time in program	14	4	15	6
Better alternatives	14	4	nr	nr

Note: nr = not reported.

Table 3. Emphasis Placed on General Subject Areas in Doctoral Program.

Subject	Current Study Mean Response of Total ($n = 32$)	EIS 1981 Study Mean Response of Total ($n = 46$)
Research skills	46%	28%
Technical competency in accounting	18%	29%
Fundamental skills (math, computer science, etc.)	16%	16%
Technical competency in other business areas	10%	18%
Teaching effectiveness	8%	6%
Other	2%	3%

reasons: (1) inadequate resources ($n = 7$, 25%), (2) lack of faculty interest ($n = 6$, 21%), and (3) inadequate marginal benefits ($n = 5$, 18%).

Emphasis on General Subject Areas

We asked coordinators to indicate the approximate weight (total = 1.0) given to research skills, technical competency in accounting, fundamental skills, technical competency in other business areas, teaching effectiveness, and other areas. Table 3 indicates that while teaching effectiveness receives only minor emphasis as in EIS, 1981, focus on research skills has increased while focus on technical competency in accounting and other business areas have decreased. The mean response of 46% to research skills may be due to a shift in emphasis from teaching the technical competencies required on the CPA exam to teaching more abstract skills such as critical reasoning and active learning. Training future teachers best cultivates these abstract skills (i.e. by training future teachers to do research). The 8% response to teaching effectiveness may be due to the cost of training in teaching effectiveness and the difficulty of measuring the results of that training.

Teaching Skills and Training Techniques

Table 4, Panel A indicates specific teaching skills taught in doctoral programs, and shows the percentage of respondents indicating the integration of training for each skill. Of 39 respondents, 22 (56%) indicated that they taught communication skills, and indicated 20 that they taught teaching methods and aids. Also, eight (21%) of respondents indicated the integration of training in learning theory.[5] Table 4, Panel A shows significant increases in teaching skill areas as

Table 4. Summary Statistics For Teaching Skills and Training Techniques.

Panel A: Teaching Skills Taught in Doctoral Programs

	Current Study		EIS, 1981 Study	
Skill	Percent Response	Number Response ($n = 39$)	Percent Response	Number Response ($n = 46$)
Teaching methods and aids	51	20	13	6
Communication skills	56	22	15	7
Motivation	31	12	11	5
Learning theory	21	8	nr	nr
Testing	33	13	11	5
Counseling and guidance	23	9	11	5
Course design	46	18	13	6
Other	8	3	20	9
None of the above	33	13	28	13

Panel B: Teaching Skills and Training Techniques

	Schools Requiring Teaching		Schools Not Requiring Teaching	
Skill	Percent Response	Number Response ($n = 22$)	Percent Response	Number Response ($n = 17$)
Teaching methods and aids	55	12	47	8
Communication skills	55	12	59	10
Motivation	41	9	18	3
Learning theory	23	5	18	3
Testing	41	9	24	4
Counseling and guidance	41	9	0	0
Course design	55	12	35	6
Other	9	2	12	2

Note: percentage response total does not equal 100 because respondents may have indicated more than one answer.
nr = not reported.

well. However, 13 (33%) of the respondents indicated a lack of integration of any of the listed skills into curricula or training. Comparing the current study results to EIS, 1981 shows that all the percentages have increased except the "Other" response. It appears that all the skills listed on the questionnaire are being covered now more than they were in 1981.

Table 4, Panel B displays the overlap between teaching skills taught and training techniques. Schools that require teaching experience and those that do not both appear to cover most teaching skills in their doctoral program except counseling and guidance, which schools with no teaching requirement do not cover.

Table 1 indicates that 28% of the respondents provide a formal teaching course, 5% provide a teaching course integrated within a practicum and 41% provide individualized teaching assistance. However, Table 4 reports that 51% of the respondents explicitly provide training in teaching methods and aids, 31% provide training in motivation, 33% provide training in testing, and 46% provide training in course design. It appears that many respondents feel they cover these skills as part of their program but are not part of formal course-work requirements. A summary interpretation of Tables 1 through 4 indicates evidence of more emphasis being placed on exposing doctoral students to: (a) teaching theory, (b) practical experience, and (c) doing research best fosters more research skills because active learning and critical thinking.

Change in Emphasis on Teacher Training

To assess anticipated future changes, we asked coordinators to indicate their perceptions of future changes within their program in emphasis on teacher training. Only 39% indicated an increasing emphasis, while 58% felt emphasis would remain unchanged (see Table 5). In EIS, 1981, 28% of coordinators indicated an increasing emphasis, and 72% felt the emphasis would remain unchanged. Speculation regarding why most of the respondents project no future changes in emphasis may lead to the following conclusions: (1) the respondents are not interested in realigning doctoral program curricula to include an increased emphasis on teacher training, (2) the respondents have distinct philosophical beliefs regarding the role of the doctoral program, (3) the respondents do not view teacher training as a good use of faculty and students' time, and/or (4) the respondents perceive the current emphasis placed on teacher training as appropriate.

Table 5. Perceived Change in Emphasis on Teacher Training in Doctoral Programs.

	Current Study		EIS, 1981 Study	
Nature of change	Percent Response	Number Response (n = 39)	Percent Response	Number Response (n = 46)
Increasing	39	15	28	13
Decreasing	3	1	0	0
Remaining unchanged	58	23	72	33

To further examine perceptions on the emphases of doctoral programs, we surveyed departmental administrators to obtain their opinions regarding the adequacy of teacher training demonstrated by faculty members and the relative emphasis that doctoral programs should give to teacher training. This was done in an attempt to compare the views of trainers and coordinators with the views of those most influential in the hiring and employment process (Administrators).

PERCEIVED NEED FOR EDUCATION TRAINING

Program Emphasis and Adequacy

Eighty-seven percent of administrators indicated that too little emphasis is placed on the development of teaching skills in doctoral programs and 46% indicated insufficient training in accounting practice (see Table 6). These perception measures of the relative emphasis placed on various topics in doctoral programs imply an "either/or" choice while there may be synergistic effects between research skills and teaching skills. That is, faculty members better prepared in terms of research skills may also have enhanced teaching skills.

We explored evidence of any possible inadequacies in the development of teaching skills in doctoral programs through inquiry to administrators regarding training in the specific teaching areas indicated in Table 7. Results were very similar to EIS, 1981. In general, Administrators perceived training in these specific areas to be inadequate. The greatest perceived inadequacy was that of Teaching Methods (81.5 %) while "only" 56.2% of the departmental administrators perceived training in Motivation to be inadequate.

Possibly, institutions offering different levels of academic degrees might have different concerns and therefore demand different levels of teaching effectiveness from faculty members. Specifically, baccalaureate degree institutions might

Table 6. Emphasis Placed on Topics in Doctoral Programs as Percieved by Departmental Administrators ($n = 356$).

Topic	Too Much (%)	Too Little (%)	About Right (%)	No Response (%)
Teaching skills	0.6	87.1	7.3	5.1
Accounting practice	2.5	46.4	46.4	4.7
Research skills	34.6	4.5	56.2	4.7
Other business subjects	3.7	33.2	58.2	4.9
Accounting theory	16.9	10.4	68.0	4.7

Table 7. Adequacy of Training in Teaching Areas as Percieved by Departmental Administrators ($n = 356$).

Area	Adequate (%)	Inadequate (%)	No Response (%)
Teaching methods	12.1	81.5	6.4
Counseling and guidance	18.5	73.6	7.9
Testing	24.2	68.5	7.3
Communication skills	29.8	63.8	6.4
Course design	21.9	71.4	6.7
Learning theory	27.0	65.5	7.6
Motivation	35.4	56.2	8.4

Note: One hundred ninety-nine respondents indicated Inadequate in every area.

be more interested in teaching skills, and less in academic research skills, than institutions offering degrees at the master's and doctorate levels (EIS, 1981). To assess any differences in demanded levels of teaching competencies by administrators at institutions offering differing levels of degrees, responses to items in Tables 6 and 7 were broken down based on the highest degree offered (bachelor's, master's, or doctorate) by the responding institution. Table 8 shows differences in administrators' perceptions of emphasis placed on topics in doctoral programs. Statistical significance of differences was determined through chi-square tests.

As in EIS, 1981, perceived differences in emphasis on various topics in doctoral programs were not large, although several were statistically significant. Seventy-four percent of doctoral granting institutions, 94% of master's granting institutions, and 85% of baccalaureate granting institutions indicated under-emphasis of teaching skills in doctoral programs. Although these differences are statistically significant, one interpretation shows that an overwhelming majority of respondents in each classification indicated under-emphasis on teaching skills. Additionally, a significant portion of respondents (43% of baccalaureate and 34% of master's) indicated an overemphasis on research skills. As institutions offering baccalaureate and master's programs outnumber doctoral granting institutions 711 to 84, these statistics indicate that employers may prefer less emphasis on research and more on teaching in doctoral programs. The results show there were no significant differences between respondent classifications regarding emphasis on accounting practice, other business subjects, or accounting theory.

Table 9 indicates differences in respondents' perceptions of adequacy of training in specific teaching areas. At least 76% of all respondents indicated

Table 8. Emphasis Placed on Topics in Doctoral Programs by Departmental Administrators.

Topic	Highest Degree Offered	Too Much (%)	Too Little (%)	About Right (%)	No Response (%)
Teaching skills	Baccalaureate (n = 150)	0.7	85.3	8.0	6.0
	Master's (n = 158)	0.6	93.7	3.8	1.9
	Doctorate (n = 38)	0	73.7	18.4	7.9
	Chi-square = 11.2 Significance = 0.025				
Accounting practice	Baccalaureate	2.7	40.7	51.3	5.3
	Master's	2.5	54.4	41.1	1.9
	Doctorate	2.6	29.0	60.5	7.9
	Chi-square = 8.9 Significance = 0.064				
Research skills	Baccalaureate	43.3	2.7	48.7	5.3
	Master's	33.5	4.4	60.1	1.9
	Doctorate	2.7	13.2	76.3	7.9
	Chi-square = 27.2 Significance = 0.001				
Other business subjects	Baccalaureate	2.0	2.7	60.0	5.3
	Master's	5.7	36.1	55.7	2.5
	Doctorate	2.7 2	1.1	68.4	7.9
	Chi-square = 5.9 Significance = 0.209				
Accounting theory	Baccalaureate	18.0	8.9	68.0	5.3
	Master's	19.0	8.9	70.3	1.9
	Doctorate	5.3	21.1	65.8	7.9
	Chi-square = 8.8 Significance = 0.065				

inadequate training in teaching, with no significant differences between classifications of institutions. Furthermore, at least 58% of respondents from each of the three categories of institutions indicated perceptions of inadequate training in all areas except motivation.[6] Less than one-third of the respondents in all categories indicated adequacy with training in any area of teaching (again excluding motivation).

Hiring and Promotion Criteria

Administrators play an important and influential role in the hiring and evaluation of faculty members (EIS, 1981). Administrator attitudes regarding the current emphasis of training areas in doctoral programs (including training

Table 9. Adequacy of Training in Teaching Areas as Perceived by Departmental Administrators in Three Program Types.

Area	Highest Degree Offered	Adequate (%)	Inadequate (%)	No Response (%)
Teaching	Baccalaureate ($n = 150$)	15.3	76.7	8.0
	Master's ($n = 158$)	8.2	89.2	2.6
	Doctorate ($n = 38$)	13.2	76.3	10.5
	Chi-square = 4.6 Significance = 0.099			
Counseling and Guidance	Baccalaureate	19.3	72.7	8.0
	Master's	16.5	78.5	5.0
	Doctorate	26.3	60.5	13.2
	Chi-square = 2.9 Significance = 0.234			
Testing	Baccalaureate	24.0	67.3	8.9
	Master's	22.2	74.1	3.7
	Doctorate	31.6	57.9	10.5
	Chi-square = 2.2 Significance = 0.328			
Communication skills	Baccalaureate	26.0	66.0	8.0
	Master's	32.9	64.6	2.5
	Doctorate	31.6	57.9	10.5
	Chi-square = 1.3 Significance = 0.532			
Course design	Baccalaureate	26.0	66.0	8.0
	Master's	19.6	77.2	3.2
	Doctorate	15.8	73.7	10.5
	Chi-square = 3.3 Significance = 0.193			
Learning	Baccalaureate	29.3	62.0	8.7
	Master's	24.1	71.5	4.4
	Doctorate	29.0	60.5	10.5
	Chi-square = 1.9 Significance = 0.384			
Motivation	Baccalaureate	36.0	54.0	10.0
	Master's	32.9	62.7	4.4
	Doctorate	44.7	42.1	13.2
	Chi-square = 3.5 Significance = 0.170			

in teaching skills) may affect both hiring and promotion decisions for new and experienced accounting faculty members. A misalignment between perceived training and perceived needs may motivate coordinators to adjust emphases on areas of educational training (EIS, 1981).

Table 10 indicates the perceived importance of various criteria for the selection of new faculty members by administrators. Teaching effectiveness, attitude

Table 10. Criteria for Selecting New Faculty as Perceived by Departmental Administrators (n=356).

Criteria	Not Important (%)	Slightly Important (%)	Important (%)	Very Important (%)	No Response (%)
Technical competency in accounting	0	1.4	21.9	74.7	2.0
Teaching effectiveness	0	0.3	11.2	87.6	0.9
Attitude and personality	0	2.0	21.4	75.6	1.0
Research skills	5.1	17.4	43.0	33.7	0.8
Technical competency in other business areas	2.3	23.6	64.0	8.4	1.7
Professional certification	5.6	19.4	47.5	26.7	0.8
Prior business experience	3.9	29.2	54.5	11.0	1.4
Prior teaching experience	4.8	27.8	49.2	17.4	0.8

Criteria	Highest Degree Offered	Not Important (%)	Important (%)	Slightly Important (%)	Very Important (%)	No Response (%)
Technical competency in Accounting						
	Baccalaureate (*n* = 150)	0	0.7	24.7	72.7	1.9
	Master's (*n* = 158)	0	1.3	17.1	79.8	1.8
	Doctorate (*n* = 38)	0	5.3	31.6	60.5	2.6
	Chi-square = 10.0 Significance = 0.041					
Teaching effectiveness						
	Baccalaureate	0	0.7	4.0	94.7	0.6
	Master's	0	0	15.2	84.2	0.6
	Doctorate	0	0	26.3	71.1	2.6
	Chi-square = 20.1 Significance = 0.001					
Attitude and personality						
	Baccalaureate	0	2.0	22.0	74.7	1.3
	Master's	0	0.7	23.4	75.3	0.6
	Doctorate	0	7.9	10.5	79.0	2.6
	Chi-square = 10.6 Significance = 0.032					
Research skills						
	Baccalaureate	9.3	28.0	46.7	15.3	0.7
	Master's	1.9	11.4	47.5	38.6	0.6
	Doctorate	0	0	13.2	4.2	2.6
	Chi-square = 85.3 Significance = 0.001					
Technical competency in other business areas						
	Baccalaureate	2.0	24.0	64.7	8.0	1.3
	Master's	1.3	22.8	65.2	9.5	1.2
	Doctorate	7.9	26.4	55.3	5.2	5.2
	Chi-square = 7.5 Significance = 0.280					

Table 10. Continued.

Criteria	Highest Degree Offered	Not Important (%)	Important (%)	Slightly Important (%)	Very Important (%)	No Response (%)
Professional certification						
	Baccalaureate	2.0	13.3	48.0	36.0	0.7
	Master's	4.4	21.5	51.9	21.5	0.7
	Doctorate	23.7	36.8	26.3	10.6	2.6
	Chi-square = 50.7	Significance = 0.001				
Prior business experience						
	Baccalaureate	2.0	24.0	63.3	9.3	1.4
	Master's	3.8	32.9	49.4	13.2	0.7
	Doctorate	10.5	36.8	42.1	5.2	5.2
	Chi-square = 15.2	Significance = 0.019				
Prior teaching experience						
	Baccalaureate	3.3	22.0	58.0	16.0	0.7
	Master's	5.1	31.6	43.0	19.6	0.7
	Doctorate	10.5	39.5	39.5	7.9	2.6
	Chi-square = 14.6	Significance = 0.023				

and personality, and technical accounting competence were considered the three most important criteria.

Attitudes and perceptions of the criteria for selecting new faculty were again broken down by type of institution (Table 10). As in EIS, 1981, research skills were considered far more important by doctoral vs. non-doctoral granting institutions. Doctoral institutions also considered teaching effectiveness, professional certification, and prior teaching experience much less important than non-doctoral institutions. However, 71% of doctoral institutions considered teaching effectiveness "very important." These results were all similar to those of EIS, 1981.

As a final analysis of the perceptions and attitudes of administrators, we asked respondents to indicate the weight given to various faculty activities in promotion and tenure decisions. We display these results in Table 11. Teaching effectiveness was the main consideration for baccalaureate and master's degree institutions, and was a major consideration for doctoral granting institutions (slightly behind research and publication). These results were again very similar to the results of EIS, 1981, and are in line with the attitudes toward criteria for selecting new faculty displayed in Table 10.

Discussion and Limitations

Survey results are subject to several caveats and limitations. One might best view doctoral degrees as an economic good in an environment of supply and

Table 11. Weight Given to Activities in Promotion and Tenure Decisions as Perceived by Departmental Administrators.

	Highest Degree Offered				
	(1)	(2)	(3)	4)	(5)
	Baccalaureate	Master's	Doctorate		
	(%)	(%)	(%)	Mean	St. Dev.
Activity	($n = 145$)	($n = 155$)	($n = 36$)	(%)	(%)
Teaching effectiveness	53.3	46.2	37.2	48.3	13.4
Research and publication	23.2	34.9	50.8	31.6	17.4
Professional service	10.0	9.1	6.6	9.2	6.9
University service	12.4	9.8	4.8	10.4	7.0
Other	1.1	0	0.6	0.5	na

demand. Presumably, accounting academics, and the suppliers (doctoral programs) of those academics, respond mainly to demand forces. Most failed attempts to achieve promotion and tenure are the result of inadequate research, not inadequate classroom instruction. It seems that the current market demand, supported by most university promotion and tenure reward structures dictates effectiveness in research efforts coupled with adequacy in classroom instruction. However, the results of this study may indicate the beginning of a change in that demand structure at least in some institutions. The AECC has expressed a profound interest in recognizing and rewarding teaching effectiveness, rather than teaching adequacy, by changing the classic reward structure to make effective teaching, as well as new and innovative approaches to teaching and curriculum design, more rewarding (AECC, 1990a). Based on our results, some administrators may now be ready to embrace this concept. As reported in this study, a majority of responding administrators were dissatisfied with current teaching methods (87% of responding administrators indicated a perceived inadequate emphasis placed on the development of teaching skills in doctoral programs). Additionally, most of the 795 institutions that hire accounting doctorates (Hasselback, 2000) are not classic "research oriented" schools. Their missions and efforts are more oriented toward teaching effectiveness and service, and less toward research productivity. We support this assertion by the 94% of responding masters granting institutions and the 85% of responding baccalaureate granting institutions indicating a perceived underemphasis of teaching skills in doctoral programs (vs. 74% of responding doctoral institutions). The classic reward structure, which has demanded mainly effective research efforts, may change based on these current environmental influences.

In examining the supply side, evidence suggests an increase in teacher training in doctoral programs since EIS, 1981. More universities offer either formal courses or indirect instruction in specific teaching skills as listed in Table 2. However, training in teaching effectiveness remains a minor portion of doctoral program emphasis even though it appears to be a major influence in hiring, promotion and tenure decisions. Many universities, including doctoral granting institutions, recognize an underemphasis of teacher training. One possible explanation might suggest that most doctoral granting institutions require doctoral students to teach, usually to obtain funding, during their tenure as students. Therefore, it is highly likely that they would remedy poor teaching or "weed-out" poor teachers.

Another explanation of the lack of teacher training is the inability of coordinators to increase emphasis on one topical area (teaching), without sacrificing emphasis on another topical area (e.g. research, technical skills, etc.). However, the perception by a significant number of Administrators from baccalaureate and master's institutions of an alleged underemphasis on teaching, and overemphasis on research suggests an area for realignment or supplementation through seminars or other methods.

Finally, research productivity may enhance teaching effectiveness, as supported by Bell, Frecka and Solomon (1993). That correlation was stronger at doctoral granting institutions.

There are several limitations to this study. A significant concern is the possibility of response bias. Administrators who are satisfied with faculty teaching abilities, or who foresee an insurmountable obstacle in attempts to change current training and reward structures, or who agree with the current structure, might have little motivation to respond. Alternatively, Administrators who perceive a current underemphasis on teaching and overemphasis on research might be strongly motivated to respond.

Another limitation is some Administrators may provide strategic answers. If public rhetoric calls for better teaching, they are obligated to state their support, whether or not in fact they do support better teaching. We cannot determine the underlying reasons for the responses of the Administrators.

Universities are heterogeneous institutions and the responses are indicative of their unique missions (i.e. how they perceive the relative importance of teaching, research, and service). Some institutions, particularly those offering doctoral programs, place a very high value on research. On the other hand, institutions offering undergraduate programs place a very high value on teaching. These responses of these two types of universities will be tempered by their different missions.

The survey may have been overly generalistic and not led to the presumed conclusion that Administrators want increased teaching training in doctoral programs. Their responses may not accurately reflect information used in making reward (promotion and tenure) decisions. Either of these may have overstated concern of Administrators regarding teaching training.

Finally, there may be some methods of teacher training used by doctoral institutions that we did not survey here. Informal mentoring may not have been reflected and therefore, led to understatement of the amount of teacher training. If such informal activities are occurring then the teacher training and effectiveness gap may be much smaller than reflected by the survey results.

This is a replication. Its primary purpose was to compare the EIS, 1981 results with results from the current study. All responses are the perceptions of the doctoral program coordinators and the departmental Administrators. This study did not measure teaching effectiveness.

CONCLUSION

Despite its limitations, this study indicates that a significant gap remains between the level of teacher training offered by doctoral programs, and teaching skills perceived necessary by departmental Administrators. Future research might explore methods of closing this gap. The costs and benefits of program realignment, and the alternative of program expansion, might serve as valid topics. Exploring the level of teacher training offered in other university doctoral programs, and the resultant satisfaction levels of Administrators, might indicate change needed, and benchmarks for which to strive. Effective measures of teaching effectiveness, and continued research regarding shifts in emphasis of reward structures, might further the general concern of teacher training in doctoral programs. If teacher training continues to become more of a concern in the academic community, feasible answers to the problems of expansion and refinement of doctoral programs will come into increasing demand.

NOTES

1. We tried to replicate the design and methods in the EIS, 1981 study to maximize the validity and reliability of making cross-study comparisons.
2. We received forty-seven total responses. Eight were unusable because they came from schools without an active doctoral program. In contrast, the EIS, 1981 study received responses from 49 out of 71 doctoral program directors for a 69% response rate.
3. We used the responses from this last area to assign responses to one of three subsamples (bachelor's, master's, and doctoral), to test for the level of teaching required by faculty acting as an intervening variable in the assessment of the importance and deficiencies of teacher training (EIS, 1981).

4. The EIS, 1981 study received responses from 155 departmental administrators out of 258 for a 60% response rate.

5. EIS, 1981 included learning theory in their questionnaire but not in the discussion of results.

6. EIS, 1981 provided evidence that some administrators hold the perception that we cannot teach motivation.

ACKNOWLEDGMENTS

The helpful comments of Edward Ketz and two anonymous referees are much appreciated.

REFERENCES

Accounting Education Change Commission (1990a). Objectives of education for accountants: Position statement number one. *Issues in Accounting Education*, *5*, 307–312.

Accounting Education Change Commission (1990b). AECC urges priority for teaching in higher education. *Issues in Accounting Education*, *5*, 330–331.

Accounting Education Change Commission (1993). Evaluating and rewarding effective teaching: Issues statement number five. *Issues in Accounting Education*, *8*, 436–439.

Albrecht, W. S., & Sack, R. J. (2000). *Accounting Education: Charting the Course Through a Perilous Future*. Sarasota, FL: American Accounting Association.

Armstrong, J. S., & Overton, T. S. (1977). Estimating non-response bias in mail surveys. *Journal of Marketing Research*, *14*, 396–402.

Bell, T. B., Frecka, T. J., & Solomon, I. (1993). The relation between research productivity and teaching effectiveness: Empirical evidence for accounting educators. *Accounting Horizons*, *7*(4), 33–49.

Edwards, J. B., Ingram, R. W., & Sanders, H. P. (1981). Developing teaching skills in doctoral programs: The current status and perceived needs. *The Accounting Review*, *56*, 144–157.

Hasselback, J. R. (2000). *Accounting Faculty Directory*. Upper Saddle River, NJ: Prentice-Hall.

Hasselback, J. R. (1997). *Accounting Faculty Directory*. Upper Saddle River, NJ: Prentice-Hall.

Schultz, J. J., Meade, J. A., & Khurana, I. (1989). The changing roles of teaching, research, and service in the promotion and tenure decisions for accounting faculty. *Issues in Accounting Education*, *4*, 109–119.

A NOTE ON EQUIVALENT UNITS CALCULATIONS: TEACHING STEPS VS. TEACHING CONCEPTS

Steve Buchheit, Denton Collins
and Austin Reitenga

ABSTRACT

We investigate the relative effectiveness of two different methods for teaching process costing equivalent units problems. We find that a time-based approach improves student test scores relative to the traditional rule-based approach that is presented in managerial accounting textbooks. Our evidence comes from a quasi-experiment conducted on 431 undergraduate students enrolled in introductory cost accounting at a major metropolitan university. Our results suggest that management accounting instructors and textbook writers should consider modifying the approach used to teach equivalent units.

1. INTRODUCTION

Manufacturing firms typically select costing systems based upon the operational characteristics of their production process (Horngren et al., 1997, p. 95). When

Advances in Accounting Education, Volume 4, pages 105–117.

ISBN: 0-7623-0856-7

distinct or unique units of output are individually produced, managers typically select a job costing system. In contrast, when homogenous or highly similar output units are produced in bulk, managers typically select a process costing system. Although process costing is intuitively simple (divide total costs by total output units), partially completed output units and the need for regular unit-cost measurement necessitate the concept of "equivalent units" of output. To illustrate, if a firm incurs $1,000 of costs in order to produce 40 finished units and 20 units that are, on average, half finished, then the equivalent units of work performed are [40 units + (0.5) × (20 units)] = 50 equivalent units of output. The corresponding unit-cost measurement is:

$1,000 of assigned costs ÷ 50 equivalent units of output = $20 per unit.

Equivalent units are necessary because failure to include partially finished output units would overstate the unit cost for completed units.

Accounting teachers typically address process costing and the equivalent units concept during the introductory cost or management accounting course. The typical pedagogical approach requires students to prepare a so-called production report that is generated through a series of well-defined steps (cf. Horngren et al., 1997 and Garrison & Noreen, 2000). Unfortunately, students frequently have difficulty successfully completing equivalent units problems (Longmore, 1994, p. 88). This note provides evidence that a teaching approach focused on the timing of physical inventory flows, as opposed to the standard teaching approach focused on step-by-step rules, improves student comprehension of equivalent units problems.

We organized the balance of this note as follows. The next section contrasts the multiple steps involved in completing a traditional equivalent units problem with a time-based approach using a numerical example. The third section describes the quasi-experiment used to compare the relative effectiveness of these two approaches and discusses the results of that experiment. The final section discusses the implications of our study.

2. COMPARING TEACHING METHODS: AN EXAMPLE

We use the following example to illustrate process costing complications caused by partially completed work in process (WIP) inventory. Assume first a simple situation with no beginning WIP inventory. Inventory units and monthly expenses are:

January Inventory Units		January Expenses
Beginning Inventory	0 units	DL $3,000
Started During January	1,000 units	DM $3,000
Completed During January	700 units	OH $2,000
Ending Inventory	300 units	Total $8,000

To accurately assess costs per unit during January, "equivalent units" of ending WIP inventory are required.[1] Assume ending units are, on average, one-third complete; this implies that there are 100 equivalent units of output in ending WIP inventory (300 units × 1/3 complete). In this case, computing unit cost is simple:

$8,000 of assigned costs ÷ 800 equivalent units of output = $10 per unit.

Determining product cost during the subsequent month (February) is more complicated because both beginning and ending WIP are partially completed. Assume WIP inventory and February expense information are:

February Inventory Units		February Expenses
Beginning Inventory	300 units	DL $4,000
Started During February	1,000 units	DM $3,500
Completed During February	1,100 units	OH $2,500
Ending Inventory	200 units	Total $10,000

Beginning inventory is, on average, one-third complete (with a recorded cost of $1,000) and ending inventory is assumed to be one-fourth complete, on average. Using the preceding information, we contrast the standard step-by-step approach with a time-based approach to calculating unit costs.

2.1 The Step-by-Step Approach

When beginning and ending inventories are partially completed, a production flow assumption is necessary. Process costing systems compute unit costs using either the weighted-average method or the first-in, first-out (FIFO) method. While some writers prefer the FIFO method (Garrison & Noreen, 2000, p. 172), most firms use the weighted average approach (Horngren et al., 1999, p. 547). Evidence presented in various cost accounting textbooks suggests that a primary reason for the prevalent use of the weighted-average approach is that the method is easier to apply and understand relative to the FIFO approach (see, e.g. Garrison & Noreen, 2000; Maher, 1997). As such, our discussion and empirical testing are focused on the weighted-average method.

We discuss the four-step approach presented in Horngren et al. (1997) to illustrate the standard equivalent units calculation. These steps are:

1. Summarize the flow of physical units or output.
2. Compute output in terms of equivalent units.
3. Compute equivalent unit costs.
4. Summarize total costs to account for and assign those costs to units completed and units in ending work in process.

These preceding steps are typical of the standard step-by-step processes suggested by textbooks. While other textbooks suggest more steps [e.g. Horngren et al. (1994) identify five steps and Copeland et al. (1998; the text used by our research subjects) identify six steps], the number of steps is not important. Instead, we argue that embedding the critical timing issue within a larger rule-based problem prevents some degree of student comprehension (discussed below). To illustrate, the step-by-step method directs students to create worksheets like the one presented in Fig. 1.

The four-step approach presented in Fig. 1 treats the critical equivalent units computation (Steps 1 and 2) as part of a larger complex set of rule-based reports. As such, students must memorize the format of each step so as to solve the problem correctly. Although this approach offers practice-based reporting, it does not specifically highlight the fundamental timing issue that underlies the concept of equivalent units.

Research suggests that learning is best accomplished in two stages (see Bonner & Pennington (1991) for a review of learning issues in auditing contexts). The first stage of learning consists of instruction in the underlying concepts that characterize a problem. The second stage consists of providing feedback to the individual as he/she executes the task at hand. While the preceding step-by-step format may guide and simplify the preparation of final management reports (such as production reports), this format may inhibit student comprehension because it does not explicitly emphasize the fundamental timing issue that provides the conceptual foundation for equivalent units calculations.

Although some teaching notes and teaching sidebars advise instructors to focus on the timing aspects of percentage of completion and equivalent units (i.e. the conceptual issues underlying the computation of equivalent units), the same texts incorporating these notes and sidebars often fail to incorporate such pedagogical suggestions into the text material, problems, and examples. Similar to the concerns expressed by Horngren et al. (1997, p. 618, teaching sidebar), we suggest that this failure may lead to student confusion and may inadvertently lead students to concentrate on memorizing the mechanics of completing the production report and not on developing a conceptual grasp of these problems. As such, we suggest a time-based approach that places greater emphasis on the timing issue.[2]

Fig. 1. Step-by-Step Method for Calculating Equivalent Units (Horngreen et al., 1997).

Flow of Production	*(Step 1)* Physical Units	*(Step 2)* Equivalent Units
Completed and transferred out during the current period	1,100	1,100
Add work in process, ending	200	50
Total accounted for	1,300	1,150
Deduct work in process, beginning	300	100
Started during the current period	1,000	
Work done during the current period		1,050

Step 3: Compute cost per equivalent unit:	Unit Costs
Equivalent unit costs of beginning work in process	
Work in process, beginning	$1,000
Divide by equivalent units of beginning work in process	÷ 100
Cost per equivalent unit of beginning work in process	$ 10.00
Equivalent unit costs of work done in current period only	
Costs added in current period	$10,000
Divide by equivalent units of work done in current period	÷ 1,050
Cost per equivalent unit of work done in the current period only	$9.524

Step 4: Summarize "Total Costs to Account For", and assign these costs to units completed and to units in ending work in process.

	Equivalent units	Cost per equiv. unit	Total Prod.
Panel A: Total Costs to Account For			
Work in process, beginning	100	$10.000	$1,000
Work done in current period only	1,050	$9.524	$10,000
To Account for	1,150	$9.565*	$11,000
Panel B: Assignment of Costs			
Completed and transferred out	1,100	$9.565	$10,522
Work in process, ending	50	$9.565	$ 478
Accounted for	1,150		$11,000

* total production costs divided by total equivalent units.

2.2 A Time-Based Approach

We suggest that equivalent unit problems be taught with a more explicit focus on the timing of inventory production. Our approach emphasizes that the equivalent units concept is needed to identify the denominator in the simple "total costs ÷ total output" calculation. Based on the preceding information and the weighted average flow assumption, students must separate "work done" into only two time periods:[3]

Work done by the end of February	Work to be done in the future
1,100 finished units 50 equivalent units of ending inventory	150 units of incomplete ending inventory

After separating the timing of production, the denominator in the "Total Costs ÷ Total Output" equation is easily identified (1,150 units). We then tell students to focus on the costs associated with this output. These costs include February's total costs ($10,000) and the cost of beginning inventory ($1,000). As such, February's unit cost is:

$$(\$10{,}000 + \$1{,}000) \div 1{,}150 \text{ equivalent units} = \$9.565 \text{ per unit}$$

Ending inventory value is determined by multiplying this cost by February's ending equivalent units of inventory. Cost of goods manufactured is determined by multiplying $9.565 per unit by the number of items completed during February.

While the above approach is mathematically identical to the approach presented in the step-by-step approach, the more explicit focus on the timing of inventory production should aid student comprehension. The following section presents our evidence on the relative effectiveness of these two approaches.

3. EVIDENCE

To compare the relative effectiveness of the preceding methods (i.e. the standard step-by-step approach vs. a time-based approach), we conducted a quasi-experiment on 431 undergraduate students enrolled in introductory cost accounting at a major metropolitan university. The introductory cost accounting course is a survey course that fills a basic education requirement for both business and non-business majors. Although the course covers a standard body of material, the course is taught at different times so as to accommodate student schedules.

During Spring 1999, there were four sections of introductory cost accounting taught by three different instructors. Each section spent three class hours (two class meetings) covering process costing and the equivalent units concept.[4] Three out of four sections were taught to solve weighted-average equivalent units problems using the traditional step-by-step approach (per-class $n = 62$, 48, and 148 for a total $n = 258$) while the fourth section was taught to solve equivalent units problems using the time-based approach ($n = 118$). The instructor using the time-based method taught only one introductory cost accounting class and informed his class that his method of instruction was an alternative to the step-by-step method presented in the textbook. Given the coordinated nature of the course, students in all sections completed identical in-class problems and were assigned identical homework problems.

After completing a total of nine class sessions, students from all sections took a uniform exam that contained 30 multiple-choice questions. All students took the exam at the same chronological time. During the spring 1999 semester, four weighted-average equivalent units problems appeared on the exam (see appendix). We present student examination results, including controls for student and instructor ability, in the following sub-section.

3.1 Test Results

Fifty-five students who took the introductory cost accounting exam subsequently withdrew from the course. We speculate that these students performed poorly on the exam and potentially were not attending course instruction. If this were the case, teaching methods would have a limited effect on student performance. As such, we suspect (and verify) that these students would add noise to our analysis and therefore exclude these students from our presented results leaving a test sample of 376 students.[5] We partitioned students between the time-based group and the step-by-step group through the use of an indicator variable (TB). We coded TB "one" if the student was in the time-based group ($n = 118$); conversely, we coded TB "zero" if the student was in the step-by-step group ($n = 258$).

We measured the effectiveness of the time-based approach using the proportion of correct answers for the four weighted-average multiple choice questions (WA). If the time-based approach is more effective than the traditional step-by-step approach, WA will be significantly larger for the time-based group. However, we recognize that differences in student ability and instructor quality could influence our results. We control for these differences by using the proportion of correct answers for all non-weighted-average multiple choice questions (MC) as a proxy for student ability and instructor quality. The rationale for using this proxy is that superior student ability and superior instructor quality will be reflected in a larger proportion of correct answers on the non-weighted average multiple choice questions. In Table 1, we perform univariate tests. In Panel A, we condition MC and WA on the teaching approach used (step-by-step or time-based). In Panel B, we report the Pearson and Spearman correlation coefficients for MC, WA and TB.

The difference in the mean proportion of correct non-weighted-average questions (MC) between the step-by-step group (66%) and the time-based group (65%) is not significant at conventional levels ($p = 0.328$, two-tailed), suggesting no difference in student or instructor ability. In contrast, the differ-

Table 1. Univariate Analysis.

Panel A
Mean MC and Mean WA conditioned on TB

	N	Mean MC	Mean WA
TB = 0	258	0.664	0.487
TB = 1	118	0.649	0.561
T-statistic for difference in means		0.97	−2.08
Two-tailed *p*-value	0.328	0.038	

* TB = 0 if the step-based approach was used; TB = 1 if the time based approach was used.

Panel B
*Correlation Coefficients (two-tailed p-values)**

	MC	WA	TB
MC	1.000	0.331	−0.025
	—	(.000)	(0.626)
WA	0.327	1.000	0.117
	(0.000)	—	(0.023)
TB	−0.051	0.107	1.000
	(0.328)	(0.038)	—

MC = proportion of correct answers for all non-weighted-average multiple choice questions.
WA = proportion of correct answers for the four weighted-average multiple choice questions.
TB = 1 if the student was exposed to the time-based teaching approach.
* Pearson (Spearman) correlation coefficients are reported in the lower left-hand (upper right-hand) off-diagonal entries.

ence in the mean proportion of correct weighted-average questions (WA) between the step-by-step group (49%) and the time-based group (56%) is significant at conventional levels ($p = 0.038$, two-tailed).[6] The lower proportion for the weighted-average questions relative to the non-weighted-average questions suggests that, overall, students had relative difficulty with weighted-average questions compared to all other exam questions. In Table 2, we assess the joint effect of TB and MC on WA by regressing WA on MC and TB using ordinary least squares and the 376 student observations.

After controlling for student ability and instructor quality, the time-based method is positively related to exam scores on the weighted average multiple choice questions and highly significant ($p = 0.011$, two-tailed). The coefficient on TB indicates that students in the time-based group had a proportion of correct answers on the weighted-average questions that was 8.5% higher than students in the step-by-step group. Given that the mean proportion of correct

Table 2. A Multiple Regression of WA on MC and TB Using Ordinary Least Squares.

Variable	Coefficient	*t*-statistic	Two-tailed *p*-value
MC	0.828	6.86	0.000
TB	0.085	2.55	0.011
Constant	−0.062	−0.76	0.448
Adjusted R-squared	0.118		
F-value for Model	25.97		
Prob > F	0.000		
N	376		

MC = proportion of correct answers for all non- weighted-average multiple choice questions.
WA = proportion of correct answers for the four weighted-average multiple choice questions.
TB = 1 if the student was exposed to the time-based teaching approach.

answers on the weighted-average questions was 51%, this suggests a material increase in performance. Additional analyses (not reported) included alternative proxies for the quality of instruction and the quality of the learning environment. These analyses produced consistent results suggesting that the time-based approach was more effective than the step-by-step approach.[7]

To test the robustness of the preceding results, the average percentage correct for each equivalent units problem was calculated for the time-based approach (52%, 49%, 83%, and 41% for questions 1 through 4, respectively) and for the step-by-step approach (41%, 33%, 79%, and 38%). To determine if one specific equivalent units question is driving the overall statistical results reported in Table 2, we estimate similarly-specified logistic regression models for each question. The dependent variable for each question takes on the value of 1 if the answer was correct and zero otherwise. In each model, the coefficient on TB was positively signed and either significant at conventional levels or marginally significant, suggesting that no single question is driving our results.

4. CONCLUSIONS

Our results suggest that the time-based method is superior to the traditional step-by-step method when teaching the equivalent units concept to undergraduate students in an introductory accounting course. Although some cost and management accounting textbooks promote time-based instruction in the teaching note or teaching sidebar (e.g. Horngren et al., 1997, p. 618), we know of no textbook that explicitly focuses student attention on the time-based aspects of equivalent unit calculations. Rather, textbooks tend to embed the timing aspect of equivalent units calculations within a larger, rule-based format for calculating process costing, equivalent units problems. While our evidence suggests that student comprehension of the equivalent units concept would be improved by moving away from a rule-based pedagogical approach and emphasizing the time-based aspects of equivalent units calculations, certain limitations related to our testing method should be acknowledged.

First, students in the time-based group had access to *both* forms of instruction given that their textbook utilized the step-by-step method. Second, our test results are based only on four multiple choice questions. Third, while we control for differences in instructor and student quality in this quasi-experiment, randomly assigning students to a teaching method and having the same instructor deliver both types of instruction (time-based vs. step-by-step) to different classes would improve experimental control. Fourth, from a broader perspective, we have only investigated the relative effectiveness between teaching methods as it pertains to solving textbook-style problems. We do not measure the extent to which the step-by-step method better prepares students for practice-based production reports. Finally, our study indicates that concept-based learning is superior to rule-based learning; however, we offer no evidence that this finding is robust to settings other than equivalent units calculations. In total, these issues offer interesting avenues for future research that compares the relative effectiveness of competing teaching methods.

NOTES

1. Equivalent units calculations are more cumbersome if direct material (DM) and conversion costs (CC) are added to the production process at different rates. Two separate equivalent units calculations must be performed in this case (one for DM and one for CC). To ease exposition, we assume DM and CC are added to the production process at the same rate.

2. Instruction focused on a time-based approach may also be beneficial because it reinforces the fundamental matching principle in accounting. Recent surveys of accounting professionals suggest that a conceptual understanding of accounting is a key success factor for students entering the accounting profession (Siegel and Sorensen 1999).

3. A simple three-time-period extension exists for the FIFO equivalent units method: separate the past period, the current period, and future periods. One note of caution does exist when the FIFO flow assumption is made: calculating COGM is not formulaic; instead, students must consider the timing of completed inventory. To illustrate using

the given example, 1,100 units were finished during February, but 100 of those units were "completed" during January. As such, 100 units receive January's $10 per unit rate while the remaining 1,000 units receive February's $9.524 per unit rate ($10,000 ÷ 1,050). Unlike the weighted-average method, we have no empirical data to support the relative effectiveness of a time-based approach when the FIFO inventory flow assumption is used. However, anecdotal feedback from advanced management accounting students suggests that the time-based approach is conceptually easier to understand.

4. Students were only responsible for learning the weighted-average equivalent units method in introductory cost accounting.

5. When all students are analyzed ($n = 431$), our results are qualitatively the same, but less significant. For example, our regression analysis significance level drops from $p < 0.01$ (reported in Table 2) to $p < 0.03$ when all students are considered. To rule out potential confounds associated with a disproportionate number of student withdraws from either of our test groups, we verified that the withdrawal rate between the time-based group and step-by-step group was not significantly different ($\chi^2 = 0.004$, $p = 0.9477$).

6. While the time-based group averaged 56% correct on all weighted average problems, the top scoring step-by-step group averaged only 51%.

7. Specifically, we re-estimated the model in Table 2 after adding each instructor's end-of-semester evaluation score as a additional proxy for instructor quality. The coefficient on TB remained positive and significant at the 0.012 level. To control for any size/quality effects associated with larger versus smaller classes, we also included the class size as an additional co-variate. Significance levels using this specification are virtually identical to those reported in Table 2 (i.e. the coefficient on TB was positive and significant at the 0.015 level).

REFERENCES

Bonner, S. E., & Pennington, N. (1991). Cognitive processes and knowledge as determinants of auditor expertise. *Journal of Accounting Literature, 10*, 1–50.

Copeland, R. M., Dascher, P. E., Strawser, J. R., & Strawser, R. H. (1998). *Managerial Accounting* (8th ed.). Houston, TX: Dame.

Garrison, R. H., & Noreen, E. W. (2000). *Managerial Accounting* (9th ed.). New York, NY: Irwin McGraw Hill.

Horngren, C. T., Foster, G., & Datar, S. (1994). *Cost Accounting: A Managerial Emphasis* (8th ed.). Upper Saddle River, NJ: Prentice-Hall.

Horngren, C. T., Foster, G., & Datar, S. (1997). *Cost Accounting: A Managerial Emphasis* (9th ed.). Upper Saddle River, NJ: Prentice-Hall.

Horngren, C. T., Foster, G., & Datar, S. (1999). *Cost Accounting: A Managerial Emphasis* (10th ed.). Upper Saddle River, NJ: Prentice-Hall.

Longmore, P. (1994). Process costing demystified. *Accountancy, 114*(October), 88–91.

Maher, M. (1997). *Cost Accounting: Creating Value for Management*. New York, NY: McGraw-Hill.

Siegel, G., & Sorensen, J. E. (1999). *Counting More, Counting Less: Transformations in the Management Accounting Profession*. Montvale, NJ: Institute of Management Accountants.

APPENDIX: ACTUAL TEST QUESTIONS

Use the following information to answer the next three questions:

The XYZ Company uses a weighted-average, process cost system. The following information is available from their records:

		Percentage of Completion	
WIP Inventory:	Units	Materials	Conversion Costs
Beginning work-in-process	20	100%	50%
Units started	?		
Units completed	80		
Ending work-in-process	40	100%	50%

The equivalent units produced during the period as to materials totaled
(a) 40 units (c) 100 units (e) none of the above
(b) 80 units (d) 120 units

The equivalent units produced during the period as to conversion costs totaled
(a) 40 units (c) 100 units (e) none of the above
(b) 80 units (d) 120 units

The number of units started during the period totaled
(a) 40 units (c) 100 units (e) none of the above
(b) 80 units (d)120 units

A company using a process costing system collected the following information for your use.

		Percentage of Completion	
WIP Inventory:	Units	Materials	Conversion Costs
Beginning work-in-process	10	40%	60%
Units started	30		
Units completed	20		
Ending work-in-process	20	100%	75%

	Total	Direct Materials	Conversion Costs
Beginning work-in-process	$ 25	$ 10	$ 15
Costs added during the period	125	70	55
Total	$ 150	$ 80	$ 70

Under the weighted-average cost flow assumption, what is the total cost per equivalent unit?

(a) \$ 3.32	(c) \$4.00	(e) none of the above
(b) \$ 3.84	(d) \$ 4.63	

TEACHING ACCOUNTING INFORMATION SYSTEMS USING PERSONAL COMPUTER MOVIES

Lois S. Mahoney and Judith K. Welch

ABSTRACT

Personal Computer Movies (PC Movies) deliver instruction of course content and application of specific skills. They are simple, flexible, and powerful multimedia applications that turn a personal computer (PC) into a VCR. Students view instructor-made movies on their PC at a convenient time and place. This paper discusses the development and making of PC Movies, the uses of PC Movies in teaching accounting, specifically an undergraduate Accounting Information Systems course, and student reaction to the use of this tool.

Each semester instructors make choices about the allocation of course time and resources to accomplish learning objectives. These decisions involve choosing material to "cover" in the lecture versus coverage by some alternative method. In the past, alternative methods included reading in textbooks or completion of homework problems designed to teach material. Today the availability of technology allows more options for presenting course content. This paper discusses a technology tool that allows presentation of content by the instructor without using class time. The specific tool, a Personal Computer Movie (PC Movie), is easy to create by the instructor and easy for students to use.

Advances in Accounting Education, Volume 4, pages 119–138.

ISBN: 0-7623-0856-7

In this paper we explain PC Movies, how to make, distribute, and view them, and how to use them. Secondly, we present student reactions and comments about using PC Movies. Finally, we make recommendations about using them.

BACKGROUND

Tomilson and Kilner (1991) and Wade et al. (1994) promote flexible learning situations that enable students to match learning activities with their learning styles. Williams et al. (1988) noted that personalized systems of instruction in which students study the course material at their own pace results in higher student achievement than traditional lecture/discussion. Fordham (1996) found out-of-class video approaches as effective as in-class lecture approaches for reviewing prerequisite accounting knowledge for an accounting systems course. Jensen and Sandlin (1992) found that students who used course management software had higher final exam scores, as well as higher quality term papers, than students enrolled in the traditional course. Jensen and Sandlin attributed these results to use of electronic technology that presents the material in an easily accessible manner. Kachelmeier et al. (1992) found that students who used a computerized pension learning aid scored higher on exams than students who did not use the aid. Butler and Mautz (1996) found more positive attitudes toward the presentation and the presenter associated with multimedia, regardless of the student's preferred presentation style.

Based upon the above studies, we conclude that technology used for instruction can be as effective as traditional lecture/discussion. In addition, many forms of technology allow students flexibility to review the material at their own pace as often as they want. PC Movies, a new learning tool, offers students the same flexibility.

PERSONAL COMPUTER MOVIES

PC Movie recorder programs offer a simple and flexible tool to create multimedia content. A PC Movie recorder converts the personal computer into a camcorder by capturing every on-screen action and sound happening on the desktop. This recording of actions on the screen creates a way to show dynamic relationships. Students watch the movie on a PC at their convenience and pause, rewind, and fast-forward through the movies similar to watching a movie on their VCR. Figure 1 shows an example frame of a PC

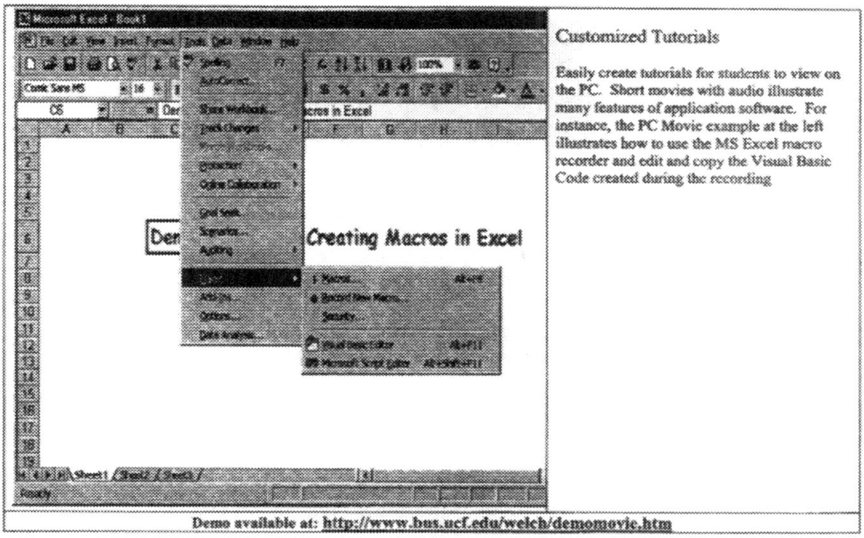

Fig. 1. PC Movie Application.

Movie about developing and using macros in MS Excel. To download this movie, visit http://www.bus.ucf.edu/welch/demomovie.htm.

PC Movies facilitate learning of both course content and application software. Any task completed on a computer can be recorded as a movie and given to students for viewing. Because movies are easy to view and create, they provide instructors a way to explain multi-step tasks and to deliver the content in the same way to all students. Not only does delivery of instruction by movies allow students to review each step as needed, it ensures all students have access to procedural instruction outside of class. Then during class students can raise questions, identify other ways of completing or analyzing a task, and identify extensions.

In addition to changing the delivery of procedural content, movies help students learn new computer applications from scratch or review instructions covered during class. They provide an excellent way to reinforce and document concepts the instructor wants the students to learn. Finally, the movies provide students with access to instruction or review of prerequisite competencies.

Creating PC Movies

Creating a PC Movie is simple. Though each vendor of recorder software has slightly different recording procedures, they operate similarly. The developer

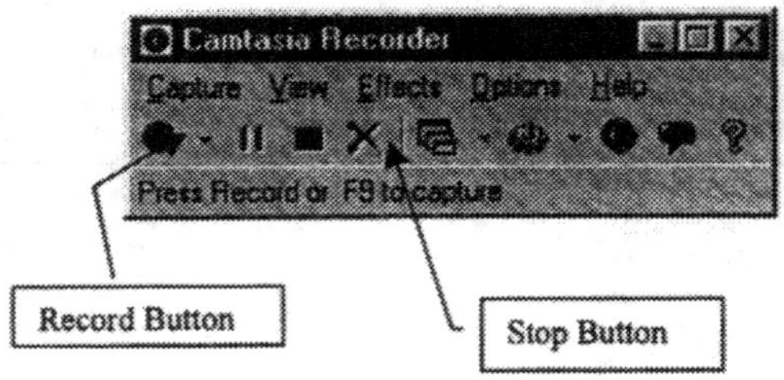

1. Acquire and install a PC Movie recorder application (see references for application specific information).
2. Select preferences concerning video and audio quality.
3. Plan the movie: identify learning objective, material/application for demonstration, and prepare outline of task.
4. Open the application (such as a spreadsheet or presentation application) and the specific file to be demonstrated during the movie. Practice the computer specific tasks and plan the audio to correspond to these tasks.
5. Open the PC Movie Recorder application and select File | New from the menu bar.
6. Click record on the PC Movie Recorder application control and perform the actions practiced in Step 3 above. Record the audio simultaneously with the actions or if preferred record the audio later.
7. Stop recording by clicking the Stop button.
8. Save the movie by selecting File | Save as . . . from the menu bar, name the file, and select an appropriate format.
9. Review the content by clicking on the Play button, and, if necessary, record the movie again.

Fig 2. Developing and Making PC Movies.

clicks on the "record" button to start recording, demonstrates the on-screen activity with appropriate narration, and stops recording when finished. After these actions, the developer saves the file using the File menu. The instructions and controls for a sample application are listed in Fig. 2.

Several vendors offer recorder applications: ScreenCam by Lotus, Camtasia Recorder and Producer by TechSmith, CameraMan by Motion Works, Windows Media Encoder by Microsoft, and HyperCam by Hyperionics. Each of these programs costs less than $150. Table 1 compares the features of these applications. Minimum system requirements should match the minimum require-ments for your operating system, and recording sound requires a sound card, speakers, and a microphone.

One of the determinants of movie file size is the compression algorithm selected by the developer. The compression algorithm is a software component that translates video or audio between its uncompressed form and the compressed form. This component is referred to as a CODEC for

Table 1. PC Movie Applications.

			Features					
Program	Developer	Web Site Information	*Full-Screen Recording*	*Playback*	*Editing*	*File Formats*	*Platform*	Price
Camtasia Recorder and Producer[1]	TechSmith	http://www.techsmith.com	Window sizing available	Stand alone or Windows AVI	Using with Producer	AVI and two streaming formats	Windows 95/98/2000/ NT	$149.95
CameraMan	Motion Works	http://www.mwg.com	Window sizing available	Windows AVI	Editor included	AVI (Win) and MOV (Mac)	Windows 95/98 and Mac	$ 69.95
Media Encoder	Microsoft	http://www.microsoft.com	Window sizing available	Windows AVI		WMV and AVI	Windows 95/98/ 2000 and NT	Free
HyperCam	Hyperionics	http://www.hyperionics.com/	Window sizing available	Windows AVI	No	AVI	Windows 95/98 and NT	$ 30.00
ScreenCam[2]	Lotus	http://www.lotus.com	Yes	Stand alone or proprietary player	Limited or AVI	Proprietary SCM Windows 95 and (non-standard)	Windows 3.1, NT Versions	$89.95

1. The TechSmith Camtasia product is more than just a movie recorder. The package includes the ability to both edit and produce movies in various file formats.

2. The Lotus ScreenCam recorder is not updated for Windows 2000 operating system and there are no plans for development. The player works on all of the following operating systems: Windows 95, 98, 98SE, 98 Millenium Edition, Windows NT4x and Windows 2000.

compressor/decompressor. The compression algorithm affects the quality and size of a PC Movie; therefore, a developer should consider the requirements of the demonstration and the availability of players on computers used by students. As a comparison, a one-minute movie with the lowest quality audio used, 256 colors, and 800X600 resolution resulted in the following file sizes using four different algorithms:

- AVI Uncompressed: 142,512 KB
- Microsoft MPEG-4 V2: 947 KB (CODEC available in Windows)
- Lotus ScreenCam: 770 KB (player required for decompression)
- Techsmith Screen Capture Compression (TSCC): 134 KB (CODEC requires installation on first use).

The developer of a PC Movie should view movies on various types of equipment to ensure students will see what the developer intends. For instance, select a window size that contains the number of pixels no greater than the "lowest" expected monitor/video card students may have. Most applications display well in the smallest number of colors a video card has available. The authors used as few as 16 colors in recording acceptable movies for MS Excel and Access. However, Web pages often use graphics containing thousands of colors and may require use of a higher number of colors to produce acceptable results.

Table 2. Comparison of Movie Sizes at Different Resolutions and Different Colors.

	Resolution		
Colors	640X480	800X600	1064X768
256	28	38	43.5
	100%	136%	155%
16-bit	42.5	41	63
	152%	146%	225%
24-bit	46	55	91
	164%	196%	325%
32-bit	54.3	88.7	108.5
	194%	317%	388%

Parameters used for this measurement:
10 second movie
Techsmith ScreenCapture Compression (TSCC codec)
5 frames per second
Audio at lowest quality
File sizes measured in KB
Base line percent is on 256 colors, 640X480 resolution.

All of the recorder applications allow the recording of both video and audio during the recording process. Recording a silent movie and adding the audio later is an alternative. The multimedia files are large, and trade-offs are necessary with respect to quality for both video and audio tracks. Selection of the lowest number of colors available on the video, a low monitor resolution, and the lowest quality of audio will result in the smallest file size. Table 2 shows comparisons of resulting file sizes based on a specific length movie (10 seconds at 5 frames per second) and a specific compression algorithm (TSCC). For a 10 second video, the file size differs by almost 400% based on the choices made by the developer. Even mindful of these choices, a five to seven minute movie may be 3–5 megabytes. The developer should select the lowest combination of these attributes that produces an acceptable result.

Consideration of audio quality requires two decisions: (1) the data speed, kilohertz, and (2) channels, mono versus stereo. In general, the greater the data speed the better the quality and the larger the file. The difference in file size of a ten second movie ranged from 109 KB for 8.00 khz and 8 bit mono to 2094 KB for 48.00 khz and 16 bit stereo. All of the movies recorded by the authors used the lowest quality settings.[1] For voice-overs, these choices produce acceptable results.

Another important decision is selection of the file format. Choosing a file format involves consideration of how the user will play the movies. Several of the recorder applications allow saving in the Windows AVI format and these movies are played using the Windows Media Player. Movies can also be packaged to play as stand-alone movies. Some of the recorder applications include the ability to save files using streaming media formats, such as Real Media (RM) or Active Streaming Format (ASF). Finally, proprietary formats, such as ScreenCam (SCM), require the distribution of a free player before a user can view the movie. Though the authors found minimal problems with students using the free player to view PC Movies, they believe that the use of stand-alone movies are even more user friendly.

Distributing and Viewing of PC Movies

Distribution of PC Movies is not difficult and can be accomplished using multiple methods. These methods include sending as an attachment by e-mail, distributing the files on a CD, downloading files from a Web site for subsequent playback or streaming from a Web server with simultaneous playback. Each distribution method requires different resources. See Table 3 for comparison of methods of delivery. Figure 3 shows a sample Internet site for downloading movies.

Table 3. Comparison of Distribution Methods.

Method	Advantages	Disadvantages	Recommendation
E-mail	Quick Familiar	File sizes are large: requires compression Download time could be excessive for students with slow connect speeds	Use for single and/or one time distribution of short movies
CD (write-once)	Portable Permanent	Requires pre-recording of all movies Requires CD-recorder and recording time Development time for the CD	Use when distributing many movies and/or long movies
Web download	Continuous updates	File sizes dictates special "packaging" for efficient download Web site development and maintenance Download time could be excessive for students with slow connect speeds	Use for distribution of a few movies and/or updates to movies
Web streaming	Continuous updates	Requires high bandwidth for smooth playback Requires additional steps for converting movies to streaming formats Web site development and maintenance	Use where students have high-speed connects

Because of the large number of PC Movies used in our Accounting Information Systems (AIS) course, both the instructors and students found CD distribution the easiest method of delivery. Each semester, the instructors create a new version of the CD with updates from the previous semester. At the beginning of the semester, CDs are produced and written for all the students registered in the AIS course. Students receive the CDs free of charge and may keep the CD. Funding for acquisition of the CD recorder and the CDs came from private sources.

For faculty members who do not have the equipment or time to copy CDs, it should be noted that many Universities provide this service for classroom purposes for the cost of a disk. CDs, including the cover, can be professionally made for under $10 each, depending upon quantity. Prices for recorders and blank CDs continue to fall, making the most significant element the

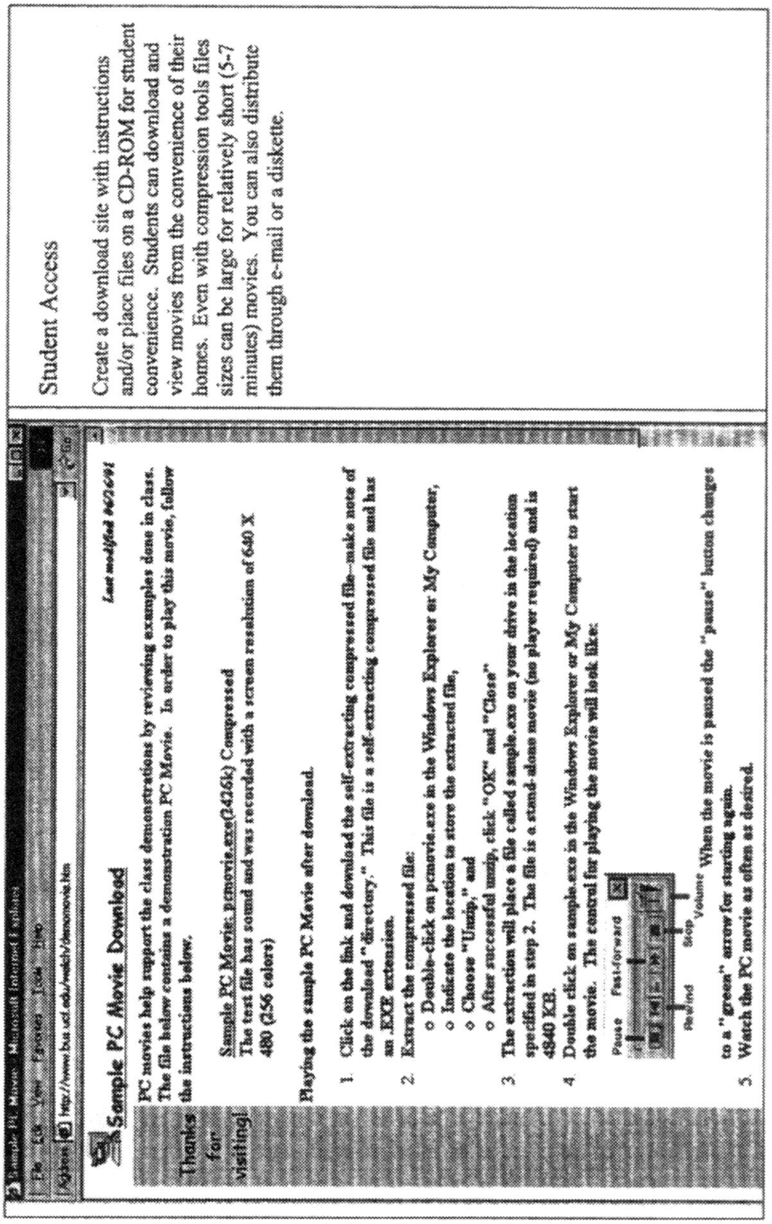

Fig. 3. Access to PC Movies.

personnel time of instructors or student assistants to record multiple copies of the CDs.

A student views a movie in one of four different ways. If the movie was recorded as a stand-alone movie then double-clicking on the file, usually an EXE file, plays the movie. If the movie was recorded as an AVI file, the student launches the Windows Media Player, opens the file and begins playing the movie by clicking on the play button. Additionally if a proprietary player is required, such as the ScreenCam player, the student completes the same sequence of activities for the appropriate player. Finally, if a streaming format from a Web server is employed, the student clicks on the link, the player loads automatically (if it is installed on the computer), and the movie begins playing. In each of these cases the learning effort for the student is low.

The application of PC Movies as course material allows each student the flexibility to learn or review the material at a convenient time and place. Students review the movies as many times as necessary to learn course concepts and skills. If the PC Movies are kept short and easily digestible, a student reviews them on an as-needed basis and does not delay other students. The delivery of content by PC Movies ensures the same explanation is available to all students. Because faculty encounter diverse student populations, the availability of one consistent explanation (especially if the transcript is available) allows for reflection and absorption time for all students.

Potential Uses of PC Movies in Accounting Courses

PC Movies can demonstrate problem-solving strategies and computer applications for any accounting course and concept.[2] Developing a movie includes the same considerations an instructor incorporates to plan any lesson. The instructor develops a learning objective, constructs a problem, develops a computer-based solution to the problem, plans the audio, and records the movie. If an instructor already has computer-based problems previously used in classroom presentations, then the additional step is simply recording the movie.

PC Movies excel at application development learning tasks or small incremental learning objectives. For example, to instruct students about present value concepts an instructor presents a problem and demonstrates the calculation of a solution via table look-up or spreadsheet functions. A valuable part of the lesson may include a demonstration of the sensitivity of results to changing values in the model. To teach students how to effectively use spreadsheet technology, an instructor can demonstrate creating and using macros for repetitive tasks or demonstrate setting up accounting worksheets with documentation. Any complex computation can be illustrated, explained, and analyzed with PC Movies.

Instructors who want students to move beyond using the computer for computational purposes can illustrate the creation of decision management tools. Not only can instructors demonstrate the computation and analysis of the cost-volume-profit model, they can show students how to turn this model into a tool to aid decision making by incorporating logic and formatting. Faculty can utilize movies to show the organization and structure of data, perform complex queries, and create forms and reports in a relational database. In sum, PC Movies can deliver any course content.

Instructor designed, developed, and narrated PC Movies may be perceived by students as personal interaction with the instructor. Some publishers have developed movies to correspond to textbook material; however, these movies tend to be generic and not specifically related to skills the instructor wants students to learn. Instructor-designed movies target specific skills students need to learn.

The undergraduate AIS course reported here uses 35 PC Movies to teach both theoretical and applied course concepts.[3] Table 4 shows a list of the topics and brief description of types of material covered. In general, these movies demonstrate computer application tasks using MS Excel, MS Visual Basic for Applications (VBA), and MS Access software. Each movie relates to a task students perform in a project or an important course concept. For example, a course project requires students to identify data tables, populate the tables, and establish relationships in an Access Database. The movies Designing Tables and Creating Relationships demonstrate how to perform these tasks. Students observe and hear how to perform computerized procedures, such as writing macros, developing user forms and building relational databases. The length of these movies ranged from 3 minutes 33 seconds to 11 minutes 27 seconds. Additional PC Movies demonstrate previous students' projects.

STUDENT REACTIONS AND COMMENTS

Student Reactions

To assess student reaction to PC Movies, students in the AIS courses completed a survey (see Appendix 1). A total of 48 out of 96 students who finished the course completed a questionnaire about the course support material provided by the instructor. Most of the questions relate to student reactions to using PC Movies. Table 5 reports the results of this survey. Overall, student comments are extremely positive. Ninety-six percent of all respondents report PC Movies were "indispensable" or "very beneficial" for learning computer applications. Eighty-six percent of the students report the use of the movies was "very useful."

Table 4. PC Movies Used in Teaching Accounting Information Systems.

Course Learning Goal	Software Used	Task Specific Movie	Length of Movie
Create a management decision-making tool using advanced spreadsheet features			
	Spreadsheet/MS Excel	Using the Forms Toolbar	4 min 10 sec
		Making Option Boxes and Check Boxes	3 min 52 sec
		Naming Cells and Ranges	5 min 53 sec
		Making Drop Down and List Boxes	4 min 44 sec
		Using Scroll Bars and Spinners	5 min 50 sec
		Making Buttons	3 min 33 sec
		Using Text Boxes and Notes	4 min 20 sec
		Creating Macros (3)	Average 5 min 20 sec
		Using Pivot Tables	5 min 58 sec
	Visual Basic for Applications	Overview of Visual Basic	6 min 33 sec
		Making Userforms (3)	Average 4 min 53 sec
Apply concepts of relational database management systems to business events			
	Desktop Database/ MS Access	Overview of Access	6 min 34 sec
		Designing Tables	5 min 7 sec
		Creating Relationships (3)	6 min 1 sec
		Creating a Mainform/ Subform (6)	Average 7 min 10 sec
		Making Simple Queries (2)	Average 9 min 24 sec
Design and implement a limited scope application controlling the user interface and applying internal controls using database technology			
	Desktop Database/ MS Access	Making Complex Queries (3)	Average 9 min 24 sec
		Creating Macros	5 min 30 sec
		Creating Password Protection	5 min 6 sec
		Making Message Boxes	5 min 44 sec
		Creating Dialog Boxes	6 min 2 sec
		Using Option Buttons	6 min 6 sec
		Calculating Totals on Forms	5 min 44 sec

Table 5. Responses to Survey Concerning Course Support Materials.

Question	Responses				
How beneficial do you believe the PC Movies are for learning about computer applications?	*Indispensible* 52%	*Very Beneficial* 44%	*Neutral* 4%	*Not Beneficial* 0%	*Worthless* 0%
How often did you view each PC Movie?	*<1* 2%	*1 time* 17%	*2–3 times* 58%	*>3* 23%	
Did you go back and review various PC Movies while working on projects?	*Very Frequently* 37%	*Frequently* 40%	*Somewhat* 19%	*Seldom* 4%	*Never* 0%
Using PC Movies is ________?	*Very Easy* 65%	*Easy* 21%	*About Average* 12%	*Difficult* 0%	*Very Difficult* 2%
How do you feel about the length of the PC Movies?	*Too Short* 6%	*Short* 19%	*Just Right* 64%	*Long* 4%	*Too Long* 0%
Of the support material given to you in class, what item was the most helpful to your learning?	*PC Movies* 73%	*Handouts* 9%	*Demonstration Files* 16%	*Previous Student Files* 2%	
Of the support material given to you in class, what item was the least helpful to your learning?	*PC Movies* 4%	*Handouts* 47%	*Demonstration Files* 4%	*Previous Student Files* 45%	
The use of PC Movies were______?	*Very Useful* 86%	*Somewhat Useful* 14%	*Not Useful* 0%	*Not Useful At All* 0%	*Never Used Them* 0%

In addition to the textbook, the students received handouts, sample student files from previous semesters, instructor demonstration files, and PC Movies. Table 5 shows students felt PC Movies were the best ancillary materials available to them for learning the course; 73% of the students thought PC Movies were the "most helpful" to their learning experience while only 4% thought they were the "least helpful."

Eighty-one percent of the students reported viewing each movie two or more times while 77% of the students said they went back and reviewed the movies while working on the projects. Students overwhelmingly reported little difficulty using PC Movies. While 21% reported that using PC Movies was "easy," another 65% reported that they were "very easy" to use. Though the length of PC Movies varied from 3 minutes and 33 seconds to 11 minutes and 27 seconds with the average movie being approximately six minutes, 64% of the students thought the length was "just right." This result suggests PC Movies used for teaching should be between 5 to 10 minutes long.

Student Comments

Forty-two percent of the respondents cited the visualization of computer applications along with the step-by-step demonstration as the feature they liked best about PC Movies. Other advantageous features cited include the ability to play the movies over and over again (29%); ability to work at their own pace when and where they wanted to (12%); and availability of reference materials at all times (8%).

In general, students expressed a desire for more detailed PC Movies (19%) and thought some of the PC Movies went fast (8%). One student mentioned version specific issues because some of the demonstrations did not work on all available "versions" of the software. Students also reported, on average, a willingness to pay $10 for the CD.

MAKING THE DECISION TO USE PC MOVIES

Making the decision to use PC Movies requires consideration of the benefits and costs both to the faculty and students. Often faculty explain certain course concepts many times during a semester and office hours. Identification of these key topics and recording of a PC Movie about these topics may reduce the burden on class time and faculty time. Especially for demonstration of computer skills, the PC Movie frees class time for questions and demonstration of applicability of that skill to course issues. For example, recording movies about breakeven analysis could explain and demonstrate the interactions that occur among the variables. While this demonstration could also occur in class, the availability of a movie a student could watch as many times as necessary to understand the relationships would increase learning. Increased learning could then lead to more complex application of course concepts.

Students benefit in multiple ways from the availability of PC Movies. Some of the potential benefits include:

- They learn "applications" by using material from multiple sources
- They gain confidence in their abilities
- They learn independent of time and place
- They learn strategies for resolving problems and finding help other than from the instructor.

Our experience shows students are able to produce a higher quality computer project with unlimited availability of explanations for problems encountered. Also, for students who like to work ahead of schedule, movies give them the necessary resources to do so.

Along with the benefits, there are costs inherent in using PC Movies. The most obvious cost is the initial development of the movies. These costs involve both dollars and time. Development time involves acquiring the software, planning and making the movies, and deciding on a distribution method. First, deciding which software to acquire may require examination of more than one tool. Most companies allow downloading their software for evaluation purposes. Planning the course topics and computerized concepts to cover in the movies and how to demonstrate them takes time, but each new movie takes less and less time as you become comfortable with the information to cover, how to cover it, and the application tool. Initially, the same movie may need to be recorded several times with different settings to see what works best. Finally, a distribution method should be selected appropriate to student needs. One of the nice things about Web distribution is the ease of updating movies as new versions of software are issued.

While the development time can be significant, there are gains that accrue after the PC Movie is made. Fewer student questions and frequent explanations on the same concepts free up class time. Students learn more independently but still feel as if the instructor is helping.

CONCLUSION AND RECOMMENDATIONS

Considering the reported ease of use by students, the perceived value as a learning aide, and the relative ease of development, faculty ought to consider the usage of PC Movies as learning tools. They reinforce key concepts, demonstrate use of computer applications, provide remedial assistance for prerequisite skills, and provide a step-by-step review of concepts demonstrated in the classroom.[4] In addition, students view movies at their own pace in a comfortable setting. Because the PC Movie player and movies can be copied free of charge, PC Movies are cost effective additions to classroom support. Use of PC Movies offers the following benefits:

- Content learned independent of time and place
- Different learning styles accommodated
- Technology-related tasks learned efficiently
- Additional time-on-task does not use class time
- Explanations repeated to those with language barriers.

PC Movies provide a practical new approach to learning. These movies can provide instructions for on-line classes. In today's society where the Internet is used increasingly to offer educational courses and even degrees, PC Movies provide an excellent way to demonstrate course material and specifically, software applications. Students using PC Movies for on-line instruction receive the same lecture/demonstration as students in the classroom and can review them as often as they like, when and where they like. The benefits of using PC Movies far outweigh the costs.

NOTES

1. For students viewing movies without audio support, transcripts of each movie are available. Students could use their own headphones in a university lab.
2. Several methods of delivery exist for presentation of "lecture" material via the computer. Using presentation graphics programs with audio is a potential presentation mode. While these applications do allow for animations, PC Movies show additional "action" unavailable through current presentation graphics technologies.
3. The ease of development means additional movies can be developed and added to Web sites for downloading by students. The number of available movies continues to grow as time passes.
4. The College of Business Administration at the University of Central Florida developed an extensive Web support site using PC movies to reinforce required computer competency skills. These PC movies are available from the College in a streaming format via the Web, printable instructions via the Web or on a CD-Rom. The Web site address is http://www.bus.ucf.edu/skills/.

REFERENCES

Butler, J. B., & Mautz, R. D. (1996). Multimedia presentations and learning: A laboratory experiment. *Issues in Accounting Education, 11*, 259–280.

Fordham, D. R. (1996). Freeing class time: Empirical evidence on the benefits of using out-of-class video segments in lieu of in-class reviews. *Issues in Accounting Education, 11*, 37–48.

Jensen, R. E., & Sandlin, P. K. (1992). Why do it? Advantages and dangers of new waves of computer-aided teaching/instruction. *Journal of Accounting Education, 10*, 39–60.

Kachelmeier, S. J., Jones, J. D., & Keller, J. A. (1992). Evaluating the effectiveness of a computer-intensive learning aid for teaching pension accounting. *Issues in Accounting Education, 10*, 39–60.

Tomilson, P., & Kilner, S. (1991). *Flexible Learning, Flexible Teaching: The Flexible Learning Framework and Current Educational Theory*. Sheffield, England: Employment Department.

Wade, W., H., Smith, K. A., & Arfield, J. (Eds). (1994). *Flexible Learning in Higher Education*. London, England: Biddles Ltd.

Williams, J. R., Tiller, M. G., Herring, H. C., & Scheiner, J. H. (1988). *A Framework for the Development of Accounting Education Research*. Sarasota, FL: American Accounting Association.

APPENDIX 1

Questionnaire

This course was offered as part of a pilot program at UCF. The format was one traditional face-to-face class and one asynchronous class using computer and Web-based activities. As part of this pilot program, I would like your comments about the course format, and any more suggestions about how the Media Enhanced part of the course could be improved. In addition to your feedback on the Media Enhanced portion of the course, several questions relate to the CD provided to you by the School of Accounting. Please respond to all questions honestly, as your responses will be anonymous, and after submission you should receive a response on the screen that you may print as confirmation of completion. Bring the confirmation sheet to the final exam for the "extra" points.

Instructions: (please respond to all questions)

Please place an X in the space next to the best answer. After completing all questions, please send the questionnaire back to me by pushing the reply and send buttons.

CD Questions

1. The CD contained several types of learning materials, put an "x" in the space next to the item that was MOST helpful to your learning:

____ Class handouts (pdf format)
____ Lotus ScreenCams on Excel and Access topics
____ Sample student files from previous semesters
____ Dr. Welch's demonstration files

2. The CD contained several types of learning materials, put an "x" in the space next to the item that was LEAST helpful to your learning:

____ Class handouts (pdf format)
____ Lotus ScreenCams on Excel and Access topics
____ Sample student files from previous semesters
____ Dr. Welch's demonstration files

3. The CD contained several types of support materials, put an "x" in the space next to the item that was MOST helpful to you:

____ Interactive application called, "Cruising the Information Superhighway"
____ Power point slides files from the textbook
____ Data files from the Grauer textbook
____ Plug-ins for your browser

4. The CD contained several types of support materials, put an "x" in the space next to the item that was LEAST helpful to you:

____ Interactive application called, "Cruising the Information Superhighway"
____ Power point slides files from the textbook
____ Data files from the Grauer textbook
____ Plug-ins for your browser

5. How much would you be willing to pay for a CD similar to this one that was designed to support accounting class assignments in several courses?

____

6. The use of ScreenCam movies were:

____ Very useful
____ Somewhat useful
____ Not useful
____ Not useful at all
____ Don't know, never tried them

7. How often did you view the ScreenCams?

____ Less than one time each
____ One time each
____ Two to three times each
____ More than three times each

8. Did you go back and review various ScreenCams while working on projects?

____ Very Frequently
____ Frequently
____ Somewhat
____ Seldom
____ Never

9. How beneficial do you believe the ScreenCams are for learning about computer applications:

____ Indispensable
____ Very Beneficial
____ Neutral
____ Not Beneficial
____ Worthless

10. How do you feel about the length of the ScreenCams?

____ Way too long
____ Long
____ Just right
____ Short
____ Too short

11. Using ScreenCams is:

____ Very difficult
____ Somewhat difficult
____ About average for computer applications
____ Somewhat easy
____ Very easy

12. What do you believe the average length in minutes of a ScreenCam should be? (Type your answer in the space.)

____

13. Do you believe there should be more or less ScreenCams used in this class? (Type your answer in the space.)

____

14. What did you like best about the ScreenCams? (Type your answer in the space below.)

____

15. What did you like least about the ScreenCams? (Type your answer in the space below.)

____

16. Anything else you want to say about the CD or the Media Enhanced format. (Type your answer in the space below.)

____

MEASURING THE PROBLEM-DEFINING ABILITY OF ACCOUNTING STUDENTS

Carol J. Normand and Richard E. Baker

ABSTRACT

This paper describes an exploratory study designed to help accounting educators address the challenge of assessing the problem-solving ability of accounting students. In this study, a method is described which is designed to produce case-based assessment tools that measure the level of problem-solving ability obtained by accounting majors. Findings from educational psychology research that indicate problem-solving ability is a cognitive process consisting of identifiable stages as well as findings from accounting research were used to develop this method. Previous accounting behavioral research has shown that, if accountants cannot adequately define and represent a problem, strategy selection and the evaluation of actions taken will be skewed, therefore, the method proposed in this paper focuses on the problem-defining stage of the problem-solving process. Statistical tests indicated that the student problem-defining scores obtained by the assessment tool produced by the proposed method do replicate prior research, are not biased towards several demographic groups, and is robust enough to assess problem-defining ability at varying levels of difficulty.

Advances in Accounting Education, Volume 4, pages 139–167.

ISBN: 0-7623-0856-7

INTRODUCTION

In the past fifteen years, numerous reports and studies issued by accounting professionals and educators have articulated a new configuration of skills and abilities necessary for success in today's accounting profession.[1] Although these reports and studies have varied in their lists of requisite skills and abilities, all have included problem-solving ability as a skill needed by entry-level accountants to achieve success in their chosen profession.

In 1993, the American Assembly of Collegiate Schools of Business (AACSB) responded to the reports and studies by including a problem-solving focus in its 1993 standards for accounting accreditation. This focus was continued in the AACSB's 1999 revision of the accounting accreditation standards. Included in these standards were the following statements:

> ... The accounting curriculum must reflect the increasing breadth and specificity of accounting services. Course work in accounting should emphasize theory, concepts, principles, problem solving and research techniques, and should prepare students to solve complex and unstructured problems (AACSB, 1999, p. 44).

> ... Discuss the effectiveness of the ... curriculum and processes in accomplishing the accounting academic unit's mission, each program's educational objectives, and in achieving quality and continuous improvement (AACSB, 1999, p. 48).

As a result of these accounting accreditation requirements, accounting educators must now develop ways of teaching problem solving that are appropriate for the missions and educational objectives of their institutions. Additionally, accounting educators must develop assessment methods that measure the level of problem-solving ability attained by accounting majors and that assist in achieving continuous improvement of accounting curricula.

To help accounting educators address the challenge of assessing the problem-solving ability of their students, we completed an exploratory study. The primary objective of this study is to demonstrate a method that could be undertaken at individual institutions to measure the problem-solving ability of accounting majors. This proposed method is based on findings from both educational psychology and accounting research. The secondary objective of our study is to offer preliminary evidence obtained from one possible assessment tool that resulted from the proposed method. Our proposed problem-solving assessment method could assist in the continuous improvement of accounting curricula by measuring the problem-solving ability obtained by accounting students before and after a curricular or pedagogical adjustment made by the accounting faculty of an institution.

Because the missions of accounting programs, the nature of students, and the focus of accounting faculty vary between institutions, the results obtained by the proposed method would also vary from institution to institution. Just as a single senior exit survey cannot be used to establish a national baseline for program excellence, our proposed method could not be used to determine a national problem-solving baseline.

In this exploratory paper, first, we present an overview of educational psychology research findings that indicate problem-solving ability is a cognitive process consisting of identifiable stages. Second, we review the ways in which accounting education research has explored problem-solving ability as well as the ways in which that research has suggested problem-solving ability be assessed. Third, we describe a method based on findings from both accounting research and cognitive psychology research that is designed to develop tools that assess the level of accounting student problem-solving ability in one stage of the problem-solving process. Finally, the ways in which accounting faculty at individual institutions can use the ideas and findings presented in this study are discussed.

An initial motivation for this study was to develop a sufficiently robust and unbiased assessment tool that could be used to determine accounting students' problem-defining abilities. This tool could be used to assess students' problem-defining and problem-solving abilities at one point in time as well as any change in those abilities that resulted from specific educational initiatives. The key point, thus, is that we needed an assessment device that provided the feedback necessary to evaluate and assess our accounting curriculum and students' educational outcomes.

THEORETICAL BACKGROUND

Problem-Solving Models

Since the 1970s, cognitive psychologists have been studying how individuals solve problems. While some of these researchers have focused on developing general theories concerning the problem-solving process (Anderson, 1983; Newell & Simon, 1972), other cognitive psychologists have focused on developing operational definitions for problem-solving ability that can be employed in educational settings. Some of these education-oriented researchers have defined problem solving as a process that involves analyzing and resolving a perplexing or difficult situation (Marzano et al., 1988, p. 145).[2] Additionally, according to these researchers, problem-solving ability is a cognitive process that has several identifiable stages (Sternberg, 1988, p. 78; Wales, Nardi & Stager, 1987, p. 9; Bransford & Stein, 1984, p. 27).

Bransford and Stein's IDEAL model (1984, p. 27) provides one set of possible stages in the problem-solving cognitive process. In this model, an easily understood progressive framework using the stages of the scientific method as the stages of the problem-solving process integrates the research findings of many cognitive psychology researchers. Each initial letter in the name of the model stands for a specific stage of the problem-solving process. The stages identified by Bransford and Stein are:

(1) **I**dentify the problem.
(2) **D**efine and represent the problem.
(3) **E**xplore possible strategies.
(4) **A**ct on the strategies.
(5) **L**ook back and evaluate the effects of the activities.

Individuals must frequently move through these stages a number of times before arriving at a satisfactory solution to the problem under consideration.

After a review of other models suggested by cognitive researchers, we chose Bransford and Stein's IDEAL model for this study for several reasons. This model has been widely used in other domains (Marzano et al., 1988, p. 47) and the authors believed its mnemonic would be a beneficial device. Additionally, models similar to the Bransford and Stein model have already been introduced into the accounting literature.

For example, in Gainen and Locatelli's 1995 assessment guide, problem-solving ability was included as a desired learning outcome for accounting programs. The authors proposed performance criteria for assessing the problem-solving ability of accounting students that are very similar to the IDEAL problem-solving model. Gainen and Locatelli's problem-solving ability performance criteria (1995, p. 86) were:

- Identifying and diagnosing the problem
- Generating alternative solutions and strategies
- Developing a plan of action
- Implementing the plan of action
- Keeping the planning process open to new information and ideas.

As indicated by their last criterion, Gainen and Locatelli believed that the problem-solving process is iterative in nature as did Bransford and Stein.

Additionally, a model developed by Langenderfer and Rockness (1989, p. 66) has been widely used to teach students how to analyze ethical situations. The seven steps in this model are:

- Determine the facts
- Define the ethical issue
- Identify major values
- Specify the alternatives
- Compare values and alternatives
- If a clear decision does not emerge, assess the consequences
- Make your decision.

A review of these steps indicates that the ethical dilemma model bears a striking resemblance to the IDEAL problem-solving model.

Importance of the "Define the Problem" Stage

In addition to developing the IDEAL model, Bransford and Stein emphasized the critical importance of the "define the problem" stage of the model (1984, p. 15). These authors cited previous research that indicated expert problem solvers develop one or more ways to represent a problem before taking action and that different representations of a problem often lead to different actions being taken. Without a thorough examination of multiple problem representations or definitions, subsequent actions taken, although perhaps not in error, might be incomplete or not as effective as possible.

Since the publication of the Bransford and Stein book, other researchers exploring the problem-solving processes of experts and novices have supported this position (Clark & Lamberts, 1997; Mumpower & Stewart, 1996; Kaplan & Simon, 1990). Additionally, cognitive psychology researchers have found that the categories novices use to define problems are more superficial and surface-feature oriented while the categories used by experts are more conceptual and principle based (Glaser & Chi, 1988, p. xviii). This difference in problem definition between experts and novices has been shown to occur across a wide variety of domains (Allison & Allison, 1993, p. 317; Smith, 1992, p. 204; Lesgold et al., 1988, p. 340; Weiser & Shertz, 1983, p. 397; Schoenfeld & Hermann, 1982, p. 491; Chi, Feltovich & Glaser, 1981, p. 150).

Some accounting behavioral researchers have utilized the findings of expert/novice cognitive psychology research as a basis for their studies. Their findings also support the importance of properly representing a problem before developing a solution (Bierstaker, Bedard & Biggs, 1999: p. 33; Phillips, 1998, p. 123; Bonner, Libby & Nelson 1997, p. 404; Stone & Shelly, 1997, p. 55; Beddard & Biggs, 1991, p. 639) and that the categories accounting experts employ to define a problem are more conceptual and more principle-based than novices (Frederick, Heiman-Hoffman & Libby, 1994, p. 18).

Because of these findings and the overwhelming extent of the entire problem-solving process, we decided that our proposed method should focus on developing assessment tools for the problem-defining stage of the problem-solving process. If accountants cannot adequately define a problem, then strategy selection and the evaluation of actions taken will be skewed. Accounting education should, therefore, place emphasis on this stage of the problem-solving process.

Additionally, from a practical viewpoint, students cannot take real actions to solve problems in classroom situations. Most case studies, therefore, only require students to present possible solutions to problems and to discuss possible actions that could be taken. Because most case studies focus on the problem-defining stage of the problem-solving process, most performance evaluations are also focused on this stage.

Problem-Solving Assessment in Accounting Education Literature

Although formal outcome assessment plans for accounting programs have been explored by several authors (Stivers, Campbell & Hermanson, 2000; Kimmell, Marquette & Olsen, 1998; Akers, Giacomino & Trebby, 1997; DeMong, Lindgren & Perry, 1994; Herring & Izard, 1992), none have focused on assessing of the level of problem-solving ability attained by accounting program graduates. Hill, Perry and Stein (1998, p. 70) did discuss the formal assessment of the degree to which an accounting program influenced the development of problem-solving abilities in its graduates, however, problem solving was only one capability included in an area identified as "intellectual skills" on a survey completed by accounting students. In this survey, students were asked to indicate the strength of their problem-solving capability as they perceived it. DeMong, Lindgren and Perry (1994, p. 15), however, indicated that student perception surveys have little or no ability to measure assessment outcomes such as critical thinking and creativity.

After reflecting on the previous assessment literature, we decided to base our proposed problem-defining assessment method on cases. This decision was based on publications by the Accounting Education Change Commission (AECC) and the assessment framework established by Gainen and Locatelli.

In its *Position Statement No. One* (AECC, 1990, p. 308), the AECC stated that the focus of accounting education should be on developing analytical and conceptual thinking and not on memorizing professional standards. In its

Position Statement No. Two (AECC, 1992, p. 250), the AECC recommended the use of case studies as one way in which this focus might be achieved.

Building on the recommendation of the AECC, Gainen and Locatelli (1995, p. 99) suggested using case studies to evaluate the problem-solving ability of accounting students. These authors suggested that student problem-solving performance on case studies could be assessed by developing specific learning objectives and using several indicators or sources of evidence to determine if the learning objectives were being achieved. One of the seven problem-solving learning objectives presented by these authors was "student correctly uses accounting principles to address the problem."

One of the five indicators or sources of evidence suggested by Gainen and Locatelli (1995, p. 101) was the "cross-grading of written case analyses using an analytical rating scale based on performance criteria." Unfortunately, the authors did not define what they meant by "cross-grading" or an "analytical rating scale" nor did they provide a detailed explanation of how this idea for a suggested source of problem-solving evidence might be operationalized.

In contrast to the assessment guide presented by Gainen and Locatelli, our exploratory paper contributes to accounting education research by describing how our proposed method designed to assess the level of problem-defining ability attained by accounting students was developed and implemented at one institution. Additionally, our paper describes preliminary evidence concerning one possible assessment tool that resulted from that method.

IMPLEMENTING THE PROPOSED PROBLEM-DEFINING ASSESSMENT METHOD

Our proposed problem-solving assessment method has the following characteristics:

- it is focused on the problem-defining stage of the problem-solving process;
- the performance criterion is "students correctly use accounting principles to address the problem."

We developed and implemented this assessment method through the following four-step process.

1. Developing the assessment materials
2. Establishing benchmarks
3. Conducting the assessment
4. Evaluating the assessment method.

Details concerning each of these steps are presented in the following sections.

Developing the Assessment Materials

For this study, we selected two Deloitte & Touche Trueblood cases dealing with revenue recognition issues. We also designed worksheets and a personal information questionnaire so that the assessment method was a simple to administer paper-and-pencil test. The two cases and one worksheet are presented in Appendix A.

Trueblood cases published by the Deloitte and Touche Foundation were utilized in this study because they are available to, and widely used by, accounting educators. Additionally, these cases were developed from experiences in the practice domain. To be selected for the study, the cases had to be short enough to be read in about five minutes and incorporate material included in a typical undergraduate accounting curriculum. In the initial implementation of the proposed method, the students took an average of 7.21 minutes to complete Case 1 and an average of 7.11 minutes to complete Case 2.

For the proposed problem-defining assessment method, we intentionally selected two Trueblood cases of varying difficulty but dealing with similar financial accounting principles. By selecting these cases, we manipulated the level of difficulty while prior knowledge of the financial accounting principles being assessed was held steady. Case 2, therefore, was more difficult than Case 1 because it involved more accounting principles as well as more years and more non-relevant information.

Establishing Benchmarks

Problem-defining benchmarks were created for each case in order to develop an analytical rating scale that could be used to grade student responses. Prior research that indicates the categories experts employ to define a problem in their domain are more conceptual and more principle-based than the categories used by novices was used in the development of these benchmarks.

The benchmarks were established through a two-step process. First, five practitioner financial accounting experts[3] read the two selected cases and indicated the set of accounting principles they used to define each case. Each expert also completed a personal-information questionnaire. The expert responses helped to establish the level of problem-defining ability that exists in practice for these cases. Because one of the goals of professional education is to move the novice to the expert level as effectively and efficiently as possible, experts can help accounting educators establish measures for this objective.

The level of familiarity with the content of the two cases that each expert reported on the personal-information questionnaire was used to review the responses provided by the experts. This level of problem familiarity was used to review the experts' responses because of concerns expressed by Bonner and Pennington (1991, p. 39). These authors suggested that time with a firm is a reasonable surrogate for expertise only if the individual had experience with the problem or problems being explored in the study.

Second, the authors used the experts' responses,[4] the teaching materials provided by Deloitte and Touche LLP and their own understanding to identify two accounting principles as issues in Case 1 (revenue recognition and full disclosure) and three accounting principles as issues in Case 2 (revenue recognition, liability recognition, full disclosure). Each accounting principle included in the two problem-defining benchmarks was assigned a two-point value. A perfect score for Case 1, therefore, was four and a perfect score for Case 2 was six. As stated above, Case 2 was considered to be a more complex representation of problem solving in financial accounting than Case 1 because of the way in which the problem material was presented and the number of accounting issues involved in defining the case.

Conducting the Assessment

Instrumentation

Each student participating in this study received copies of the two case studies, worksheets on which they indicated the set of accounting principles they employed to define each case, and a personal-information questionnaire. We tested these materials in a pilot study before they were distributed to the students. Because all materials were distributed to the students at the same time, the students selected which case they read first.

Sample Selection

For this exploratory study, a voluntary sample of 46 students was obtained from a population of 120 accounting students graduating from a large Midwestern AACSB-accredited university. To be included in the sample, the students had to be graduating in May or August of the year in which the data were collected and have less than five years of accounting-related work experience.

Additionally, because this study focused on the level of problem-defining ability obtained by graduating accounting majors, students must have successfully completed the following accounting courses to participate in the study: intermediate financial accounting I and II, intermediate cost accounting, accounting systems, auditing theory, and taxation. The students who volunteered to complete the research materials responded to requests from the authors as well as other faculty members and received no compensation (money or points towards a grade) for their participation.[5]

Students entering the accounting program were not included in this study. The degree to which an individual can solve problems in a specific domain is highly dependent upon the level of domain-specific knowledge an individual has acquired (Choo, 1996, p. 340; Libby & Luft, 1993, p. 429). Individuals beginning the accounting undergraduate program, therefore, might not have learned enough domain-specific knowledge to participate effectively in this exploratory study.

The student sample used in this study was not random because the sample consisted of voluntary subjects who were recruited using a variety of methods. To establish the validity of the sample, F tests and Student t tests were performed using data for several demographic variables: university grade point average, gender, native versus transfer status, commuting versus campus resident status, and age. The findings showed that the sample, although not random, was representative of the population at this university for these demographic variables.[6]

Because the stated purpose of this study is to begin the development of a an assessment method that could be used by accounting educators to determine the level of problem-defining ability obtained by accounting graduates, the authors felt that a sample size of 46 is sufficient for this study. The size of graduating accounting classes at many institutions is not large so assessment tools developed through the proposed method must be appropriate for smaller sample sizes.

Measurement of Student Problem-Defining Abilities

The problem-defining ability of each student was measured by developing evidence for the performance criterion "student correctly uses accounting principles to address the problem." This evidence was obtained by assigning a value based on the benchmark analytical scale to the set of accounting principles that each student reported using to define each case. In this exploratory study, each author independently assigned a score based on a comparison of the student answers for each problem to the appropriate benchmark. The scores assigned by each author were compared and differences were discussed until consensus was achieved.

A score was assigned to the set of financial accounting concepts selected by a student by comparing the set of accounting principles included in the appropriate benchmark to the student's set of accounting principles. Scores from 0 through 4 were assigned for Case 1, and scores 0 through 6 were assigned for Case 2. If none of the accounting concepts selected by the student matched those included in the benchmark, the student received a score of "0". If the set of accounting concepts selected by the student was identical to the benchmark, the student received a score of "4" for Case 1 and a score of "6" for Case 2.

For example, for Case 1, the student answer "sale of land with boot involved" received a score of "0" because the answer only repeated information given in the problem. The student answers "reporting a letter of credit & reporting/disclosing a sale" and "footnote" received a score of "1" because the students did indicate an understanding of the financial statement components involved in the answer but not the underlying principles. The student answer "sales-revenue recognition" received a score of "2". Some students, therefore, scored low because they did not list accounting principles. Table 1 presents descriptive statistics for the student problem-defining scores developed for Case 1 and Case 2.

Because this paper describes the initial implementation of the proposed assessment method, these scores form the baseline of problem-defining ability for the students graduating from this institution. Comparative evidence would be accumulated concerning the level of student problem-defining ability achieved by this program if students from future graduating classes also complete this particular assessment tool.

Evaluating the Assessment Method

If accounting educators are going to use the problem-defining assessment method proposed in this paper to measure the level of problem-solving ability

Table 1. Descriptive Statistics for Student Problem-Defining Scores.

Distribution of Student Scores	Case 1	Case 2
0	10	21
1	14	6
2	22	15
3	0	2
4	0	2
5	n/a	0
6	n/a	0
Median	1.00	1.00
Mean	1.26	1.09
St. Dev.	0.80	1.17

obtained by the students at their institutions, the effectiveness of the method should be explored. One way in which that effectiveness can be investigated is by performing statistical tests using the data collected through one of the possible assessment tools developed with the process. The following questions could be answered by these tests.

(1) Does the assessment tool produce student problem-defining data that is consistent with prior research? This research indicates that the categories experts employ to define a problem in their domain are more conceptual and more principle-based than the categories used by novices (students).
(2) Does the assessment tool produce data that is biased towards one or more demographic groups?
(3) Do the student problem-defining scores obtained by the assessment tool reflect the differing level of difficulty between Case 1 and Case 2?

For these analyses, the dependent variable consisted of the student problem-defining scores obtained by the assessment tool designed for this study. To perform statistical analyses, data for two independent variables (accounting-related work experience, and accounting grade point average) and two covariants (gender and age) were developed.[7] Details concerning these variables are presented in Exhibit 1 and details concerning the statistical analyses performed are presented in Appendix B.

We selected these two variables and two covariants[8] because we wanted to determine if the proposed assessment tool was robust and not biased by student attributes that are readily determinable in the composition of most accounting classes. Additionally, we wanted to explore variables that some accounting educators might expect to influence the problem-defining ability of students.

For example, some educators may feel that some accounting-related work experience may improve a student's ability to define accounting problems because of the "real-world" experience they have gained. Some accounting educators may have an a priori feeling that students with higher accounting grade point averages may have better problem-defining skills in accounting cases than students with lower accounting grade point averages. Age might be related to higher problem-defining skills because of older students' life experiences. Finally, we included gender because of the virtually equal mix of male and female students in today's accounting classrooms.

One limitation of this statistical analysis is the variety of variables that were not explored but might impact student problem-defining ability. Examples of variables that could affect how the students defined the cases presented and how thoroughly they completed the research instruments are: level of

Exhibit 1. Description of Variables.

Accounting-Related Work Experience	
Literature Supporting the Examination of the Variable	Shelton 1999; Choo 1996; Nelson, Libby & Bonner, 1995; English & Koeppen 1993; Bonner & Pennington 1991; Knechel & Snowball 1987; Hayes 1985; Bloom 1982
Measurement of Variable	Student reported no internship or accounting-related work experience (15 students) Student reported only an accounting-related internship experience (23 students) Student reported less than five years of accounting-related work experience (8 students)
Comments on Measurement of Variable	Six students who reported both an internship and less than five years of accounting-related work experience were assigned to category 2. Students in category 2 had an average of 2.5 years of accounting-related work experience in addition to any internship experience.
Mean Student Score (Standard Deviation) per Category	No work experience: Case 1 – 1.13 (0.74); Case 2 – 1.13 (1.19) Internship experience: Case 1 – 1.30 (0.93); Case 2 – 0.87 (1.06) Some work experience: Case 1 – 1.38 (0.53); Case 2 – 1.63 (1.41)

Accounting Grade Point Average (AGPA)	
Literature Supporting the Examination of the Variable	Almer, Hopper & Kaplan 1998; Ahadiat & Smith 1994; Dinius & Rogow 1988; Pasewark, Strawser, & Wilkerson 1988; Lewis, Shimerda, & Graham 1996
Measurement of Variable	Low AGPA - 2.20 to 2.65 (17 students) Medium APGA - 2.66 to 3.15 (15 students) High AGPA - 3.16 to 4.00 (14 students)
Comments	The mean of the AGPA data was calculated as 2.97 with a standard deviation of .52 and a range of 2.20 to 4.00. The 33rd percentile of this data was 2.65 and the 66th percentile was 3.15.
Mean Student Score (Standard Deviation) per Category	Low GPA: Case 1 – 1.00 (0.79); Case 2 – 0.71 (0.92) Medium GPA: Case 1 – 1.60 (0.63); Case 2 – 1.20 (1.15) High GPA: Case 1 – 1.21 (0.89); Case 2 – 1.43 (1.40)

Exhibit 1. Continued.

Gender	
Literature Supporting the Examination of the Variable	Brazelton 1998; Buckless, Lipe, & Ranscroft 1991
Measurement of Variable	25 males 21 females
Mean Student Score (Standard Deviation) per Category	Male: Case 1 – 1.16 (0.85); Case 2 – 1.08 (1.15) Female: Case 1 – 1.38 (0.74); Case 2 – 1.10 (1.22)
Age	
Literature Supporting the Examination of the Variable	Graham 1998; Howard & Henney 1998; Richardson & King 1998; Wooten1998; Bowden & Merritt 1995;
Measurement of Variable	Students 22 to 24 years old – 33 Students 25 years or older – 13
Mean Student Score (Standard Deviation) per Category	Traditional students: Case 1 – 1.24 (0.83); Case 2 – 1.03 (1.16) Non-traditional students: Case 1 – 1.31 (0.75); Case 2 – 1.23 (1.24)

cognitive development, learning style, personality type, level of reading comprehension, motivation for participating in the study (self-selection bias), level of fatigue while completing the research instruments, and previous exposure to problem-solving or problem-defining methods. Nevertheless, we believe that the students' problem-defining skills were impacted the most by the four major variables that were included in the analysis.

According to the statistical analyses performed, the student problem-defining scores as measured by the possible assessment tool were consistent with prior problem solving research and expert/novice research. This analysis indicated that, for each case, the student problem-defining scores were significantly lower than the benchmarks that were developed using expert responses, the teaching materials provided by Deloitte and Touche LLP, and the authors' understanding of the issues involved in each case. The categories students used to define the two cases, therefore, were less conceptual and principle-based than the expert categories.

Additionally, statistical analyses seemed to indicate that the student problem-defining scores as measured by the possible assessment tool were not biased towards one or more demographic groups. These analyses indicated that neither the main effects of the variables nor the interactions between accounting-related work experience and grade point average when controlled for age and for gender were significant. These findings are important to the accounting educators at this institution because they suggest that the proposed problem-defining method will produce assessment tools that are not biased by prior work experience, accounting GPA, gender or age. The accounting educators at this institution, therefore, can use cases to measure students' problem-defining abilities for assessment purposes. These findings might not generalize to other accounting programs because the relationships between student work experience, accounting GPA, age, and gender might differ across programs.

Finally, the assessment tool developed using the proposed problem-defining method is apparently sufficiently robust enough to reflect the differing level of difficulty between cases. According to the statistical analyses performed, the student problem-defining scores differed significantly between Case 1 and Case 2 for all variable categories except students with some accounting-related work experience and students with high AGPAs. For these students, the decline in their ability to use accounting principles to define specific accounting problems as the case situation became more complex was not significant. For all other categories of students, the ability to use accounting principles to define specific accounting problems declined significantly as the case situation became more complex.

An important aspect of these findings is that gender was not significant in any of the analyses performed. The fact that the benchmark for each case was developed using responses from five male experts apparently did not adversely affect the scoring assigned to the problem-defining ability of the female students as measured by the assessment tool. Additional research can be conducted to confirm this important finding.

DISCUSSION AND RECOMMENDATIONS

As stated at the beginning of this paper, the primary motivation for this exploratory study was to suggest a method by which a robust and unbiased assessment tool that determined accounting students' problem-defining abilities could be developed. The assessment tool produced by this method had to provide information feedback at one fixed point in time as well as provide a mechanism for developing comparative data over time. Because of previous accounting education literature and because many accounting courses frequently use cases, we were hopeful that a case-based assessment tool could be developed and easily integrated into accounting curricula.

As promising as our findings are after the first implementation of our proposed problem-defining assessment method, we realize that much work remains to refine the proposed method. For example, because assigning a problem-defining score to the student responses involves some subjective judgments, a larger panel of scorers could be involved in the method. Additionally, to insure conscientious student participation, the assessment tool could be included in a required accounting course. Obtaining conscientious student participation was the most difficult aspect of this first implementation of the proposed method.

Another adaptation to the method as it is described in this paper is the inclusion of practitioner experts from organizations other than large public accounting firms when developing the benchmarks. Accounting educators need to determine if the participation of appropriate experts from diverse backgrounds modifies the nature of the benchmarks.

Additionally, rather than mailing the materials to the experts, we believe asking practitioners to fill out the materials when they are on campus would increase the number of completed forms. These expert responses provide an important, practice-based perspective on the problem-defining stage of the problem-solving process and this perspective is not generally a part of the background of most accounting faculty members.

In addition to our adaptations of the process, other accounting educators need to use the proposed method to develop problem-defining assessment materials at their institutions. These studies would determine if the proposed method can be used to develop assessment tools appropriate for other institutions. For example, these studies would determine if the proposed method can be employed to develop assessment tools appropriate for varying sample sizes. Additionally, these studies would determine if the main effects and interactions between accounting-related work experience, grade point average, gender, and age are not significant for other samples regardless of the difficulty level of the problem. Also, if additional problem-defining assessment materials can be developed, they can be shared at meetings of accounting academics or other sharing forums.

Research also needs to be conducted to determine if the proposed method can be used to develop assessment tools appropriate for other areas of the accounting domain such as cost/managerial, systems, auditing, and taxation. Assessment tools, therefore, need to be developed using cases from those areas. Additionally, the effect of other variables such as learning type, level of cognitive maturity, and personality type on the student problem-defining scores that result from instruments developed from the suggested process should be explored.

Finally, accounting researchers need to determine the most efficient and effective format for the assessment tools that result from the proposed method. For example, researchers need to determine if the proposed method can be conducted using only one financial accounting case or if more cases should be used. Additionally, research will need to be continued concerning when and where in the educational process student problem-solving assessment should occur.

Suggestions for Problem-Solving Pedagogies

Accounting educators cannot teach students to be accounting problem-solving experts. Our graduates can become experts at solving problems in the accounting domain only over time with appropriate experience. We can help our students become better problem-solvers, however, by using the research described in this study to develop problem-solving-focused pedagogies.

One way in which accounting educators could develop problem-solving-focused pedagogies would be to integrate into core accounting courses units that teach a specific generic problem-solving model such as the IDEAL model before they assign case studies. Because the model can be taught in classrooms, students would learn to approach case studies in an effective and efficient manner by understanding and implementing the five stages of the problem-solving model. While discussing a generic problem-solving model such as the IDEAL model, the value of defining a problem could be emphasized and students would learn to take more time at the critical, early stages of the problem-solving process. Taking the time to build multiple representations of a problem rather than immediately attempting to solve the problem could be emphasized in class discussions with all of the students.

Once the value of developing multiple representations is presented, the accounting educator could then discuss how to use appropriate accounting concepts to develop alternate courses of actions so that the students' analysis of financial accounting problems was at a more principled level. Such courses of action could be developed for each representation as a group so that students could develop some skill in using the accounting principles and concepts being taught before they attempted to solve a case study individually. This pedagogical approach would help students learn how to use the accounting concepts and principles currently being taught in accounting curricula when faced with developing solutions to a challenging, unstructured financial accounting problem.

Finally, the assessment method suggested in this paper could be used to grade case studies. This method is based upon the students' defining the problems presented in the case rather than solely supplying a proposed solution. By following these grading procedures, accounting educators would emphasize the problem-defining stage of the problem-solving process and not just the development of one right answer. If this emphasis was integrated and coordinated across each required course in a curriculum, each student's progress in learning to define financial accounting problems could be measured through a portfolio assessment technique.

By encouraging students to take the time to build multiple representations of problems using appropriate accounting concepts and principles as well as using the assessment method described in this paper, accounting educators could help students develop an awareness that single, correct "answers" rarely exist and that issues can be considered from several perspectives. Such curricular activities would help to narrow the gap between what accountancy students are currently doing to solve problems in accounting and what they need to be doing to build a firm foundation upon which problem-solving expertise in accounting can be developed.

The realization that problem-solving ability can be defined as a cognitive process with identifiable and quantifiable stages is an important first step in the development of appropriate pedagogies to teach problem-solving ability to accounting students and assessment methods designed to determine the levels of problem-defining ability achieved by students. These pedagogies and assessment methods, when integrated across an accounting curriculum, will help accounting educators better prepare their students for successful twenty-first century careers in accounting by enhancing their students' problem-solving abilities.

ACKNOWLEDGMENTS

The authors wish to acknowledge Dr. Jean Pierce for her guidance with this research project. Without her expertise in cognitive psychology and novice/expert studies, the theoretical foundation of this study would have been considerably weaker. We would also like to thank the late Dr. Patrick Delaney, Dr. John Simon, and John McDougald for their assistance in persuading students to complete the research materials. Without their help, the student sample would have been considerably smaller. Finally, we would like to thank the anonymous reviewers for their many helpful comments.

NOTES

1. See, for example, the Bedford Report (AAA, 1986), the Perspectives on Education White Paper by the then Big-8 public accounting firms (1989), *Position Statement No. 1* by the AECC (AECC, 1990), and the *AICPA Core Competency Framework for Entry Into the Accounting Profession* (AICPA, 1999).

2.Marzano et al. (1988, p. 48), defined the decision-making process as a cognitive process involving the selection of one alternative from two or more competing alternatives. Based on this definition, the decision-making process is used within all stages of the problem-solving process.

3. All five of the practitioner experts were from two large public accounting firms. Three of the experts were partners, one was a senior manager, and one was a manager. Their years of experience ranged from eighteen years to thirty-five years. Two of the partners had master degrees while the other three had only bachelor degrees. A total of thirty-five sets of research materials were distributed to practitioners who had been identified as experts, however, only five were returned completed.

4. Because the practitioner experts had taken an average of 8.60 minutes to complete Case 1 and an average of 11.20 minutes to complete Case 2, the times taken to define each case by the students and experts involved in this study duplicate early cognitive psychology research (Larkin, 1981; Paige & Simon, 1966). This research found that experts take longer to define problems than novices. Although this finding has been widely accepted in cognitive psychology (Glaser & Chi, 1988, p. xix), the authors could find no recent research exploring this difference between expert and novice problem defining.

5. Because of these criteria, non-traditional students with extended accounting work experience as well as graduate students who voluntarily participated in this study were excluded from the sample. Based on a review of the personal-information questionnaires, ten students who had voluntarily completed the research materials were excluded from the sample while forty-six were included.

6. Although the sample was representative of the student population for significant demographic variables, there might have been some self-selection bias caused by the way in which the sample was obtained. Not controlling for psychological variables, therefore, is a limitation of this study.

7. Because this study used four variables, the collinearity of the variables was tested. A Spearman correlation coefficient was calculated for each possible pair of variables. None of the p values calculated were less than 0.05; therefore, none of the two-way relationships between the four variables are significant at conventional levels. Consequently, collinearity was not a significant concern in this study.

8. One concern with these analyses is that the variables involved are both continuous and discrete. For example, the student problem-defining scores for both cases are discrete variables. For Case 1, the scores were represented by "0", "1", "2", and "3"; for Case 2, the student problem-defining scores were represented by "0", "1", "2", "3", and "4". Additionally, gender and work experience are discrete variables having two and three categories respectively. The only continuous variables included in these analyses, therefore, were age and AGPA. To complete appropriate statistical tests, therefore, the variables age and AGPA were converted to discrete variables.

9. Because neither the expert data nor the student data for the variables under investigation were normally distributed, an F test was not used to determine if the sample variances were equivalent. Levene's test for equality of variances tests for the equality of group variances without assuming the data are normally distributed.

10. Although the experts performed quite well on Case 1 as indicated by their mean score of 3.60 compared to a maximum benchmark score of 4.00, they did not perform as well on Case 2 as indicated by their mean score of 4.00 compared to a maximum benchmark score of 6.00. This decreased performance may be a reflection of their differing levels of experience with the subject matter of Case 1 and Case 2. For Case 1, the experts self-reported an average experience level of 4.00 on a Likert scale in which 7 was labeled "extensive experience". For Case 2, the experts self-reported an average experience level of only 3.60. The idea expressed by Bonner and Pennington (1991, p. 39) that time with a firm is a reasonable surrogate for expertise only if the

individual has had experience with the problem being explored, therefore, seems to be demonstrated by these expert responses.

11. The paired-samples *t* test is a statistical test that can be used when the observations for two variables can be paired in some way. For example, this test can be used when the same person is observed before and after a treatment or to compare two scores of the same person. Pairing is used to make the data in the two variables as similar as possible. Observed differences between the groups can then be attributed more readily to the independent variable.

REFERENCES

AACSB – The International Association for Management Education (1999). *Accounting Standards*. St. Louis, MO: AACSB.

Accounting Education Change Commission (AECC) (1990). Objectives of Education for Accountants: Position Statement Number One. *Issues in Accounting Education*, *5*(2), 307–312.

Accounting Education Change Commission (AECC). (1992). The First Course in Accounting: Position Statement Number Two. *Issues in Accounting Education*, *7*(2), 49, 252.

Ahadiat, N., & Smith, K. J. (1994). A Factor-Analytic Investigation of Employee Selection Factors of Significance to Recruiters of Entry-Level Accountants. *Issues in Accounting Education*, *9*(1), 59–79.

Akers, M. D., Giacomino, D. E., & Trebby, J. P. (1997). Designing and Implementing an Accounting Assessment Program. *Issues in Accounting Education*, (Fall), 59–80.

Allison, D. J., & Allison, P. A. (1993). Both Ends of a Telescope: Experience and Expertise in Principal Problem Solving. *Educational Administration Quarterly*, *29*(3), 302–322.

Almer, E. D., Hopper, J. R., & Kaplan, S. E. (1998). The Effect of Diversity-Related Attributes on Hiring, Advancement and Voluntary Turnover Judgments. *Accounting Horizons*, *12*(1), 1–17.

American Accounting Association, Committee on the Future, Structure, Content and Scope of Accounting Education (The Bedford Committee) (1986). Future Accounting Education: Preparing for the Expanding Profession. *Issues in Accounting Education*, *1*(1), 160–195.

American Institute of Certified Public Accountants (1999). *The AICPA Core Competency Framework for Entry into the Accounting Profession*. New York: AICPA.

Anderson, J. R. (1983). *The Architecture of Cognition*. Cambridge, MA: Harvard University Press.

Bedard, J. C., & Biggs, S. F. (1991). Pattern Recognition, Hypotheses Generation, and Auditor Performance in an Analytical Task. *The Accounting Review*, *66*(3), 622–642.

Bierstaker, J. L., Bedard, J. C., & Biggs, S. F. (1999). The Role of Problem Representation Shifts in Auditor Decision Processes in Analytical Procedures. *Auditing: A Journal of Practice and Theory*, *18*(1), 18–36.

Bloom, B. S. (1982). *The Role of Gifts and Markers in the Development of Talent. Exceptional Children*, *48*(6), 510–522.

Bonner, S. E., Libby, R., & Nelson, M. W. (1997). Audit Category Knowledge as a Precondition to Learning from Experience. *Accounting, Organizations, and Society*, *22*(5), 387–410.

Bonner, S. E., & Pennington, N. (1991). Cognitive Processes and Knowledge as Determinants of Auditor Expertise. *Journal of Accounting Literature*, *10*, 1–50.

Bowden, R., & Merritt, R. (1995). The Adult Learner Challenge: Instructively and Administratively. *Education*, *115*, 426–433.

Bransford, J. D., & Stein, B. S. (1984). *The IDEAL Problem Solver*. New York: Freeman.

Brazelton, J. K. (1998). Implications for Women in Accounting: Some Preliminary Evidence Regarding Gender Communication. *Issues in Accounting Education, 13*(3), 509–530.

Buckless, F., Lipe, M., & Ravenscroft, S. (1991). Do Gender Effects of Accounting Course Performance Persist After Controlling for General Academic Attitude? *Issues in Accounting Education, 6*, 248–261.

Chi, M. T. H., Feltovich, P. J., & Glaser, R. (1981). Categorization and Representation of Physics Problems by Experts and Novices. *Cognitive Science, 5*, 121–152.

Choo, F. (1996). Auditors' Knowledge Content and Judgment Performance: A Cognitive Script Approach. *Accounting, Organizations and Society, 21*(4), 339–359.

Clark, V. J., & Lamberts, K. (1997). Strategy Shifts and Expertise in Solving Transformation Rule Problems. *Thinking and Reasoning, 3*(4), 271–290.

DeMong, R. F., Lindgren, J. H., Lindgren, Jr., & Perry, S. E. (1994). Designing As Assessment Program For Accounting. *Issues in Accounting Education*, (Spring), 11–27.

Dinius, S. H., & Rogow, R. B. (1988). Application of the Delphi Method in Identifying Characteristics Big Eight Firms Seek in Entry-Level Accountants. *Journal of Accounting Education, 6*, 83–101.

English, D. M., & Koeppen, D. R. (1993). The Relationship of Accounting Internships and Subsequent Academic Performance. *Issues in Accounting Education*, (Fall), 292–299.

Frederick, D. M., Heiman-Hoffman, V. B., & Libby, R. (1994). The Structure Of Auditors' Knowledge Of Financial Statement Errors. *Auditing: A Journal of Practice & Theory, 13*(1), 1–21.

Gainen, J., & Locatelli, P. (1995). *Assessment for the New Curriculum: A Guide for Professional Accounting Programs*. Sarasota, FL: American Accounting Association.

Glaser, R., & Chi, M. T. H. (1988). Overview. In: M. T. H. Chi, R. Glaser, & M. J. Farr (Eds), *The Nature of Expertise* (pp. xv–xxviii). Hillsdale, N.J.: Lawrence Erlbaum Associates.

Graham, S. W. (1998). Adult Growth in College: The Effects of Age and Educational Ethos. *Journal of College Student Development, 39*(3). 239–250

Hayes, J. R. (1985). Three problems in teaching general skills. In: S. Chipman, J. Segal & R. Glaser (Eds), *Thinking and Learning*, Vol. 2. (pp. 391–405). Hillsdale, NJ: Lawrence Erlbaum Associates.

Herring, H. C., III, & Izard, C. D. (1992). Outcomes Assessment of Accounting Majors. *Issues in Accounting Education*, (Spring), 1–17.

Hill, N. T., Perry, S. E., & Stein, D. M. (1998). Using Accounting Student Surveys in an Outcomes Assessment Program. *Issues in Accounting Education, 13*(1), 65–78.

Howard, J. R., & Henney, A. L. (1998). Student Participation and Instructor Gender in the Mixed-Age College Classroom. *The Journal of Higher Education, 69*(4), 384–403.

Kaplan, C. A., & Simon, H. A. (1990). In Search of Insight. *Cognitive Psychology, 22*, 374–419.

Kimmell, S. L., Marquette, R. P., & Olsen, D. H. (1998). Outcomes Assessment Programs: Historical Perspective and State of the Art. *Issues in Accounting Education*, (November), 851–868.

Knechel, W. R., & Snowball, D. (1987). Accounting Internships and Subsequent Academic Performance: an Empirical Study. *The Accounting Review*, (October), 799–807.

Langenderfer, H. Q., & Rockness, J. W. (1989). Integrating Ethics into the Accounting Curriculum: Issues, Problems, and Solutions. *Issues in Accounting Education, 4*(1), 58–69.

Larkin, J. H. (1981). Cognition of Learning Physics. *American Journal of Physics, 49*, 534–541.

Lesgold, A., Robinson, H., Feltovich, P., Glaser, R., Klepfer, D., & Wang, Y. (1988). Expertise in a Complex Skill: Diagnosing X-Ray Pictures. In: M. T. H. Chi, R. Glaser, & M. J. Farr (Eds), *The Nature of Expertise* (pp. 311–342). Hilldale, NJ: Lawrence Erlbaum Associates.

Lewis, T. D., Shimerda, T. A., & Graham, G. (1996). What the Academic Advisor Needs to Know About Job Placement. *Journal of Accounting Education*, (Fall), 135–142.

Libby, R., & Luft, J. (1993). Determinants of Judgment Performance in Accounting Settings: Ability, Knowledge, Motivation, and Environment. *Accounting, Organizations and Society, 18*(5), 425–450.

Marzano, R. J., Brandt, R. S., Hughes, C. S., Jones, B. F., Presseisen, B. Z., Rankin, S. C., & Suhor, C. (1988). *Dimensions of Thinking: A Framework for Curriculum and Instruction.* Alexandria, VA: Association for Supervision and Curriculum Development.

Mumpower, J. L., & Stewart, T. R. (1996). Expert Judgement and Expert Disagreement. *Thinking and Reasoning,. 2*(2/3), 191–211.

Nelson, M. W., Libby, R., & Bonner, S. E. (1995). Knowledge Structure and the Estimation of Conditional Probabilities In Audit Planning. *The Accounting Review, 70*(1), 27–47.

Newell, A., & Simon, H. A. (1972). *Human Problem Solving*. Englewood Cliffs, N.J.: Prentice Hall.

Paige, J. M., & Simon, H. A. (1966). Cognition Processes in Solving Algebra Word Problems. In: B. Kleinmuntz (Ed.), *Problem Solving* (pp. 51–119). New York: Wiley.

Pasewark, W. R., Strawser, J. R., & Wilkerson, J. E., Jr. (1988). Empirical Evidence on the Association Between Characteristics of Graduating Accounting Students and Recruiting Decisions of Accounting Employers. *Issues in Accounting Education, 3*(21), 388–401.

Arthur Andersen & Co., Arthur Young, Coopers & Lybrand, Deloitte Haskins & Sells, Ernst & Whinney, Peat Marwick Main & Co., Price Waterhouse, and Touche Ross (1989). *Perspectives on Education: Capabilities for Success in the Accounting Profession* (the White Paper). New York, NY.

Phillips, F. (1998). Accounting Students' Beliefs About Knowledge: Associating Performance with Underlying Belief Dimensions. *Issues in Accounting Education, 13*(1), 113–126.

Richardson, J. T. E., & King, E. (1998). Adult Students in Higher Education: Burden or Boon? *Journal of Higher Education, 69*(1), 65, 88.

Schoenfeld, A. H., & Hermann, D. J. (1982). Problem Perception and Knowledge Structure in Expert and Novice Mathematical Problem-Solvers. *Journal of Experimental Psychology: Learning, Memory, and Cognition, 8*(5), 484–494.

Shelton, S. W. (1999). The Effect of Experience on the Use of Irrelevant Evidence in Auditor Judgment. *The Accounting Review, 74*(2), 217–224.

Smith, M. U. (1992). Expertise and the Organization of Knowledge: Unexpected Differences Among Genetic Counselors, Faculty, and Students on Problem Categorization Tasks. *Journal of Research in Science Teaching, 29*(2), 179–205.

Sternberg, R. J. (1988). *The Triarchic Mind: A New Theory of Human Intelligence*. New York: Penguin Books.

Stivers, B. P., Campbell, J. E., & Hermanson, H. M. (2000). An Assessment Program for Accounting: Design, Implementation, and Reflection. *Issues in Accounting Education, 15*(4), 553–581.

Stone, D. N., & Shelley, M. K. (1997). Educating for Accounting Expertise: A Field Study. *Journal of Accounting Research, 35*(Supplement), 35–61.

Wales, C. E., Nardi, A. H., & Stager, R. A. (1987). *Thinking skills: Making a Choice. Morgantown,* WV: Center for Guided Design.

Weiser, M., & Shertz, J. (1982). Programming Problem Representation in Novice and Expert Programmers. *International Journal of Man-Machine Studies, 19*, 391–398.

Wooten, T. C. (1998). Factors Influencing Student Learning in Introductory Accounting Classes: A Comparison of Traditional and Non-traditional Students. *Issues in Accounting Education, 12*(2), 357, 373.

APPENDIX A

Problem No. 1

Name: Time You Began to Read:

On January 15, 1997, Sweetooth Corp, which has a March 31 year-end, entered into a transaction to sell the land and building from which it operates a candy factory for a total selling price of $22,500,000. The book value of the land and the building was $3,532,000. The final closing is not expected to occur until sometime between June 1998 and March 1999.

On March 15, 1997, Sweetooth received an irrevocable letter of credit, issued by a major bank, for $5,850,000, which represented more than 25% of the sales price. Sweetooth would collect the $5,850,000 and would keep the property even if the buyer decides not to complete the transaction. The letter of credit has an option for an extension for up to one year for the total period of two years. At closing, the entire selling price will be paid in cash.

Sweetooth is going to continue to operate its candy factory in the building and will continue to be responsible for all normal occupancy costs until final closing when it would move to another location. After the sale, the building will be torn down and replaced by a major office building complex.

Required: *How should Sweetooth account for this transaction?*

Time you stopped reading:

Please use this space for any diagrams of the information presented in this problem that you wish to make.

(Case 92–93. Copyright 1991 Deloitte & Touche Foundation)

Problem No. 2

Name: Time You Began to Read:

Hi-Tech is a publicly-owned research and development company, which is not involved in manufacturing or distributing products. It has obtained patents for two newly developed synthetic building materials and has entered into long-term license agreements that permit other companies to produce and market these materials. Hi-Tech will receive a royalty based on a percentage of product sales.

You have been consulted by Hi-Tech's CFO about the accounting for a transaction under which Hi-Tech would sell to New Inventions, Corp. the right to receive a portion of the future royalties. New Inventions has provided Hi-Tech with R&D financing in the past. New Inventions would pay Hi-Tech $2 million in 1998 and another $1.3 million in 1999 for the right to receive 5% of the royalties received by Hi-Tech on sales of those materials during 2000 to 2005. The agreement also specifies that if cumulative payments exceed $20 million, the rate will drop from five percent to one percent.

Based on Hi-Tech's projections, New Inventions will receive a 32% rate of return on the investment. However, Hi-Tech does not guarantee that New Inventions will receive any royalties. For example, if the market for these synthetic materials disappears before 2000, New Inventions will receive no payments. Further, the agreement is not cancelable; there is no minimum guaranteed amount; and New Inventions has no recourse against Hi-Tech. New Inventions is only entitled to receive the specified percentage of actual future royalties, if any.

Hi-Tech has no involvement in generating the royalties and has no specific performance requirements under the terms of the arrangement other than to defend the related patents against infringement.

Required: *How should Hi-Tech account for this transaction on its 1997 financial statements?*

Time you stopped reading:

Please use this space for any diagrams of the information presented in this problem that you wish to make.

(Case 93–5. Copyright 1993 Deloitte & Touche Foundation)

Worksheet No. 1
Name: Time you began worksheet:

REMEMBER: I AM NOT LOOKING FOR A SOLUTION. I AM TRYING TO FIND OUT HOW YOU DEFINE THIS SITUATION.

(1) What kind of financial accounting problem is Problem No. 1?
(2) Please prioritize the factors you used to determine what kind of problem this is.
  Most Important:
  Second Most Important:
  Third Most Important:
(3) Time at which you stopped working on this worksheet:

Note: The title for the Case 2 worksheet was "Worksheet No. 2" and question 1 read "What kind of financial accounting problem is Problem No. 2?" All other wording on the Case 2 worksheet was identical to the worksheet for Case 1.

APPENDIX B

Formal hypotheses were not developed for the statistical analyses that were performed because this study was exploratory in nature. The following research questions, however, did guide the explorations:

Question 1: Did the student problem-defining scores obtained by the assessment tool differ from the practitioner expert problem-defining scores?

Question 2: Is the problem-defining ability of graduating accounting students as measured by the assessment tool related to accounting-related work experience, accounting grade point average (AGPA), gender, or age for each case?

Question 3: Is the problem-defining ability of graduating accounting students as measured by the assessment tool related to accounting-related work experience when controlled for gender and for age for each case?

Question 4: Is the problem-defining ability of graduating accounting students as measured by the assessment tool related to accounting grade point average (AGPA) when controlled for gender and for age for each case?

Question 5: Is the problem-defining ability of graduating accounting students as measured by the assessment tool related to accounting-related work experience, accounting grade point average (AGPA), gender, or age between cases?

For these analyses the dependent variable consisted of the student problem-defining scores obtained by the assessment tool. To perform statistical analyses for research questions two through five, data for two independent variables (accounting-related work experience, and accounting grade point average) and two covariants (gender and age) were developed. The analysis of covariance design was used for Questions 4 and 5 in order to statistically control any student demographic differences based on gender and age that might confound differences between the three accounting-related work experience groups and the three accounting grade point average groups.

Analysis of Research Question 1

Previous expert/novice research has indicated that while both experts and novices use categories to define a problem in a domain, experts' categories are more conceptual and more principle-based. To determine if the proposed problem-defining method replicated previous expert/novice research, a Levene test[9] and a two-tailed Student *t* test were used to test the equivalency of the scores achieved by the accounting experts and the students for both cases.

Because the Levene's test statistics indicated that the variances of the expert scores and the student scores were equivalent for both cases (0.709 and 0.467 respectively), a two-tailed Student *t* test assuming equivalent variances was conducted for each case.

These tests produced a Student *t* statistic for Case 1 of 6.140 and 5.189 for Case 2; the *p* values were 0.000 for both cases. These statistics indicate that both Student *t* tests were significant at the 0.05 level. According to these tests, therefore, there was a difference between the set of accounting concepts selected by the students and by the experts to define the cases regardless of the difficulty level of the case.

Additionally, the means of the sets of accounting concepts selected by the experts (3.60 and 4.00)[10] were higher than the means of the sets selected by the students (1.26 and 1.09) to define each case. The experts, therefore, used more appropriate financial accounting concepts to define the problems than did the students as measured by the proposed method. The expert and student (novice) problem-defining abilities as measured by the proposed method, therefore, were consistent with prior research.

Analysis of Research Questions 2, 3 and 4

To determine if the proposed method is biased towards one or more demographic groups, several analyses were performed using the student problem-defining scores for Case 1 and Case 2 as dependent variables. In these analyses, the data developed for accounting-related work experience, AGPA, gender, and age were used as independent variables.

To analyze research question 2, a MANOVA was calculated to determine if the main effects of any of the four variables (accounting-related work experience, AGPA, gender, and age) were related to the problem-defining ability of graduating accounting majors as measured by the proposed method for each case. The first panel in Table 2, MANOVA Without Covariants, presents the F values and the respective *p* values for each variable in this analysis.

As seen in Table 2, none of the *p* values are below 0.05; therefore, none of the variables is significantly related to the level of student problem-defining ability as measured by the proposed method for either case at this level of significance. For Case 1, however, the *p* value for AGPA was 0.099

Table 2. Relationship between Student Problem Defining Scores and Independent Variables for Each Case.

Variable	Covariate	Case 1 F Value	p Value	Case 2 F Value	p Value
MANOVA Without Covariants					
Work Experience		0.170	0.844	1.863	0.169
AGPA		2.460	0.099	2.170	0.128
Gender		1.181	0.284	0.030	0.864
Age		0.186	0.669	0.000	0.982
MANOVA With Covariants					
Work Experience	Gender	0.171	0.843	1.013	0.373
Work Experience	Age	0.255	0.777	0.838	0.441
AGPA	Gender	0.806	0.455	0.051	0.951
AGPA	Age	1.352	0.272	0.112	0.895

which is significant at a 0.10 significance level. These findings indicate that accounting-related work experience, gender, or age by themselves are not significantly related to the problem-defining abilities of the graduating accounting students in our study for either case. The variable, AGPA, however, does appear to have some relationship to the student problem-defining abilities for Case 1.

To analyze research questions 3 and 4, a MANOVA was calculated to determine if accounting-related work experience and AGPA were related to the problem-defining ability of graduating accounting majors when controlled for gender and for age for each case. Panel two in Table 2, MANOVA With Covariants, presents the F values and the respective p values calculated by this analysis.

As seen in Table 2, none of the p values are below 0.05; therefore, none of the interactions between the variables are significantly related to the level of student problem-defining ability as measured by the proposed method for either case at this level of significance. These findings suggest that even after controlling for a potential difference in student problem-defining abilities based on the interaction between age or gender with prior work experience or APGA, there are no significant differences in the problem-defining abilities of students as measured by the proposed case-based assessment method for either case. The relationship between student problem-defining scores and AGPA for Case 1 appears to be mitigated by the interaction between AGPA and gender as well as by the interaction between AGPA and age.

Analysis of Question 5

To determine if any of the four independent variables (accounting-related work experience, AGPA, gender, and age) were related to the problem-defining ability of graduating accounting majors as measured by the proposed method between each case, paired-samples *t* tests[11] were calculated. Exhibit 1 presents descriptive statistics for the variables and Table 3 presents the *t* values and respective *p* values for these analyses.

To perform the paired-samples *t* tests, a percent of benchmark score was calculated for the student problem-defining score of each student. Because a perfect score for Case 1 was four and a perfect score for Case 2 was six, the students could have achieved a higher problem-defining score on Case 2 than on Case 1 and, in reality, performed worse. A percent of benchmark was calculated for each student so that the scores for each case could be compared. The percent of benchmark calculations, therefore, effectively common-sized the scores for each student.

As can be seen in Table 3, the mean percent of benchmark calculations indicate that the mean student scores for each variable category were higher

Table. 3. Student Problem-Defining Scores Between Cases.

Variable Categories	*N*	CASE 1 (Benchmark: 4) Mean Percent of Benchmark (Mean Student Score/ Benchmark)	CASE 2 (Benchmark: 6) Mean Percent of Benchmark (Mean Student Score/ Benchmark)	*t* statistic	*p* value
Work Experience					
None	15	28.3%	18.8%	2.200	0.045
Internships	23	32.5%	14.5%	3.122	0.005
Some	8	34.5%	27.2%	0.956	0.371
AGPA					
Low	17	25.0%	11.8%	2.672	0.017
Medium	15	40.0%	20.0%	4.054	0.001
High	14	30.3%	23.8%	0.803	0.437
Gender					
Male	25	29.0%	18.0%	2.499	0.020
Female	21	34.5%	18.3%	2.896	0.009
Age					
22–24	33	31.0%	17.2%	3.120	0.004
25 & above	13	32.8%	20.5%	2.333	0.038

for Case 1 than for Case 2. The student problem-defining ability as measured by the proposed method for the other variable categories was as expected – problem-defining ability was higher for Case 1 than for Case 2. This finding was expected because Case 2 was considered to be a more complex representation of problem defining ability than Case 1 due to the presentation of the case material and the number of accounting issues involved in the case.

Additionally, as seen in Table 3, all but two of the p values are below 0.05; thus, the student problem-defining scores differed significantly between Case 1 and Case 2 for all variable categories except students with some accounting-related work experience and students with high AGPAs. Students with some work experience and students with high AGPAs did perform more poorly on Case 2, although the differences are not significant.

This finding suggests that students with some work experience and students with high AGPAs performed relatively about the same on Case 1 as they did on Case 2. For all other categories of students, the ability to apply accounting principles to a specific situation is relatively higher for Case 1, the less complex case, than for Case 2, the more complex case. The proposed assessment method did produce a tool, therefore, that did measure the students' problem-defining ability at difference levels of problem difficulty again indicating the robustness of the proposed case-based problem-defining assessment method.

BUDGETING FOR SNOW REMOVAL COSTS USING MONTE CARLO SIMULATION: A CLASSROOM PROJECT

Eleanor G. Henry, Dean Crawford and Roberta M. Lipsig

ABSTRACT[1]

The project focus is a budgeting scenario for a municipality that must plan expenditures for future snow removal costs. The project contains an actual historical data set for area snowfall and several years of variable cost data for snow removal furnished by the city. Monte Carlo simulation produces a probability distribution for snow removal costs given the uncertainty of future amounts of snow. The simulation results have direct applications in budget preparation and in performance evaluations. The project provides several benefits to students including: exposure to real-world data and budgeting problems; a review of budget preparation and variance calculation; an introduction to simulation models; practice using simple statistical methods; and reinforcement of computer and spreadsheet skills. The Monte Carlo simulation uses standard Excel functions. The project is appropriate for an upper-division undergraduate or graduate course in Cost, Managerial, or Non-profit Accounting.

Advances in Accounting Education, Volume 4, pages 169–188.

ISBN: 0-7623-0856-7

INTRODUCTION

A series of research studies by the Institute of Management Accountants identifies budgeting as an important topic for accounting educators. In the 1994 study, budgeting ranked first on a list of accounting knowledge, skills and abilities (KSAs) for which entry-level accountants were least prepared (Siegel & Sorensen, 1994, p. 5). In the 1995 follow-up study, short-term budgeting ranked fifth on a list of the most critical work activities for accountants (Siegel & Sorensen, 1996, p. 9). The most recent research report confirms the relevance of the KSAs identified in the earlier studies (Siegel & Sorensen, 1999, pp. 5–6). In addition, the report emphasizes strategic planning and process improvement as the two most critical work activities for company success. However, the report states that accounting curricula provide coverage for neither strategic planning nor process improvement.

An entity's internal value chain consists of both major and supporting processes (Morse et al., 2000, pp. 176–177). One major process is the delivery of services to a client. Supporting processes include accounting, design, finance, human resources, and maintenance. To the extent that the accounting and finance function is a supporting process, enhancements to the budgeting activity are process improvements. This project demonstrates how Monte Carlo simulation (MCS) can improve the budgeting process and the internal value chain. The project also adds value to existing accounting courses that cover the budgeting topic.

Because budgeting is an integral part of strategic planning and subsequent performance evaluation, the budgeting activity is important to a wide cross section of business entities. The topic appears in cost, managerial, and non-profit or governmental accounting courses. Budgets provide a useful and necessary framework for establishing standards or norms for inputs of resources as well as outputs of product or service. Budget variances, differences between actual and planned costs, can offer important explanatory information in the performance evaluation phase. Budget variances also quantify factors over which the entity has no control, including weather and other environmental phenomena that impact the activities and costs of a service entity.

The classroom project is a budgeting scenario for a municipality in northern New York that must plan expenditures for future snow removal costs. The student user of the project plays the role of the budget preparer or budget analyst. The project supplies the budget preparer with an actual historical data set for area snowfall and several years of variable snow removal costs. Using the Excel regression analysis function, the budget preparer estimates a variable cost function using inches of snowfall and numbers of snow days as independent variables and snow removal cost as the dependent variable. Monte Carlo simulation produces an estimated probability distribution for snow removal costs given the uncertainty of future amounts of snow. Standard Excel functions provide the tools for the computer simulation.

Budget preparation and the later performance evaluation are more accurate if the municipality can identify costs related to uncontrollable weather factors. The budget preparer makes several calculations in sequence. The first step is a static budget amount for snow removal. This calculation incorporates the simulated probability distribution of snow removal costs. Second, the budget preparer calculates a flexible budget amount using actual snowfall and snow days in the budgeted cost function.

Subsequently, the budget preparer calculates a flexible budget variance and a volume variance. The volume variance isolates a portion of the total cost variance attributable to snowfall that is more or less than planned. The budget preparer then directs attention to the flexible budget variance and the differences between actual and planned variable costs given the actual level of snowfall.

BACKGROUND AND PREVIOUS RESEARCH

Although MCS dates back to government defense programs of the 1940s, simulation techniques gained practicality and popularity during the 1960s when computer programs and mainframe computers made rapid data calculations and analysis possible (Hertz, 1964, pp. 95–106). A major practical advantage of MCS today is that it requires only simple spreadsheet tools.

MCS aids in modeling the effects of random events on outcomes of interest. Knowles (1994, p. 10) reported on the value of MCS models in predicting the costs of damages to property from hurricanes and earthquakes. Chau (1995, pp. 369–383) constructed an MCS model to project construction costs. Various business decisions also feature MCS applications. Sheel (1995, pp. 18–26) presented an MCS model for hoteliers in estimating the effects of customer mix and room rates on total profits. Brabazon (1997, pp. 36–38) described the usefulness of MCS to the management accountant in cost-volume-profit analysis.

Static (deterministic) budgets reflect one level of sales or, in the case of cost budgets, one cost driver. Flexible budgeting introduces a degree of realism in preparing static budgets for an expected range of sales or costs. If two or more variables in the budget vary simultaneously, the number of potential static budgets increases rapidly (Nordhauser & Chau, 1997, p. 105). For example, five levels of unit sales, three possible tax rates, five interest rates, four wage rates, and two potential prices for raw materials produce 600 possible budgets. Electronic spreadsheets simplify the budget calculations, but increase the amount of data that the decision maker must analyze. MCS can produce a stochastic flexible budget.

MCS uses a sampling procedure that draws from the possible ranges of expected variables to produce a number of trial budgets. The combined budget trials form a cumulative probability density function from which the decision maker can make inferences about the likelihood of achieving a budgeted number.

MCS has an obvious advantage in simplifying the analysis of data. The extent of its usefulness depends on a number of factors (Chau, 1995, pp. 369–383; Brealey & Meyers, 1996, 247–255). First, the reliability of the simulation depends on the validity of the assumptions regarding the probability distribution of the cost driver (Chau, 1995, p. 369). Second, if more than one cost driver is present in the model, the validity of the simulation requires recognition of the interdependence among cost drivers.

Finally, the value of the simulation model in actual practice depends on its costs and complexity (Brealey & Meyers, 1996, p. 254). Achieving realism in a simulation may require a very complex model. If the model is so complex that the decision maker does not understand it, he or she cannot rely on it. Although discussions of MCS appear in the literature, few accounting texts provide training in the procedure (Nordhauser & Chau, 1997, p. 103).[2] A major purpose of this student project is to provide exposure to sophisticated budgeting techniques.

PROJECT DESCRIPTION AND DATA

The subject of analysis is a municipality in northern New York State. The city's accounting year is the calendar year. Each autumn the office of the mayor prepares a budget based on estimates of the city's revenues and expenditures for the upcoming year. In December, the city council receives the budget for approval or suggested revisions. The mayor's office bases its expenditure estimates on the budget requests from the city department managers.

The City Street Department's total expenditures for snow removal have both fixed and variable components. Examples of the fixed expenditures are regular wages paid to the snow removal crews and scheduled maintenance and upkeep of the snowplows. Variable expenditures consist primarily of overtime for the snow removal crews, the cost of supplies such as rock salt and cinders, and the cost of "shovels," the replacement blades on the front of the snowplows.

This project uses MCS to budget a city's expenditures for snow removal. This particular budgeting problem has two distinguishing features. First, the amount of snow that the city will experience in the coming year is an uncontrollable phenomenon. Second, the best predictors of the variable component of the city's snow removal expenditures are the city's snowfall in inches and the number of days with measurable accumulation. The city has approximately 60 snow days and receives about 119 inches of snow each year. However, both variables can vary widely from year to year. Descriptive statistics for the city's calendar year snowfall and the total number of snow days appear in Panel A of Table 1.

The city's budgeting problem with respect to snow removal costs involves two related weather factors. The variable component of next year's snow removal expenditures depends on the amount of snow that the city will receive and the number of days that the city will need to plow the streets. Thus, the probability distribution of the variable expenditures is a function of the probability distributions of the city's total snowfall and number of snow days. However, the two variables are clearly correlated, so a statistical treatment must consider the distributions jointly and not in isolation. The interdependency of

Table 1. Annual Snow Fall 1926–1997.[5]

Panel A: Descriptive Statistics

Statistic	Snow Days	Snowfall (inches)
Mean	59.94	119.04
Median	58.00	101.35
Mode	58.00	74
Standard Deviation	14.57	47.63
Skewness	−0.03	0.79
Range	60.00	227.80
Minimum	28	41.60
Maximum	88	269.40
Observations	72	72

Panel B: Equation 1: Snowfall (inches) = $\beta_0 + \beta_1 \times$ Snow Days

Regression Statistics

R-Square	0.60		
Standard error	30.28		
Intercept coefficient	−32.98	t-statistic: −2.17	p-value: 0.03
Snow Days coefficient	2.54	t-statistic: 10.28	p-value: 0.00
Observations	72		

Note: The National Climatic Data Center provided the Snowfall data.

the two distributions makes it difficult for city officials to form reliable estimates about the likely range of variable snow removal costs and the probability that the actual expenditures will fall inside that range. We make three assumptions to streamline the data analysis. First, the number of snow days is approximately normally distributed. Second, the number of inches of snowfall is conditional on the number of snow days. Third, a linear regression equation will model the interdependency between snow days and inches of snow, in which inches of snow are dependent on the number of snow days.

$$\text{Snowfall Inches} = \beta_0 + \beta_1 \times \text{Snow days} \quad (1)$$

Panel B of Table 1 presents the results of the ordinary least-squares regression model using 72 observations of snow days and inches of snowfall for the period 1926 through 1997. The relatively high R^2 of 0.60 indicates a good fit of the model to the data. The coefficients are statistically significant as well. However, the regression equation captures better the expected value of snow inches with the addition of an error term or estimated residual.

Table 2. Analysis of Residuals.

Panel A: Descriptive Statistics	
Mean	0.00
Median	−7.01
Mode	na
Standard Deviation	30.07
Kurtosis	0.55
Skewness	0.66
Minimum	−64.29
Maximum	86.82
Observations	72

Panel B: Cumulative Probability Distribution

Interval of Inches	Frequency	Probability %	Cumulative Probability %
−64.29	1	1.39	1.39
−64.29 to −45.40	2	2.78	4.17
−45.40 to −26.51	9	12.50	16.67
−26.51 to −7.62	24	33.33	50.00
−7.62 to 11.27	10	13.89	63.89
11.27 to 30.16	16	22.21	86.10
30.16 to 49.05	4	5.56	91.66
49.05 to 67.93	3	4.17	95.83
67.93 to 86.82	3	4.17	100.00

Table 2 presents descriptive statistics for and the distribution of the residuals from the regression analysis. The residuals are relatively large ranging from −64.29 to +86.82 snow inches. The statistics show evidence of skewness and kurtosis suggesting that the residuals are not normally distributed. We assume a discrete distribution to model the error terms. The dependent relationship of snowfall in inches on snow days is expressed as follows:

$$\text{Snowfall Inches} = -32.98 + 2.54 \times \text{Snow days} + \text{Residual Estimate} \quad (2)$$

MCS is well suited for variable costs when the distributions of the underlying cost drivers are uncertain. The first step is to specify the functional relationship between the variable snow removal expenditures and the underlying random variables (number of snow days and inches of snowfall). A multivariate, ordinary least-squares regression equation describes the functional relationship. The next step is to obtain a representative set of observations of the random variable, the number of snow days in a calendar year. The assumptions implicit in using this set are that next year's snow days is a random draw from a theoretical normal distribution with the parameters described in Panel A of Table 1.

The simulation consists of a series of trials. In each trial, a number of snow days is a random draw on which snowfall in inches is conditional. Similarly, the estimated residual term is a random draw from a discrete distribution of actual residuals or error terms. The conditional amount of snowfall is calculated from the regression equation (2) above.

The budget preparer computes the variable snow removal expenditure using a cost equation that incorporates snow days and inches of snowfall. Additional trials repeat the procedure of randomly drawing a snow days number, residual estimates, and computing the variable costs for that year's snow. The result is a series of variable snow removal expenditure amounts. From the simulation results, the budget preparer estimates the most likely expenditure and the range of possible expenditures. The next section develops the variable cost equation and illustrates the MCS procedures in the snow removal problem.

ESTIMATING VARIABLE SNOW REMOVAL COSTS WITH MCS

Three expenditure accounts contain the accumulated variable snow removal costs: Street Department Overtime, Garage Overtime, and Snow Removal Contracted Costs. The last account represents the city's expenditures for salt, sand, cinders, and shovels. Table 3 shows the monthly expenditures in these three accounts for the years 1993 through 1997. The table also shows the city's monthly snowfall and number of snow days for these years. The budget preparer uses the data from Table 3 to estimate the following ordinary least-squares regression:

$$\text{Variable cost} = \beta_0 + \beta_1 \times \text{Snow days} + \beta_2 \times \text{Inches} \tag{3}$$

Table 3. Monthly Snowfall and Variable Snow Removal Costs 1993 to 1997.

Calendar Year	Snow Days	Snowfall (Inches)	Street Department Actual Overtime	Garage Actual Overtime	Actual Contracted Costs	Total Variable Snow Removal Costs
January	17	29.1	$ 10,975	$ 18,777	$ 71,835	$ 101,587
February	19	65.3	18,113	24,041	73,529	115,683
March	13	34.1	10,671	13,746	32,002	56,419
April	4	4.8	1,831	658	1,547	4,036
November	5	8.0	2,639	3,414	4,383	10.436
December	14	35.6	6,771	9,364	44,732	60,867
Total 1993	72	176.9	$ 51,000	$ 70,000	$ 228,028	$ 349,028
January	24	93.8	$ 25,044	$ 34,697	$ 56,804	$ 116,545
February	16	40.2	10,044	15,394	38,898	64,336
March	12	18.6	8,633	12,601	1,365	22,599
April	2	7.6	651	967	14,546	16,164
November	3	5.6	2,328	2,305	3,281	7,914
December	6	9.0	4,300	4,036	528	8,864
Total 1994	63	174.8	$ 51,000	$ 70,000	$ 115,422	$ 185,422
January	15	16.2	$ 7,524	$ 15,023	$ 17,160	$ 39,707
February	18	58.5	14,138	17,598	69,727	101,463
March	3	8.1	4,114	2,754	5,236	12,104
April	3	2.1	1,199	1,174	289	2,662
November	17	27.3	9,663	9,098	42,404	61,165
December	20	69.9	17,962	38,353	117,098	173,413
Total 1995	76	182.1	$ 54,600	$ 84,000	$ 251,914	$ 335,914
January	22	56.4	$ 17,902	$ 23,712	$ 66,403	$ 108,017
February	14	24.9	6,068	14,667	30,604	51,339
March	12	26.2	9,021	12,187	52,191	73,399
April	2	1.0	1,157	417	6,034	7,608
November	15	35.2	10,683	13,985	57,936	82,604
December	20	36.9	9,769	19,032	80,164	108,965
Total 1996	85	180.6	$ 54,600	$ 84,000	$ 293,332	$ 377,332

Table 3. Continued.

Calendar Year	Snow Days	Snowfall (Inches)	Street Department Actual Overtime	Garage Actual Overtime	Actual Contracted Costs	Total Variable Snow Removal Costs
January	16	39.2	$ 13,060	$ 15,533	$ 23,969	$ 52,562
February	23	71.0	19,692	25,388	54,524	99,604
March	9	7.7	3,749	9,411	11,740	24,900
April	4	3.4	2,033	4,139	17,206	23,378
November	3	0.7	849	665	23,626	25,140
December	22	51.9	18,827	34,414	59,736	112,977
Total 1997	77	173.9	$ 58,210	$ 89,550	$ 190,801	$ 280,351

Before estimating the regression, it is necessary to ascertain that the underlying amounts are an accurate reflection of the city's true costs. Table 3 indicates that the city's Street Department Actual Overtime was exactly $51,000 in calendar 1993 and 1994 and exactly $54,600 in calendar 1995 and 1996. Similarly, Garage Actual Overtime was $70,000 in 1993 and 1994 and $84,000 in 1995 and 1996. Because deficit spending is undesirable, the budgeted amount constrains actual expenditures. However, budget numbers may contain a certain amount of slack. Department managers have incentives to spend budget excesses to ensure that next year's budget amount will not be smaller. The size of the budget excess, if any, is apparent in the late months of the year. If this is true for the Street Department, then the expenditures for the months of November and December may not reflect true costs. The budget preparer should estimate the regression over the months of January through April only to control for this possibility. The regression produced the following formula for estimated variable snow removal costs:

$$\text{Variable cost} = -\$850.90 + \$2{,}822.46 \times \text{Snow days} + \$676.03 \times \text{Inches} \quad (4)$$

The *t*-statistics on the coefficients of the independent variables were 2.14 and 2.45 respectively. Both coefficients are significant at the 0.05 level. The R^2 of the entire model was 0.87.

Estimating the Cost Equation with Excel

The budget preparer performs regression analysis in Excel 2000 by selecting Tools from the menu bar and Data Analysis and Regression from the sub menus.

There are 20 observations of total variable snow removal cost, snow days, and snowfall inches from Table 3 for the months January through April for years 1993 through 1997. The preparer should record these observations in three adjacent spreadsheet columns.

The dialogue box for Regression asks for input data ranges for the dependent variable Y (total variable cost) and the independent variables X_1 and X_2 (snow days and snow inches). The input data range for the independent variables includes both snow inches and snow days. The input range should begin with the first row of the first column and end with the last row of the second column. The output range in the dialogue box is a cell address in the spreadsheet. The cell address is the upper left-hand corner of a seven-column blank area in the spreadsheet in which the regression output will appear. The regression function will generate the necessary statistics for the cost function as described above.

Obtaining Random Numbers for MCS

The Monte Carlo simulation portion of the project is easy to construct using the function "Random Number Generation" and "Normal" distribution type for snow days. Estimating the residuals requires the random number generation function and "Discrete" distribution type. These features are available on most spreadsheet packages.[3] A suggested spreadsheet begins with the following format:

	A	B	C	D
1	Random Snow Days	Random Residual	Snowfall Inches	Estimated Cost
2				

The first step in constructing the spreadsheet is to obtain a set of random numbers for snow days. This example uses 50 trials. The spreadsheet preparer should go to Excel Tools, Data Analysis and select Random Number Generation from the menu box. If Data Analysis does not appear on the pull-down menu, the spreadsheet preparer must add in the feature by clicking on Add-Ins and checking the Analysis ToolPak box.

Figure 1 displays the dialog box for the Excel random number generator. The dialogue box asks for number of variables which is "1" to represent the single snow days variable. The number of random numbers is 50 to represent the desired number of trials. The spreadsheet preparer should select "Normal" from the menu of distribution types and enter the parameters from Panel A of Table 1, using a mean of 59.94 days and a standard deviation of 14.57 days. Selecting

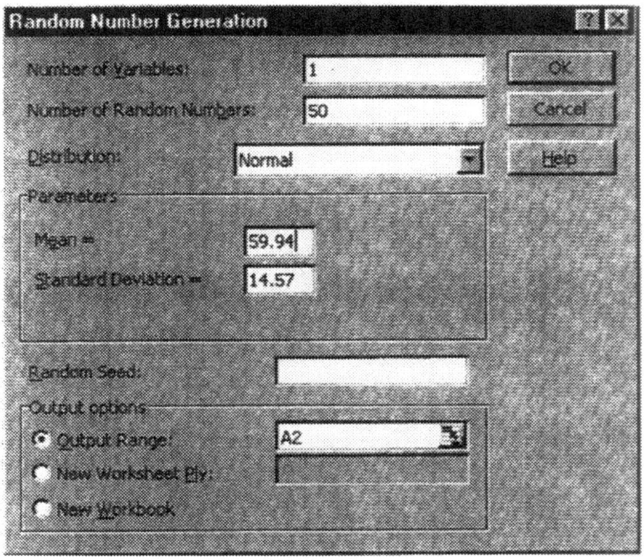

Fig 1. Excel Random Number Generator Dialog Box.

the output range as A2 will fill column A with 50 random numbers of snow days. The random numbers are truncated to obtain an integer value for snow days. By entering an integer in the "Random Seed" box, a user or multiple users will obtain the same sets of random numbers in different spreadsheets.

Excel generates also random numbers for estimated residuals. The spreadsheet preparer should go to Tools, Data Analysis, Random Number Generation, and view the dialogue box. The dialog box requires entering "1" for the number of variables, "50" for the number of trials, and selecting "Discrete" from the menu of distribution types. Panel A of Fig. 2 shows the dialog box.

The dialogue box will ask for the spreadsheet address for the discrete values of the expected residuals and the probability that each will occur. Panel B of Table 2 provides that information. Column 1 of Panel B lists nine discrete intervals. The right-hand value of the interval range is the discrete value. The probability of obtaining a residual in each of the nine discrete categories appears in column 3 of Panel B. The spreadsheet preparer must record the right-hand values and corresponding probability in two adjacent columns in a convenient area of the spreadsheet. The spreadsheet address for the dialogue box begins with the first row of the first column and ends with the ninth row

Panel A: Random Number Generator Dialog Box.

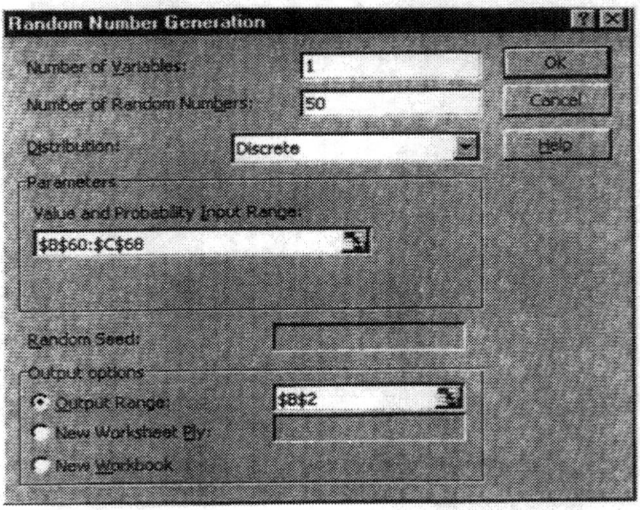

Panel B: Spreadsheet Entries for Dialog Box.

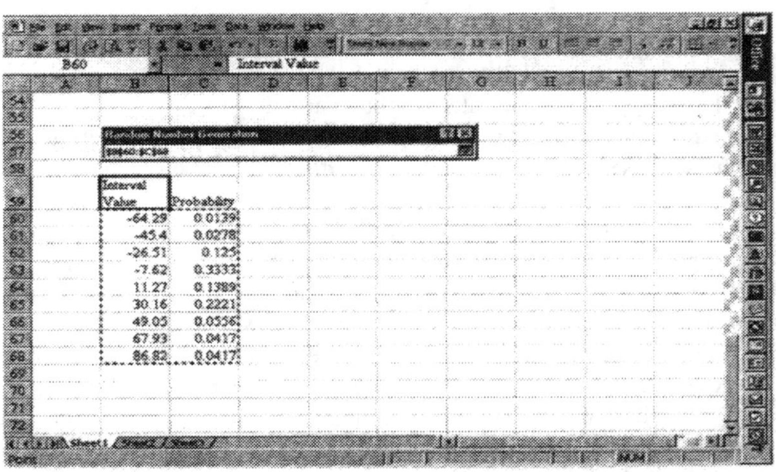

Fig 2. Random Number Generation for Discrete Distribution.

of the second column. The output address is B2. Panel B of Fig. 2 shows the spreadsheet entries and the cell addresses for the dialog box.

With this information, Excel will generate 50 random residual estimates to fill column B of the spreadsheet. For simplicity, we rounded the residual estimates to two decimal places. Columns A and B are filled with random numbers. Columns C and D require formulas to use the random numbers.

Completing the Simulation

The spreadsheet requires the following formulas in cells C2 and D2:

	A	B	C	D
1	Random Snow Days	Random Residual	Snowfall inches	Estimated Cost
2	79	−7.62	= −32.98 + 2.54*A2 + B2	= −5105.40 + 2822.46*A2 + 676.03*C2

The formula in cell C2 is an expression of equation (2). The formula in cell D2 uses the regression coefficients reported in equation (4) to compute the expected variable snow removal costs from the amounts in A2 and C2.

Note that the intercept term in cell D2 is −$5,105.40, although the intercept term from equation (4) is −$850.90. The reason for the change is that the regression coefficients reflect monthly snowfall and cost data, but the formula in D2 estimates variable snow removal costs for the entire year. The intercept term was increased by a factor of six to account for the six months of the year in which the city experienced measurable snowfall.

After entering the formulas in cells C2 and D2, the budget preparer copies the formulas 49 times to create a set of 50 trials. The assumption underlying the simulation is that the distribution of variable snow removal costs in cells D2 through D51 is the distribution describing next year's variable snow removal costs. Figure 3 displays an example of a completed spreadsheet.

Analyzing the MCS Results

The results of the 50 simulated costs from column D of Fig. 3 appear in Table 4. The trials do not constitute a sample from an unknown population or "reality" from which one makes inferences about the population characteristics. More accurately, the collective trials represent an imitation or duplicate of a real-world situation from which one can make inferences and draw conclusions about the results of the simulation. The simulation is a mathematical

	A	B	C	D
1	Random Snow Days	Random Residual	Snowfall inches	Estimated Cost
2	79	−7.62	160.06	$326,074.30
3	78	−26.51	138.63	$308,764.52
4	73	11.27	163.71	$311,607.05
5	61	49.05	171.01	$282,672.55
6	70	49.05	193.87	$323,528.74
7	83	86.82	264.66	$408,076.88
8	53	−45.4	56.24	$182,504.91
9	63	−7.62	119.42	$253,441.08
10	62	49.05	173.55	$287,212.13
11	67	−26.51	110.69	$258,829.18
12	60	−7.62	111.80	$239,822.35
13	75	−26.51	131.01	$295,145.79
14	66	−45.40	89.26	$241,519.40
15	73	−26.51	125.93	$286,066.64
49	58	86.82	201.16	$294,587.47
50	50	−45.40	48.62	$168,886.18
51	52	−7.62	91.48	$203,505.74

Fig. 3. Example of a Monte Carlo Spreadsheet and Estimation of Variable Snow Removal Costs.

representation of reality. If the results exhibit a normal, bell-shaped distribution, the budget preparer may make use of the properties and characteristics of normal distributions. However, summarization of the results in the form of a cumulative probability distribution is appropriate for a wide variety of distributions including normal distributions. Rouse (1993, p. 120) and Polimeni et al. (1991, p. 907) use a cumulative probability distribution to summarize results such as those in Fig. 3. Excel 2000 provides the mechanics for constructing a cumulative probability distribution that appears in Table 4.

On the basis of the simulated distribution of costs, the budget preparer can draw several useful conclusions. For example, a preparer may expect costs to range from $99,095 to $421,405, with a 44% probability of costs not exceeding $250,000. Given a reliable cost function, a budget of $350,000 would provide assurance that the probability of an unfavorable variance would be approximately 10%. Similarly, the probability of actual costs exceeding $400,000 is approximately 6%.

This project uses only 50 trials for demonstration purposes and to make the spreadsheet more manageable for the student. Increasing the number of trials improves the precision of the simulation results. Expanding the trials to 1,000

Table 4. Results of the Monte Carlo Simulation of Variable Snow Removal Costs.

	50 Trials		1000 Trials	
Cost Interval	Frequency	Cumulative %	Frequency	Cumulative %
$0 - $100,000	1	2.00	12	1.20
$125,000	1	4.00	20	3.20
$150,000	5	14.00	49	8.10
$175,000	4	22.00	66	14.70
$200,000	4	30.00	104	25.10
$225,000	2	34.00	128	37.90
$250,000	5	44.00	127	50.60
$275,000	6	56.00	130	63.60
$300,000	9	74.00	127	76.30
$325,000	5	84.00	95	85.80
$350,000	3	90.00	63	92.10
$375,000	1	92.00	36	95.70
$400,000	1	94.00	27	98.40
$425,000	3	100.00	10	99.40
$450,000	0	100.00	5	99.90
$475,000	0	100.00	1	100.00
Total Trials	50		1,000	
Minimum		$99,095		$71,858
Maximum		$421,405		$462,552
Mean		$253,323		$249,918

yielded the results summarized in Table 4. The probability of costs not exceeding $250,000 increases to 51%. The probability of costs greater than $400,000 approximates 1.6%. The results of the two sets of trials are similar, but not identical. Because of the random number generator, replications of the simulation will produce slightly different results. Therefore, individual projects and spreadsheets will not be identical, unless one specifies a random seed in generating the random numbers.

Excel 2000 will produce a cumulative probability distribution as well as a chart that allows the user to visually inspect the distribution of simulation results. Column D in the spreadsheet contains the simulated costs generated by the MCS operation. It is necessary to type into an adjacent column the interval ranges into which Excel will sort the results. An example is the set of cost intervals shown in Table 4. Excel refers to the intervals as "Bins." To perform the sorting step, the budget preparer should select Tools from the menu bar and Data Analysis and Histogram from the sub menus. The input data range in the Histogram dialogue box is the column of simulated costs. The Bin Range is the column of cost intervals typed in the spreadsheet. The output range is the upper left-hand corner cell address for the desired cumulative probability distribution output. Necessary additional output options include "Cumulative percentage" and "Chart Output." Activating the chart in the spreadsheet allows the budget preparer to select a chart type, edit the title and axes, and print the chart. Selection of "Descriptive Statistics" from the Data Analysis sub menu will provide access to additional statistical measures.

MCS APPLICATIONS TO PERFORMANCE EVALUATION

The budget preparer will select a budget amount from the MCS results that is consistent with the level of risk he or she is willing to assume for budgeting purposes. The calculation and disclosure of cost variances at the end of the year would increase the extent to which budgets can provide information for performance measurement. The model for the variable costs of snow removal equation (4) provides a means of recognizing uncontrollable factors in a variance calculation. For example, assume that the budget preparer estimated snow removal costs for 60 snow days and 119 inches of snow. Equation (4) produces an annual budgeted cost of $244,690.[4] Actual expenditures for variable costs of $290,000 in a year with 65 snow days and 150 inches of snow create an unfavorable static budget variance of $45,310. Part of this variance is attributable to snow in excess of the planned amount, the volume variance. Using equation (4) to calculate a flexible-budget amount based on actual inches of snow and snow days ($279,759) permits the budget preparer to isolate the volume variance and the flexible-budget variance. Thus, the total unfavorable cost variance of $45,310 consists of $35,069 as an unfavorable volume variance and $10,241 as an unfavorable flexible-budget variance. The budget preparer or budget analyst would likely proceed with investigating the flexible-budget cost variance. The unfavorable volume variance would quantify the explanations related to uncontrollable weather factors.

The MCS approach described here allows the governmental agency to estimate the probability or risk of actual expenditures exceeding the budgeted amount. The simulation model provides valuable information to enhance the planning phase of the budget process and subsequent performance evaluation. The model has applications for insurance coverage in other settings influenced by weather conditions such as hurricanes, earthquakes, rain and flooding, and severe changes in temperature. Electric and gas utility companies may find the technique useful to estimate the portion of demand driven by seasonal temperatures. Additional applications include repairs and maintenance budgets for random breakdowns and failures in processes, machines, or services.

IMPLEMENTATION IN THE CLASSROOM

This project is appropriate for an advanced undergraduate or graduate-level course in managerial, cost, or governmental accounting. In fact, the project evolved from five semesters of earlier class projects that applied MCS to cost-volume-profit and capital budgeting analyses in an advanced managerial accounting course. The major learning objective in this and the earlier projects was to incorporate uncertainty and the concept of a probability distribution of potential outcomes in a decision-making context.

In addition to developing the students' facility in using uncertainty in business decisions, the specific student learning objectives include constructing the variable costs portion of a budget, applying variance analysis, and refining computer and spreadsheet skills. An assumption is that student project users will have a basic understanding of simple statistics and spreadsheets. Because most business programs require a course in basic statistics and computer applications, the assumption seems reasonable. However, the project gives detailed instructions for composing the spreadsheet and using Excel functions should the instructor wish to distribute those with the project data.

We designed this project as an outside-of-class assignment to complement the coverage of budgeting. We introduced the project during class and explained the purpose of the Excel functions including the random number generator and the histogram needed to produce a cumulative probability distribution. We drew the layout of the spreadsheet on the blackboard and used transparencies to emphasize the functional nature of sections of the spreadsheet. We found this approach effective because we could explain the project in a visual format and provide a project overview at the same time. The class presentation required approximately 45 minutes. At the end of the class period, the majority of students had a clear idea of the necessary components in the spreadsheet and how it should look.

In addition to the class time devoted to the project, we offered a special computer laboratory session for the group as a whole and office hours to individuals who needed extra help or troubleshooting. Fewer than 25% of the students required extra help. Most were able to complete the spreadsheet without help in less than two hours. The project time requirements were reasonable and did not result in deletions of topics or reduced coverage of existing ones in the course.

We found it helpful to remind students to use the copy command as much as possible to shorten the spreadsheet preparation time and to set the auto-save feature. Students may need to add-in the Excel Analysis Toolpak, if Data Analysis does not appear on the Tools menu.

At the end of the semester, we asked open-ended questions and solicited comments from the students about the value of the project. The student feedback on the project was very positive from undergraduates, especially about the sense of accomplishment in completing a detailed spreadsheet. A small number of students commented that the MCS spreadsheet was the most valuable portion of the entire course. Graduate students commented positively and more frequently about the useful applications to problem solving and the acquired expertise with spreadsheets. We received no negative comments related to the length, difficulty, or relevance of the project.

The project flexibility allows instructors to tailor the length and complexity to a level that seems appropriate. Tables 1, 2, and 3 provide the basic snowfall and variable snow removal cost data. Instructors can shorten the project by providing the students with the regression cost function equation (4) and omitting the requirement to produce charted results. If including the regression analysis step for the cost function is desirable, instructors should advise the students to treat November and December costs of each year (Table 3) as potential outliers. In other words, if the goal is to develop an equation to predict costs under normal operating conditions, the budget preparer should exclude observations that reflect abnormal costs.

Chapter 20 of Polimeni et al. (1991, pp. 894–950) presents a detailed discussion of MCS along with sample problems and exercises for anyone who desires additional explanation of the topic. Instructors can enhance the project with questions requiring written responses or questions for discussion.

We used an earlier version of the project in both an undergraduate and graduate course in governmental accounting. The assignment had specific applications to service efforts and accomplishments (SEA) disclosures from state and local government entities (GASB, 1994). We asked discussion questions about possible measures of SEA. Service efforts include categories of financial and non-financial resources, such as actual cost, man-hours worked, and amounts of material used. Service accomplishments encompass both quantities of outputs, such as lane-miles of roads plowed, and efficiency measures such as clock-hours for snow removal and citizen satisfaction with road cleaning. The budget volume variance from the class project would provide quantitative supplementary information disclosures related to the impact of uncontrollable weather factors.

Instructors of a governmental accounting course may wish to refer students to the GASB web site (http://www.rutgers.edu/Accounting/raw/gasb/seagov/home.html) for current information on the issue of accountability, issues related to SEA, and news releases on reporting standards. The web site is informative and friendly to student users.

Instructors of cost and managerial accounting courses could ask questions about the budget computations and the preparation of the simulation model. Questions about ethical issues related to budgetary slack might also be appropriate. For example, students might identify those variables that drive total variable costs such as supplies, labor, and weather conditions. Students might discuss the managerial behavioral factors involved in cost estimation including risk aversion and the desire for a favorable performance evaluation. Finally, students might discuss the ethical implications of building slack into a budget. Texts that provide coverage of the ethical conduct standards for practicing accountants and financial managers would support class discussions of ethical situations in budgeting.

ACKNOWLEDGMENTS

We are grateful to Bill N. Schwartz (the Co-Editor) and two anonymous reviewers for their many helpful comments and suggestions.

NOTES

1. The cost and budget data used in this project are publicly available information from an anonymous city. The specific geographical location and the financial information have been disguised to protect the identity of the city. However, we retained the important facts and relationships among the data to present the situation accurately and to provide a reliable basis for analysis and discussion.

2. One reason for the lack of text coverage may be new trends in the 1990s. Boer (2000, pp. 320–322) states that the emphasis in accounting techniques and topics has shifted from mathematical and operations research techniques popular in the 1980s to activity-based costing and management decision making. Another possible explanation is that instructors are not aware of the ease and simplicity with which new versions of spreadsheets can perform simulations.

3. Using basic spreadsheet packages such as Excel or Lotus is attractive as a result of the wide availability to students on home computers or in computer laboratories. More sophisticated software includes programs such as Crystal Ball and @Risk. These programs run as "add-ins" in Lotus or Excel. The program user can select from a menu of distribution types, e.g. normal, discrete, or uniform. These programs also offer enhanced graphics and built-in sensitivity-analysis features. Simulation software is available through campus bookstores and Internet retailers. For example, Rock Ware, Inc. (http://www. rockware.com) advertises Crystal Ball at $199.

4. The annual estimate produced by equation (4) must include an adjustment to the intercept as explained previously. Variable cost = −$5,105.40 + $2,822.46 × Snow Days + $676.03 × Inches.

REFERENCES

Boer, G. B. (2000). Management accounting education: Yesterday, today, and tomorrow. *Issues in Accounting Education, 15*(2) (May), 313–334.

Brabazon, T. (1997). Using simulation in business decisions. *Management Accounting* (London, UK), *75*(2), 36–38.

Brealey, R., & Meyers, S. (1996). *Principles of Corporate Finance* (5th ed.). New York:McGraw-Hill.

Chau, K. W. (1995). Monte Carlo simulation of construction costs using subjective data. *Construction Management and Economics, 13*, 369–383.

Governmental Accounting Standards Board (GASB) (1994). Service efforts and accomplishments reporting. *Concepts Statement No. 2.* Norwalk, CT:GASB.

Hertz, D. B. (1964). Risk analysis and capital investment. *Harvard Business Review* (January-February), 95–106.

Knowles, R. (1994). Computer models can help RMs weather storms. *Property & Casualty/Risk & Benefits Management, 98*(20) (May), 10, 18.

Morse, W. J., Davis, J. R., & Hartgraves, A. L. (2000). Value chain analysis and activity-based management. In: *Management accounting: A strategic approach*, 2e (pp. 168–193). Cincinnati, OH: South-Western College Publishing.

Nordhauser, F., & Chau, C. T. (1997). Beyond flexible budgeting: Performing stochastic simulation with a spreadsheet add-in. *Accounting Educators' Journal, 9*(1), (Spring), 100–114.

Polimeni, R., Fabozzi, F., & Adelberg, A. (1991). *Cost Accounting* (3rd ed.). New York: McGraw-Hill, Inc.

Rouse, P. (1993). Constructing Monte Carlo simulations in lotus 1-2-3. *Journal of Accounting Education, 11*(1), (Spring), 113–132.

Siegel, G., & Sorensen, J. (1994). *What Corporate America Wants in Entry-level Accountants.* Montvale, NJ: The Institute of Management Accountants.

Siegel, G., & Sorensen, J. (1996). *The Practice Analysis of Management Accounting*. Montvale, NJ: The Institute of Management Accountants.

Siegel, G., & Sorensen, J. (1999). *Counting More, Counting Less-transformations in the Management Accounting Profession.* Montvale, NJ: The Institute of Management Accountants.

Sheel, A. (1995). Monte Carlo simulations and scenario analysis-decision-making tools for hoteliers. *Hotel and Restaurant Administration Quarterly, 36*(5), (October), 18–26.

AN EXPLORATORY STUDY OF STUDENT BELIEFS IN THE RESPONSE RELIABILITY OF TEACHING EVALUATION INSTRUMENTS

Brian Patrick Green, Thomas G. Calderon and Michael Harkness

ABSTRACT

Student evaluations represent the most commonly used source of information in assessing faculty teaching performance. However, faculty members frequently question the reliability and validity of student evaluations (SEs) as a medium for assessing effective teaching. Some contend that SE ratings are not reliable because students base their responses on factors that do not reflect an instructor's effectiveness as a teacher. This problem might be further complicated if the information providers (students) view the evaluation process as being futile, invalid, or unreliable. This paper examines students' perceptions of the reliability of information they supply through SE instruments. The results show that most students believe they can objectively evaluate effective teaching and can respond to items on an SE instrument without inferring beyond their experiences. Students indicate that factors identified in prior studies as

Advances in Accounting Education, Volume 4, pages 189–204.

ISBN: 0-7623-0856-7

potential sources of bias, such as student characteristics, class characteristics, and instructor characteristics, do not affect their evaluations. However, they are not aware of how SE ratings are used, and many say they do not trust the teaching evaluation process. The results suggest that when administering SEs, accounting faculty and administrators should very carefully explain to students the purpose and importance of the SE process, and the need for objectivity in the process.

INTRODUCTION

Faculty members often express concern about the reliability and validity of SEs as a medium for assessing effective teaching (Calderon, Gabbin, & Green, 1996; Seldin, 1993; Kemp & Kumar, 1990; Marsh, 1987, Marsh, 1982; White & Ahmadi, 1986). A major concern is the large number of factors beyond an instructor's control that might influence student ratings of teaching effectiveness. Motivated by this concern, Calderon, Green and Reider (1997) investigated whether administrators of accounting departments believed that their student evaluation (SE) instruments focus on aspects of faculty teaching performance that students can validly and reliably assess. They found that most administrators of accounting programs believe that SEs are good measures of effective teaching, that students can competently evaluate instructor performance, and that questions on their SE instruments are relevant to their business programs. Overall, most administrators reported that they trust SE results. The perception of students' capacity to evaluate effective teaching objectively is the single most important factor in explaining administrators' trust in SE ratings. However, many administrators also believe that factors that do not necessarily relate to an instructor's classroom performance influence SE ratings, including class grade distribution, students' grade expectations, class rigor, instructors' age, gender, rank, race, and national origin. Calderon et al. (1997) suggest that administrators cope with potential biases in SE data through awareness and by using multiple types of evidence that supplement SEs.

While their research offers insights into administrators' perceptions of SEs, it does not consider the beliefs of students as information providers in the process of assessing an instructor's classroom effectiveness. More specifically, information from SEs may lack credibility if students indicate that factors that do not necessarily relate to an instructor's classroom performance influence their responses to questions on SE instruments. Similarly, if students have doubts about the validity and reliability of SEs as a basis for assessing faculty teaching effectiveness, it is possible that those beliefs will adversely affect their responses. If such problems do exist, administrators would not be able to compensate by using multiple types of information. Such problems could taint the information provided by students and make their input unsuitable for use in assessing instructors' classroom effectiveness. This is a significant issue as SEs are the most commonly used source of information in assessing faculty teaching performance (Seldin, 1993; Yunker & Sterner, 1988).

This paper extends and complements Calderon et al. (1997) and Yunker and Sterner (1988) by examining students' perceptions about the credibility of SEs, and offering insight into whether their beliefs are consistent with the views of accounting program administrators. The paper also explores the degree to which students believe faculty should trust SE results, and investigates whether students believe that their responses are influenced by factors that the literature suggests may be unrelated to instructors' classroom effectiveness. The paper should be of interest to faculty members and administrators who are considering the role of SEs in assessment activities.

The next section of the paper presents a brief overview of the literature relating to the validity of SEs in assessing teaching performance. Then we describe the research questions and the methods used in the study. The third section presents and discusses the results. A summary of the results and a discussion of the limitations and implications of the findings conclude the paper.

PRIOR RESEARCH

The literature suggests that properly designed SE instruments can provide valid and reliable information about selected aspects of faculty teaching performance (Calderon et al., 1996; Cohen, 1981; Marsh, 1984, 1987; Marsh & Ware, 1982; Murray, 1983; Seldin, 1984). A properly designed SE instrument will include only those questions that students can validly assess (Green et al., 1998; Seldin, 1993). Among the areas that students are able to assess are: (1) the extent of learning and the value they attach to it, (2) instructor enthusiasm, (3) organization skill of instructor, (4) extent of group interaction in classes, (5) instructor rapport with students, (6) breadth of coverage, (7) examination content, evaluation methods and extent of feedback, (8) extent to which assignments contribute to course understanding, and (9) course difficulty and workload (Marsh, 1982; AECC, 1993). Seldin (1993) recommends that SEs should require students to assess what they have learned in a course and to report on such aspects as the professor's ability to communicate at the student's level, ethical and professional behavior in the classroom, rapport with students, and ability to stimulate interest in the subject. On the other hand, several studies indicate that students may not be able to judge performance factors such as sufficiency of course content and instructor knowledge of the subject matter (Cashin, 1983; Lowman, 1984; McKeachie, 1971; Moore, 1990; Trahan & Swindle, 1988).

Although there is a fair amount of consensus in the literature on the aspects of faculty teaching performance that students can and cannot validly evaluate, students, as information providers, have not been subjects of those studies. There is no evidence to indicate what they believe they can or cannot evaluate. Thus, a research issue examined in this paper is whether students believe they can provide reliable responses to the items that make up the SE instrument used by their Colleges, and whether they believe that SEs are good indicators of effective teaching.

Biases in Student Evaluations

A survey of the literature suggests that several factors that are not indicative of effective teaching may be associated with student rating of their instructors. Most of these factors fall into the following three categories:

(1) student-related characteristics such as disposition toward instructors and courses, effort in and enthusiasm for the course, and grade expectation;
(2) instructor-related characteristics, including gender, experience, personality traits and classroom performance skills, teaching style, and research productivity; and
(3) characteristics of the class such as actual grade distribution, class size, and class rigor.

Research findings related to those factors are not consistent, and many authors differ in their interpretation of findings that appear to be consistent. The relationship between SE ratings and expected course grade, one of the most frequently examined issues in this line of research, aptly illustrates this point. Although a few researchers (e.g. Frey, 1973; Miller, 1988; Palmer, Carliner & Romer, 1978) found no relationship between students' expected grades and SE ratings, most studies report a positive association between expected grade and SE ratings (Anikeeff, 1953; Arnett, Arnold & Cochran, 1989; Bausell & Magoon, 1972; Brandenburg, Slinde & Batista, 1977; Centra, 1977; DuCette & Kenney, 1982; Ellis, 1985; Feldman, 1976; Goldberg & Callahan, 1991; Heilman & Armentrout, 1936; Kemp & Kumar, 1990; Marsh, 1984; Sclul & Crivelli, 1973; Sullivan & Skanes, 1974; Weaver, 1960). Some studies, such as Marsh (1987), interpret course grade as evidence of learning and conclude that the positive association between grade and SE ratings is warranted and expected. Others, such as Ellis (1985), refer to the relationship between grade and SE ratings in the context of grade buying, grade inflation, and leniency.

Other factors that have received extensive attention in the literature, with mixed results, include: students' gender, age, and major; instructors' gender, age, and rank; and class size and rigor. Calderon et al. (1997) indicate that many administrators of accounting programs believe that these factors, as well as expected grade, affect students' rating of instructors' classroom effectiveness. Neither Calderon et al. (1997), nor the extensive list of studies they reviewed, makes it clear whether students perceive those factors as influencing their responses to SE ratings.

METHOD

The specific research questions addressed in this paper are:

(1) What are students' general beliefs about the credibility and usefulness of SEs in assessing effective teaching?
(2) Do students believe that SE ratings are influenced by student characteristics such as gender, age, academic major and grade expectation?
(3) Do students believe that SE ratings are influenced by class characteristics such as expected grade, class size, and class rigor?
(4) Do students believe that SE ratings are influenced by instructor characteristics such as gender, age, and rank?
(5) Do SE ratings reflect how much students learned in a class?

The Instrument

We adapted the survey instrument from Calderon et al. (1997) and modified it to focus on students rather than administrators. The questions included in the survey, shown in Table 1, should elicit responses in the following areas: (1) whether student characteristics influence their evaluations; (2) whether class characteristics influence student's evaluations; (3) whether instructor characteristics influence student's evaluations; and (4) student perceptions of factors influencing the usefulness and credibility of student evaluations. We scaled students' responses with the five point Likert scale shown in Table 1. The instrument also solicited information on students' degree program, academic standing, major, age and gender. Designed as an interactive web document, the instrument captured and stored student responses directly into a Microsoft Access database.

Table 1. Survey Questions.

Student respondents were asked to indicate their level of agreement with the following statements using the scale 5 = strongly agree, 4 = agree, 3 = no opinion, 2 = disagree, 1 = strongly disagree.

General Perceptions Concerning Student Evaluations

- I can answer most questions on the student evaluation form using my own experience.
- I am sometimes asked to infer beyond my own experience to answer questions on the student evaluation form.
- Most questions on the student evaluation are relevant to the business program.
- Most questions on the student evaluation are relevant to my major/concentration.
- Overall, student evaluations are good measures of effective teaching.
- Overall, student evaluations reflect how much I learned in class.
- Some student evaluation questions cause a negative response.
- I can objectively evaluate effective teaching.
- I know students who cannot objectively evaluate effective teaching.
- Student evaluations should be completely trusted by faculty.

Perceptions Relating to Student, Class and Instructor Characteristics

The factors listed below DO NOT affect my evaluation of an instructor.

- My gender
- My age
- The course is part of my major
- The grade I expect to receive
- The instructor's gender
- The instructor's age
- The instructor's rank
- Class size
- Class rigor

The factors listed below DO affect other students' evaluation of an instructor

- My gender
- My age
- The course is part of my major
- The grade I expect to receive
- The instructor's gender
- The instructor's age
- The instructor's rank
- Class size
- Class rigor

The Sample

A sample of 246 students, enrolled in accounting courses at two midwestern universities, participated in the survey for course credit. Both universities are located in an urban setting and had total enrollments of 8,800 and 26,000 non-residential students, with approximately 1,000 undergraduate and 500 graduate business (including accounting) students. The courses surveyed were undergraduate Introductory Principles of Accounting, Accounting Information Systems, Auditing, and an MBA-level Principles of Accounting. As shown in Table 2, students came from a wide cross-section of degree programs, academic majors, and levels of academic standing. The average age of respondents is approximately 25, and most are accounting majors.

Table 2. Student Demographics.

Degree Program	*Percent*
BS	29.63
BA	48.97
MBA	14.40
Other	7.00
Academic Standing	
Freshman	1.63
Sophomore	18.37
Junior	32.25
Senior	33.47
Graduate	14.29
Age (years)	
Lowest	18.00
Highest	51.00
Mean	24.66
Standard Deviation	6.64
Major	
Accounting	41.22
Accounting Information Systems	3.27
Finance	15.92
MIS	6.12
Management	13.06
Human Resources	0.41
Marketing	7.76
Other	12.25
Gender	
Male	50.62
Female	49.38
Total sample size	246

RESULTS AND DISCUSSION

General Perceptions

Table 3 presents students' perceptions of the usefulness and credibility of SEs. Over 90% of the students believe they can answer most questions on student evaluation instruments using their own experience. It is evident that students were discriminating when responding to this question. While they can respond effectively to most questions, it is apparent that there may be some items on the SE instrument they are unable to answer based on their own experience.

Table 3. Perceived Usefulness and Integrity of Student Evaluations.

	N	Median	Mean	Std. Dev.	*Percent of Respondents* Strongly Disagree	Disagree	Neutral	Agree	Strongly Agree
I can answer most questions on the student evaluation form using my own experience.	245	4.00	4.18	0.72	0.41	4.08	4.08	60.00	31.43
Sometimes I am asked to infer beyond my experience to answer questions on the student evaluation.	246	3.00	2.79	0.97	6.10	39.43	25.20	27.64	1.63
Most questions on the student evaluation are relevant to the business program.	245	4.00	3.38	0.86	0.00	22.04	20.82	53.88	3.27
Most questions on the student evaluation are relevant to my major.	246	3.00	3.07	0.93	2.44	31.30	24.80	39.84	1.63
Overall, student evaluations are good measures of effective teaching.	244	4.00	3.31	1.13	5.74	24.59	13.93	44.67	11.07
Overall, the student evaluations reflect how much I learned.	245	3.00	2.89	1.08	6.53	41.22	12.25	36.33	3.67
Some student evaluation questions cause a negative response.	246	4.00	3.45	0.84	0.00	17.07	26.42	50.81	5.69
I can objectively evaluate effective teaching.	246	4.00	3.99	0.81	0.81	6.10	9.76	59.76	23.58
I know other students who cannot objectively evaluate effective teaching.	244	4.00	3.60	0.85	1.23	9.02	29.92	48.36	11.48
Student evaluations should be completely trusted by faculty.	246	2.50	2.80	1.08	7.32	42.68	18.29	26.02	5.69

In excess of 25% of students indicate that in order to respond to certain SE items they must make inferences that are beyond their knowledge and experience. This response suggests that students generally believe that they can answer most, but not all, of the questions on the student evaluation instruments. This finding is consistent with the findings of Green et al. (1998), which reports that SE instruments used in accounting departments had at least one question to which students could not objectively respond. While the current study does not offer insight into how students respond to items they do not believe they can answer, it draws additional attention to a potential problem that could adversely affect the reliability of SE instruments.

Despite some disagreement over the inferences they are required to make when rating their instructors' teaching performance, many students agree that SE's are relevant to both their business programs and their majors (57 and 40%, respectively). Considering that SEs are used to draw inferences about the performance of business faculty, it is intriguing that at least 22% of the students surveyed feel that SE instruments are relevant to neither the business program nor their majors. This result suggests that some students feel that they cannot comment adequately on the performance of instructors in their specific disciplines. Tailoring SEs to specific majors or degree programs may lead to better assessment of outcomes. Such tailoring, however, might exacerbate the difficulty of making comparisons of SE ratings among departments or across different programs within the same department.

Responses to questions that ask students whether SEs are good measures of effective teaching or whether they and their peers can evaluate effective teaching are contradictory and students harbor doubts about their ability to evaluate effective teaching. Forty-five percent of students indicate some degree of doubt that SEs are good measures of effective teaching. Although a substantial majority (83%) agree that they can objectively evaluate effective teaching, close to 60% say they know other students who cannot objectively evaluate effective teaching. Though this statistic is high, it is not clear from the study whether these students are referring to either a small minority or a majority of their peers who cannot objectively evaluate teaching. Nonetheless, the belief that some of their peers cannot effectively evaluate teaching could affect students' confidence in the teaching evaluation process. Thus it is not surprising that only 32% of students believe that faculty should trust SE results.

Like administrators (Calderon et al., 1997), most students disagree or remain neutral with the statements that SE's reflect their level of learning. About 60% were neutral or indicated that SE's do not reflect how much they learned. This appears to run counter to some of the reported findings in the literature, such as Cashin (1990), which suggest that student ratings are correlated with measures of student learning and may be a good measure of student learning. On the other hand, this result is consistent with Centra's (1993) observation that SE ratings are not appropriate measures of student learning and that administrators should use other indictors of learning to supplement SE results.

Several positive observations from the study counterbalance the negative findings and interpretations discussed above. For example, a majority of students believe they can respond to most items on the SE instrument based on their personal experience and background, that SEs are good measures of effective teaching, that SE content is relevant to the business program, and that they can evaluate effective teaching. Many students (40%) also indicate that SE ratings reflect how much they learned in a class.

Perceived Biases: Student Characteristics

Table 4 presents students' beliefs about factors that the literature cites as possible sources of bias in SE ratings. At least 90% of students believe that their age and gender do not affect their evaluations. However, approximately a quarter of the students surveyed felt that these characteristics affect the ratings of other students. When asked if the course being a part of their major would affect their evaluation, 76% indicated it would not. On the other hand, 45% felt this characteristic biased the evaluations of their peers. Similarly, 69% indicate that grade expectations do not affect their SE ratings. Conversely, 58% believe grade expectations influence other students' ratings of their instructors.

The high proportion of students who indicate that extraneous factors do not affect their own ratings of an instructor's teaching effectiveness, but would affect other students' ratings suggests that students lack confidence in the objectivity of at least a subset of their peers. Many students do not believe that their peers would be objective in evaluating their instructors. The interpretation of the relationship between SE's and grade expectations is somewhat ambiguous. The literature suggests a link between SE results and grade expectations. Some researchers suggest that such a relationship does not reflect bias; rather, the link indicates a connection between SE ratings and student learning (Marsh, 1987; Centra, 1993). One may also contend that grade expectations reflects expected grading leniency, which is unrelated to learning (Ellis, 1985). Similarly, the apparent relationship between the course being a part of the student's major and grade expectations may also indicate an expectation (perhaps unmet) on the part of the student to do well in these courses. Thus, students' grade expectations in courses that are part of their majors may affect their evaluation and be unrelated to the extent of learning that has occurred.

Table 4. Perceived Bias Resulting from Student and Class Characteristics.

		N	Median	Mean	Std. Dev.	Percent of Respondents: Strongly Disagree	Disagree	Neutral	Agree	Strongly Agree
Gender	Does not affect my evaluation	245	4.00	4.35	0.69	0.00	2.45	4.90	47.76	44.90
	Affects other students' evaluations	246	2.00	2.56	1.04	14.63	38.62	25.20	19.11	2.44
Age	Does not affect my evaluation	245	4.00	4.22	0.85	0.00	8.16	3.27	47.35	41.22
	Affects other students' evaluations	246	3.00	2.68	1.05	13.01	34.55	25.61	24.80	2.03
The course is part of major										
	Does not affect my evaluation	245	4.00	3.81	1.06	1.63	17.55	4.90	50.20	25.71
	Affects other students' evaluations	246	3.00	3.17	1.02	4.88	24.39	25.61	39.02	6.10
The grade expected to be received										
	Does not affect my evaluation	245	4.00	3.60	1.09	2.45	22.04	6.53	51.02	17.96
	Affects other students' evaluations	246	4.00	3.41	1.01	3.25	19.92	18.70	49.19	8.94
The instructor's gender										
	Does not affect my evaluation	245	4.00	4.31	0.72	0.41	1.63	7.76	46.53	43.67
	Affects other students' evaluations	246	2.00	2.57	1.05	14.23	37.81	29.27	13.82	4.88
The instructor's age										
	Does not affect my evaluation	245	4.00	4.22	0.77	0.41	2.86	9.80	47.76	39.18
	Affects other students' evaluations	245	3.00	263	1.03	12.65	35.92	30.61	17.14	3.67
The instructor's rank										
	Does not affect my evaluation	245	4.00	4.20	0.76	0.00	4.90	6.12	52.65	36.33
	Affects other students' evaluations	246	3.00	2.66	1.04	12.20	36.59	27.64	19.92	3.66
Class size										
	Does not affect my evaluation	245	4.00	3.78	1.03	1.63	15.92	8.57	50.20	23.67
	Affects other students' evaluations	243	3.00	2.93	0.99	6.58	30.04	30.45	30.04	2.88
Class rigor										
	Does not affect my evaluation	245	4.00	3.34	1.14	1.63	31.43	14.69	35.51	16.74
	Affects other students' evaluations	244	4.00	3.33	0.97	3.69	18.03	26.23	45.49	6.56

Perceived Biases: Instructor Characteristics

In general, students agree that an instructor's gender (90%), age (88%), and rank (89%) do not affect their SE ratings. This is consistent with the views of accounting program administrators who, according to Calderon et al. (1997), believe that neither gender (74%) nor age (71%) affects SE ratings. When asked whether these characteristics affected the SE ratings of their peers, about one half of all respondents indicated that they did not believe that instructors' gender, age, and rank affected the SE ratings of their classmates. Though the literature generally reports inconsistent findings relating to the association between instructor characteristics and SE ratings, it is noteworthy that students believe that instructor characteristics do not influence their own ratings of instructors' classroom effectiveness, but it affects their peers' SE ratings. This echoes students' belief that they can objectively evaluate effective teaching, but that some of their peers may not be as objective.

Perceived Biases: Class Characteristics

Seventy-four percent and 53% of students believe that class size and rigor do not affect SE's, respectively. In contrast, 33% and 52% believe that class size and rigor affect their peers' SE ratings. Overall, these results imply that many students, albeit not a majority, feel that class size and rigor affect SE's. In particular, students suggest that both they and their peers consider class rigor when evaluating their instructors. The proportion of students who appear to consider class rigor when evaluating their instructors mirrors the proportion of administrators who believe that class rigor affects student ratings (Calderon et al., 1997). While this paper does not address the direction in which students may alter their ratings in response to class rigor, the finding that students consider class rigor when evaluating their instructors appears to be consistent with the literature. Centra's (1993) observed that course difficulty adversely affects SEs. Marsh (1982), on the other hand, compared class pairs taught by a single instructor and found the more difficult class (higher perceived workload and difficulty) received higher student ratings.

SUMMARY AND CONCLUSION

This study finds that most students believe they can objectively evaluate effective teaching; they can respond to most SE items (but not necessarily all) without having to infer beyond their own background and experience; SEs are a good measure of effective teaching; and SE items are relevant to the business program. Students also indicate that factors such as student characteristics, class characteristics, and instructor characteristics, identified in prior studies as possible sources of bias, do not affect their own evaluations. On the other hand, with the exception of instructor and student gender, most believe that these factors affect the way in which other students' rate their instructors. Most students believe gender had little effect on SE results. Despite these results, students do not appear to have much confidence in SE results. Only 32% of students believe that faculty should trust SE results.

At least three observations from the study might explain the low level of student confidence in SE ratings. First, effective teaching is a nebulous concept, and many students are uneasy about the concept of effective teaching as well as the media used to solicit their input about instructors' classroom performance. Second, students appear to have reservations about the objectivity of the process. In particular, students indicate that while they do not let factors such as class size, class rigor, and instructor demographic characteristics affect their assessment of faculty teaching effectiveness, these factors might influence the ratings of other students. Although it is not clear from the survey whether students believe that these factors affect the judgment of the majority of their peers or just a small group, it seems plausible that students' beliefs about this issue might affect their level of trust in the teaching evaluation process. Third, students believe that administrators and others do not use SE instruments to assess the classroom effectiveness of instructors.

A follow-up open discussion with 38 student respondents provided additional insight into students' beliefs and possible reasons for their low level of confidence in SE ratings. Students noted that they generally responded fairly to SE items. However, many acknowledged that they had, at one time or another, given positive or negative evaluations for reasons other than effective teaching. Most viewed SEs as an exercise in futility as negative evaluations appeared to have little effect on an instructor's future performance. Most students believed that SE results went into a black hole, never to reappear. They all were greatly surprised when the discussion leader stated that administrators of accounting programs and business school deans used summary SE data as input in calculating faculty pay raises. The most interesting point brought out in the discussion was that students rated instructors relative to their experiences with other instructors. Students did not use an absolute scale to assess effective teaching. Instead, they tended to anchor SE responses on recent experiences with other instructors. We suggest additional research to explore those issues.

This paper deals with students' perceptions and beliefs about their evaluation of faculty teaching performance. It complements and extends prior studies, such as Calderon et al. (1996, 1997) and Yunker and Sterner (1988). However, the sample consists of students from only two universities and the findings may not necessarily apply to other institutions. Further research that involves a much wider cross-section of subjects is required before we can make generalizations about students' perceptions of SEs. In addition, the study considers only students' beliefs and perceptions. Because we do not know whether those beliefs and perceptions translate into actual behavior, we suggest additional research to examine the link between perceptions and beliefs about SEs and actual student ratings of faculty teaching effectiveness.

Despite its limitations, this study points to some interesting issues. First, although it is not known whether they consider course learning objectives when evaluating their instructors, students appear to make a connection between learning outcomes that they value and effective teaching. Second, students relate their perceptions about SEs as a good measure of effective teaching to how much they learned in a class, their ability to respond to SE items based on their backgrounds and experiences, their capacity to be objective, and the opportunity to comment on items related to their major. This observation has important implications for both the design and administration of SEs. As pointed out in the literature, SEs should include only items to which students can respond based on their background and experience (Seldin, 1993; Calderon et al., 1996; Green et al., 1998). It appears also, that where possible, administrators might consider including in SEs items that give students an opportunity to reflect on their major and on the amount and quality of learning that took place in the class. In all cases, before administering SE instruments, instructors should make students aware of the purpose of the evaluation process, the ways in which faculty and administrators will use the information they supply, and the need for objectivity in responding to SE items.

Finally, it is evident that students are concerned about the potential for "other students" to interject bias into their SE ratings. Students are evidently concerned that despite their ability to evaluate effective teaching, some of their peers do not exercise responsibility when evaluating their professors and may allow extraneous factors to influence their judgment. We recommend further research to clarify the nature of this belief and its impact on SE ratings. Nonetheless, administrators who use SEs for summative evaluation should be cognizant of it and should make students aware of the need for and importance of objectivity when rating their instructors' teaching performance. Overall, the study provides additional justification for the use of faculty teaching portfolios for evaluating faculty teaching effectiveness. Significant benefits would accrue from the use of a portfolio of information that sheds light on the attainment of class and program learning objectives, and details activities and accomplishments related to the dimensions of effective teaching.

REFERENCES

Accounting Education Change Commission (1993). *Evaluating and Rewarding Effective Teaching, Issues Statement No. 5.* Torrance, CA: AECC.

Anikeeff, A. M. (1953). Factors Affecting Student Evaluation of College Faculty Members. *Journal of Applied Psychology, 37*, 446–464.

Arnett, K., Arnold, D. R., & Cochran, D. S. (1898). Improving Business School Student Evaluation of Faculty Performance. *Journal of Education for Business, 64*, 268–270.

Bausell, R. B., & Magoon, J. (1972). Expected Grade in a Course, Grade Point Average, and Student Ratings of the Course and the Instructor. *Educational and Psychological Measurement, 5*, 29–33.

Brandenburg, D. C., Slinde, J. A., & Batista, E. E. (1977). Student Ratings of Instruction: Validity and Normative Interpretations. *Research in Higher Education, 7*, 67–78.

Calderon, T. G., Gabbin, A. L., & Green, B. P. (1996). *A Framework for Encouraging Effective Teaching*, Harrisburg, VA: Center for Research in Accounting Education, James Madison University.

Calderon, T. G., Green, B. P., & Reider, B. P. (1997). Perceptions and Use of Student Evaluations by Heads of Accounting Departments. *The Accounting Educators' Journal*, (Fall), 1–27.

Cashin, W. E. (1990). Assessing Teaching Effectiveness. In: P. Seldin et al. (Ed.), *How Administrators Can Improve Teaching* (pp. 89–103). San Francisco: Jossey-Bass.

Cashin, W. E. (1983). Concerns about Using Student Ratings in Community Colleges. In: A. Smith (Ed.), *Evaluating Faculty and Staff: New Directions for Community Colleges*. San Francisco: Jossey-Bass.

Centra, J. A. (1993). *Reflective Faculty Evaluation*. San Francisco: Jossey-Bass.

Centra, J. A. (1977). Student Ratings of Instruction and Their Relationship to Student Learning. *American Educational Research Journal, 14*, 17–24.

Cohen, P. A. (1981). Student Ratings of Instruction and Student Achievement: A Meta-Analysis of Multisection Validity Studies. *Review of Educational Research, 51*, 281–304.

DuCette, J., & Kenney, J. (1982). Do Grading Standards Affect Student Evaluations of Teaching? Some New Evidence on an Old Question. *Journal of Educational Psychology, 74*, 308–314.

Ellis, R. S. (1985). Ratings of Teachers by Their Students Should be Used Wisely or Not at All. *Chronicle of Higher Education, 30*, 88.

Feldman, K. A. (1976). Grades and College Students' Evaluations of Their Courses and Teachers. *Research in Higher Education, 4*, 69–111.

Frey, P. W. (1973). Student Ratings of Teaching: Validity of Several Rating Factors. *Science, 182*, 83–85.

Goldberg, G., & Callahan, J. (1991). Objectivity of Student Evaluations of Instructors. *Journal of Education for Business, 66* (July/August), 377–378.

Green, B. P., Calderon, T. G., & Reider, B. P. 1998. A Content Analysis of Teaching Evaluation Instruments Used in Accounting Departments. *Issues in Accounting, 13*, 15–30.

Heilman, J. D., & Armentrout, W. D. (1936). The Rating of College Teachers on Ten Traits by Their Students. *Journal of Educational Psychology, 27*, 197–216.

Kemp, B. W., & Kumar, G. S. (1990). Student Evaluations: Are We Using Them Correctly? *Journal of Education for Business*, *65* (November/December), 106–111.

Lowman, J. (1984). *Mastering the Techniques of Teaching*. San Francisco: Jossey-Bass.

Marsh, H. W. (1982). SEEQ: A Reliable, Valid, and Useful Instrument for Collecting Student Evaluations of University Teaching. *British Journal of Educational Psychology*, *52*, 77–95.

Marsh, H. W. (1984). Students' Evaluations of University Teaching: Dimensionality, Reliability, and Validity, Potential Biases, and Utility. *Journal of Educational Psychology*, *76*, 707–754.

Marsh, H. W. (1987). Students' Evaluation of University Teaching: Research Findings, Methodological Issues, and Directions for Future Research. *International Journal of Educational Research*, *11*, 253–388.

Marsh, H. W., & Ware, J. E., Jr. (1982). Effects of Expressiveness, Content Coverage, and Incentive on Multidimensional Student Rating Scales: New Interpretation of the Dr. Fox Effect. *Journal of Educational Psychology*, *74*, 126–134.

McKeachie, W. J. (1971). Student Ratings of Faculty: A Reprise. *Academe*, *65*, 384–397.

Miller, R. I. (1988). *Evaluating Faculty for Promotion and Tenure*. San Francisco: Jossey-Bass.

Moore, R. (1990). Student Evaluations of Teaching. *The American Biology Teacher*, *52*, 260–262.

Murray, H. G. (1983). Low-Inference Classroom Teaching Behaviors and Student Ratings of College Teaching Effectiveness. *Journal of Educational Psychology*, *75*, 856–865.

Palmer, J., Carliner, G., & Romer, T. (1978). Leniency, Learning, and Evaluations. *Journal of Educational Psychology*, *70*, 855–863.

Sclul, A. J., & Crivelli, M. A. (1973). Animad Version Error in Students' Evaluations of Faculty Teaching Effectiveness. *Journal of Applied Psychology*, *58*, 259–260.

Seldin, P. (1984). *Changing Practices in Faculty Evaluation*. San Francisco: Jossey-Bass.

Seldin, P. (1993). The Use and Abuse of Student Ratings of Professors. *The Chronicle of Higher Education*, (July), A40.

Sullivan, A., & Skanes, G. (1974). Validity of Student Evaluation of Teaching and the Characteristics of Successful Instructors. *Journal of Educational Psychology*, *66*, 584–590.

Trahan, C. M., & Swindle, B. (1988). A Good Accounting Instructor: A Student Perspective. *Journal of Education for Business*, *63*, 216–219.

Weaver, C. H. (1960). Instructor Ratings by College Students. *Journal of Educational Psychology*, *51*, 21–45.

White, C. S., & Ahmadi, M. (1986). A Novel Approach to the Analysis of a Teacher-Evaluation System. *Journal of Education for Business*, *61*, 24–27.

Yunker, P. J., & Sterner, J. (1988). A Survey of Faculty Performance Evaluation in Accounting. *Accounting Educators' Journal*, (Fall), 63–71.

www.ingramcontent.com/pod-product-compliance
Lightning Source LLC
LaVergne TN
LVHW010648300926
849161LV00005B/1067